CELEBRATING AMERICA

Masterworks from Texas Collections

CELEBRATING AMERICA

Masterworks from Texas Collections

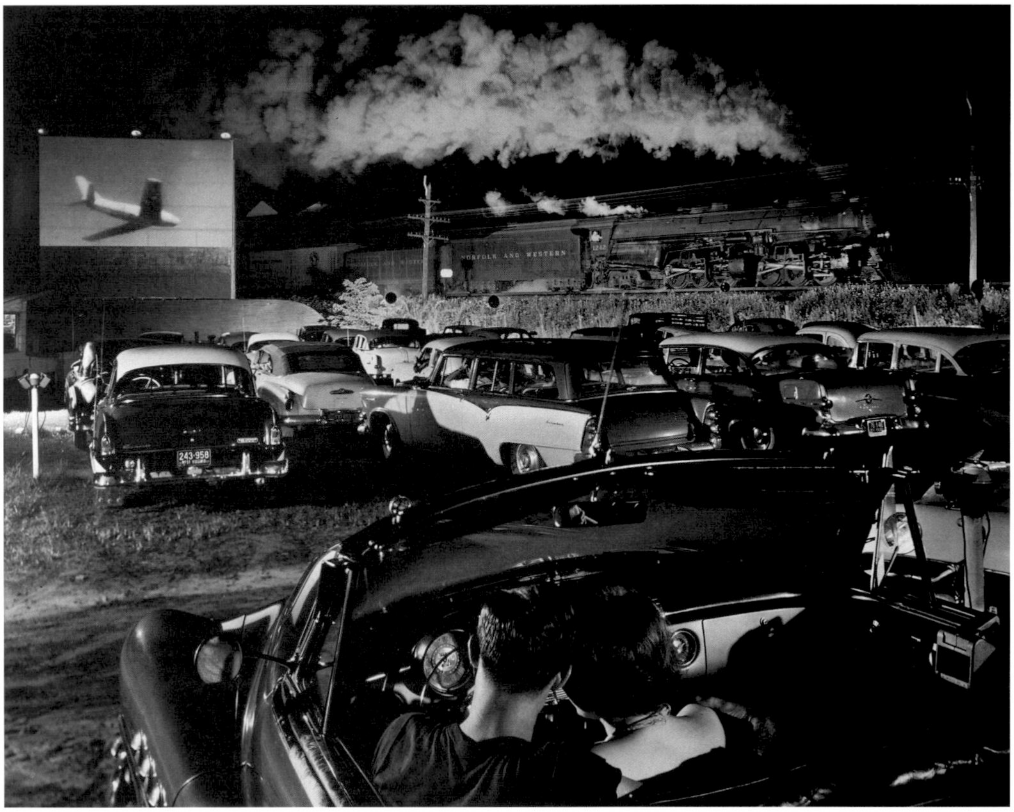

AMON CARTER MUSEUM

First Edition

3501 Camp Bowie Boulevard
Fort Worth, Texas 76107–2695
817.738.1933
www.cartermuseum.org

General Editor: Will Gillham

Manuscript Editors and Proofreaders: Will Gillham and Peter Keefe

Designer: Keely Edwards

Printer: Liberty Graphics

Published on the occasion of the exhibition held at the Amon Carter Museum, September 14 through November 17, 2002.

ISBN: 0–88360–096–X

Library of Congress Control Number: 2002107714

FRONT COVER: Winslow Homer (1836–1910), *The Woodcutter* (detail), 1891, Watercolor and graphite on paper, Collection of Fayez Sarofim

BACK COVER: George L. K. Morris (1905–1975), *Crescendo*, 1936, Oil on canvas with collage, Private Collection, Dallas, Texas

TITLE PAGE: O. Winston Link (1914–2001), *Hot Shot Eastbound, Iaeger, West Virginia*, 1956, Gelatin silver print, Copyright O. Winston Link Trust, Courtesy of SBC Communications Inc.

Table of Contents

Foreword

THIS EXHIBITION HAS BEEN CONCEIVED AS A CELEBRATION of several things. First, it celebrates the opening of the Amon Carter Museum's spacious and beautiful new galleries, designed by the museum's original architect, Philip Johnson. Second, it celebrates the richness and diversity of American art, which has been the *raison d'être* of this museum from the beginning. Third, by bringing together outstanding works by artists in all media, this exhibition celebrates the philosophy of quality that has governed the Carter's collecting activities since its inception. Lastly, and perhaps most importantly, this exhibition celebrates the public and private collections in the state of Texas, where the study and appreciation of American art have flourished for more than a century.

This celebration could not have been possible without the generous support of the many institutions and individuals in Texas who agreed to lend some of their most prized possessions to this exhibition. On behalf of the museum's Board of Trustees, I offer our heartfelt gratitude to all who have participated. Larger exhibitions like this always test the limits of a museum's resources, and it is gratifying indeed to know that there are people in the world of business who know the value of art for their communities. We are particularly indebted to Wells Fargo for their special generosity in underwriting this exhibition.

Finally, *Celebrating America* was the brainchild of Jane Myers, the museum's chief curator. She and her colleagues traveled throughout the state to view works for the project. Without their tireless efforts, we would not have such a wonderful array of works to view together in new ways. For many of us, this experience alone is worth celebrating.

Rick Stewart, *Director*

August 2002

Acknowledgments

Four years ago, while brainstorming about a special exhibition to commemorate the reopening of the expanded Amon Carter Museum, Director Rick Stewart and I landed on the idea of a loan exhibition that would bring together an assembly of American masterworks to both echo and complement the Carter's holdings. At Rick's suggestion, I began searching for possibilities by considering works of art housed in the state of Texas. Along with my colleagues in this endeavor—Curator of Paintings and Sculpture Patricia Junker, who joined me in some of my regional travels, and Curator of Photographs Barbara McCandless, who curated the photography component of this exhibition—I soon realized that the depth and quality of American art in Texas is extraordinary. Our search took us no farther than the state's borders, and the exhibition quickly evolved into a celebration of American art collecting in Texas—a most fitting acknowledgement of the occasion.

Celebrating America: Masterworks from Texas Collections could not have been realized without the dedication and support of many individuals. On behalf of the Amon Carter Museum's Board of Trustees, Director Rick Stewart, and my colleague and cocurator of the exhibition, Barbara McCandless, I thank the lenders to this exhibition, all of whom graciously allowed us into their homes, offices, and storage vaults, displaying not only warm cordiality but a willingness to part for a time with their cherished works of art.

Barbara and I thank especially the other contributors to the catalogue, our colleagues at the Carter, Rebecca Lawton, Patricia Junker, and Rick Stewart, as well as independent scholar Shirley-Reece Hughes, all of whom brought new insights to their individual essays.

Each member of the Carter's staff helped to ensure that this project was brought to fruition. I would like to single out Libby Cluett, school and youth programs coordinator; Sam Duncan, associate librarian and cataloguer; Helen Plummer, curatorial associate; Jane Posey, curatorial administrative assistant; and Karin Strohbeck, archives and library assistant, for their facilitation of exhibition research.

Members of the collections management area, including Courtney DeAngelis, associate registrar; Rynda Lemke, photographer; Melissa Thompson, registrar; Callie Morfeld Vincent, registrar's assistant; and Steven Watson, associate photographer, helped to arrange special photography and coordinate the shipment of artwork.

Will Gillham, director of publications, admirably managed the entire publication project with the assistance of Miriam Hermann, publications assistant, along with production consultant Bill Maize and photographer Steven Watson. Keely Edwards, graphic designer and publications production coordinator, created this handsome presentation.

Lucy Hyden, development consultant; Carol Noel, public relations coordinator; and Claire Barry, chief conservator of paintings, provided essential support in their individual areas of expertise.

A special thanks goes to Wendy Haynes, exhibition manager, for her tireless and enthusiastic efforts to support the exhibition in its various aspects, and to my fellow members of the museum's management committee—Rick, Jeff Guy, and Bob Workman—who remained consummate professionals while seeing the project through a frenzied period of facility relocation and the reopening of the museum following the two-year expansion.

Many museum professionals, dealers, scholars, collectors, and other enthusiasts of American art helped locate works of art for this exhibition and facilitated the subsequent research. Without their generous support, *Celebrating America* would not have been possible. My gratitude goes to Anne Adams, Claude Albritton, Michael Banschbach, Mr. and Mrs. Larry Berk, Nancy Blomberg, Sarah Boehme, Ben Breard, Jan Brenneman, Lillian Brenwasser, Suzanne Burris, Charles Butt, William Carruth, Stephen Clark, John Cleary, David Coleman, Patricia Decoster, Donald Dow, Matthew Drutt, Sam and Valerie Dunnam, Carla Ellard, Betsy Fahlman, Cynthia Farah, Motrja P. Fedorko, Burt and Missy Finger, Richard Fitzgerald, Roy Flukinger, Debra Force, Barbara French, Alan Govenar, Michael Grauer, Jim Haines, Eleanor Jones Harvey, Tracy Holmes, Amy Kelly, John and Karen Kelsey, Keri Koljian, Heather Lammers, James Maloney and Beverly Ann Young, Patrick McCracken, Joan Morganstern, Amy Munger Morris, James Munisteri, Reilly Nail, Emily Ballew Neff, Burt Nelson, George W. Neubert, Michael Nye, Ron Peshock and Gail Dickinson, Christian Peterson, Becky Duval Reese, Marilyn Richardson, Richard A. Russack, Ruth Carter Stevenson, Rodney and Gail Susholtz, Steve and Nenetta Tatum, Mark Thistlethwaite, William R. Thompson, Connie Todd, Anne Tucker, Kevin and Cheryl Vogel, Barry Walker, Chip Ware, Nancy Weekly, Morris Weiner, Clint Willour, Lyle Williams, and Richard York.

In addition to the lenders, who kindly granted permission to reproduce these works from their collections, the following institutions, organizations, and individuals granted permission to reproduce the various works herein for which they hold copyright: the Ansel Adams Publishing Rights Trust; Aperture Foundation, Inc., Paul Strand Archive; Paul Caponigro; Center for Creative Photography; Imogen Cunningham Trust; Robert Frank, Pace/MacGill Gallery; Estate of Arshile Gorky, Artists Rights Society (ARS), New York; O. Winston Link Trust; Josephine Morris; the Georgia O'Keeffe Foundation; Aaron Siskind Foundation; Joanna T. Steichen; Minor White Archive, Trustees of Princeton University; Estate of Garry Winogrand, Fraenkel Gallery; and VAGA, New York, NY.

This exhibition has been made possible by a generous gift from Wells Fargo, which agreed that this fascinating look at important collections of American art in our own backyard was worthy of celebration.

Jane Myers, *Chief Curator*

August 2002

Introduction

In the early 1770s John Singleton Copley painted the portraits of two distinguished citizens, Jabez and Sarah Bowen (pp. 26–29), who maintained influential social, political, and educational ties to their native Rhode Island. Their portraits remained together for over 200 years, including a period of extended loan to the Museum of Art at the Rhode Island School of Design in Providence. In the early 1980s the two paintings were sold separately through Kennedy Galleries of New York, making their way to Texas, where they now reside in private collections 600 miles apart. Little could the Bowens have imagined, while sitting for the renowned Boston portraitist, that their countenances would someday come to rest in a region that during their lifetimes was a Spanish colony in which the Native American and Hispanic populations maintained an uneasy balance with each other. The westward journey of these two paintings marks a well-worn path for numerous artworks located in the outstanding collections that have been assembled in Texas since the turn of the twentieth century, when the citizens who populated the state's burgeoning communities began a series of earnest campaigns to bring art to the prairies.

The nature of this catalogue and exhibition of fifty-nine paintings, sculptures, watercolors, and photographs is informed by the Amon Carter Museum's own collecting philosophy. The museum was founded in 1961 to house Amon G. Carter Sr.'s (figure 1) collection of 400 works by Frederic Remington and Charles M. Russell. Since that time, the museum has greatly broadened its collecting perspective, seeking out the finest examples of American art and in the process building a collection of masterworks—each with its own emotional, aesthetic, and intellectual associations—that emphasizes key moments in American art and culture. Today, the Carter's collection includes approximately 200 paintings, 170 sculptures, 600 drawings and watercolors, 3,500 prints, and 230,000 photographic objects. The museum's photography holdings grew rapidly throughout the 1970s and 1980s, with acquisitions of both historical

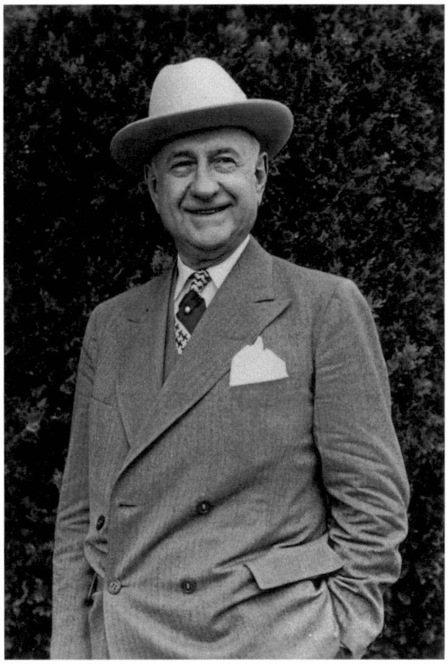

(Figure 1) Amon G. Carter Sr., ca. 1950

collections and individual masterpieces. Considered one of the finest collections of American photography anywhere, the holdings include more than 30,000 exhibition-quality prints and the archives of several major photographers, among them Laura Gilpin, Eliot Porter, and Karl Struss.

Celebrating America: Masterworks from Texas Collections commemorates the inaugural year of the museum's expanded facilities. Designed by architect Philip Johnson, the new addition—in conjunction with the original 1961 building—increased the gallery space in which to showcase the museum's collections and special exhibitions of American art to nearly 30,000 square feet (fig. 2). This exhibition and catalogue also celebrate the achievements of those institutional, private, and corporate collectors in Texas whose holdings reflect the essential nature of this country's unique character. Although the works assembled here are a small representation of the profusion of American art located throughout the state, they manifest a century-long desire to collect and share through public display the finest examples of American creative expression.

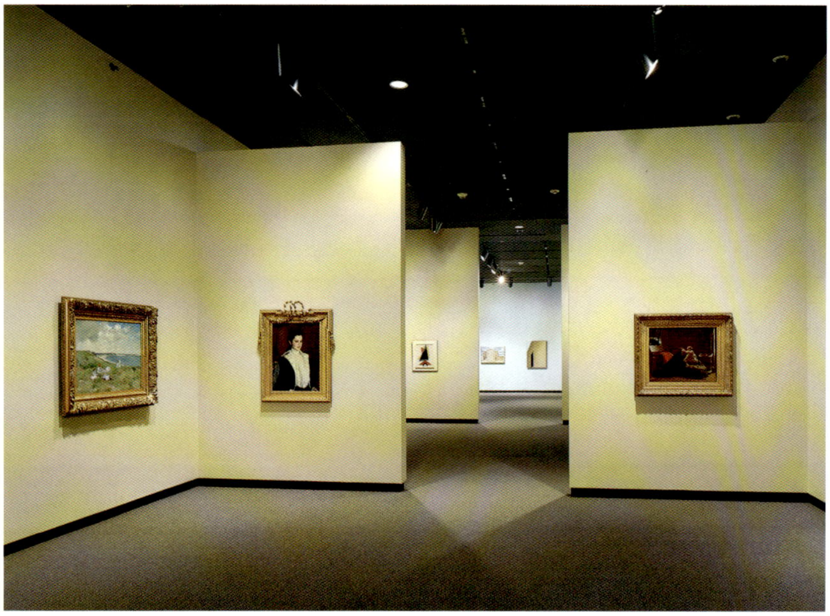

(Fig. 2) The west wing of the Carter's expanded paintings and sculpture galleries.

Celebrating America spans nearly 200 years of American art history, beginning with John Singleton Copley's portraits of Jabez and Sarah Bowen (ca. 1771–74) and closing with Garry Winogrand's 1969 photograph *Los Angeles, California* (pp. 140–141). In addition to revealing the remarkable collecting acumen of those Texas collectors, both historic and more recently established, who have enriched the state's cultural heritage, the works in this exhibition both complement and augment the Carter's own holdings. While the colonial paintings by Copley offer an earlier perspective on American portraiture than the Carter has traditionally represented, twentieth-century works by Arshile Gorky (pp. 122–123), Wayne Thiebaud (pp. 136–137), and Winogrand point to abstract and realist strains strongly represented in the Carter's collection by such works as Stuart Davis' overpowering abstraction, *Blips and Ifs* (fig. 3), and recent photographs like Terry Falke's *Mitchell Butte, Arizona/Utah Border* (fig. 4).

In the forty years since the Carter's opening, the collecting of American art has benefited from unprecedented growth in scholarship, in which connoisseurship has continued to play an indispensable role. At the same time, there has been an attendant rise in prices for American art. Photography in particular has seen an extraordinary market increase in the past five years, with early daguerreotypes and twentieth-century masterworks now commanding prices that approach those of major paintings. Despite widespread interest and intellectual scrutiny, however, many masterworks of American art still require thoughtful examination. Fitz Hugh Lane's maritime masterpiece *Sunset at Gloucester Harbor* (pp. 36–37), Raymond Jonson's *Abstract Two* (pp. 94–95), and George L. K. Morris' dynamic *Crescendo* (pp. 112–113), for example, demand more attention.

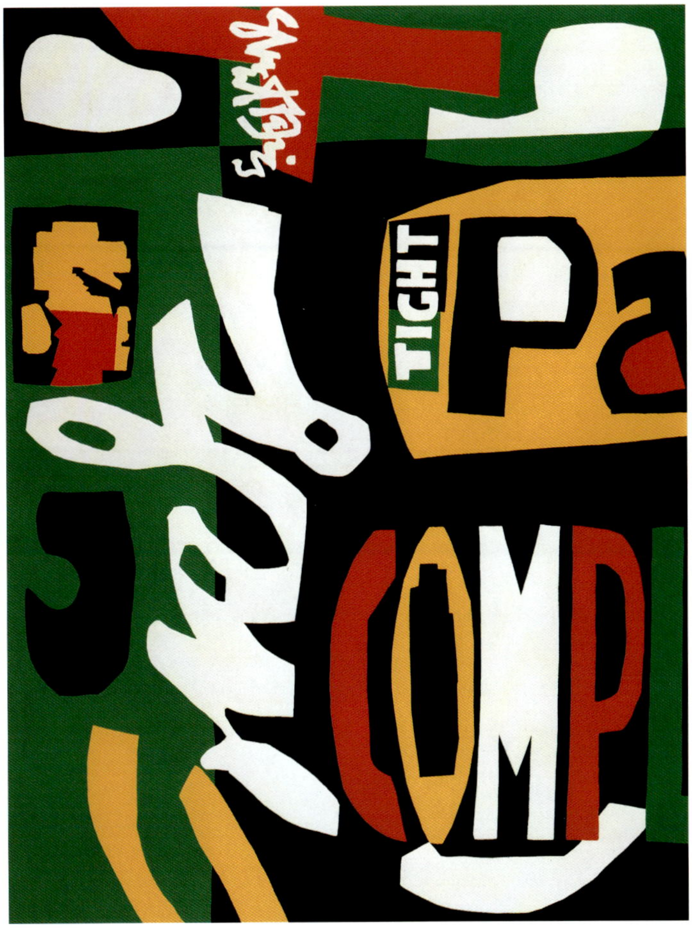

(Fig. 3) Stuart Davis (1892–1964), *Blips and Ifs*, 1963–64, oil on canvas, Acquisition in memory of John de Menil, Trustee, Amon Carter Museum, 1961–69, 1967.195

One special opportunity afforded by this exhibition involves the comparison of loaned objects with works from the Carter's own holdings. As an example, two paintings by Marsden Hartley, the Carter's *American Indian Symbols* (fig. 5) and the McNay Art Museum's *Portrait Arrangement* (pp. 74–75), were both executed in 1914, a pivotal and productive year for the artist, who was then living in Berlin. The Fort Worth picture embodies Hartley's American identity, expressed through references to Native Americans whose cultural heritage could be seen in Berlin's extensive ethnographic collections. With the advent of World War I, however, Hartley's work shifted to imagery prevalent in such works as the equally metaphorical *Portrait Arrangement*, a tribute to the death of a German soldier. In another instance, a fascinating association exists between two nineteenth-century genre pictures by Thomas Hovenden (fig. 6) and Helen Corson (pp. 48–49)—the former in the Carter's collection, the latter owned by Wells Fargo. Such a comparison provides scintillating insight into this husband and wife's sympathetic working environment in their Pennsylvania studio, where, with restrained sensitivity, they explored the

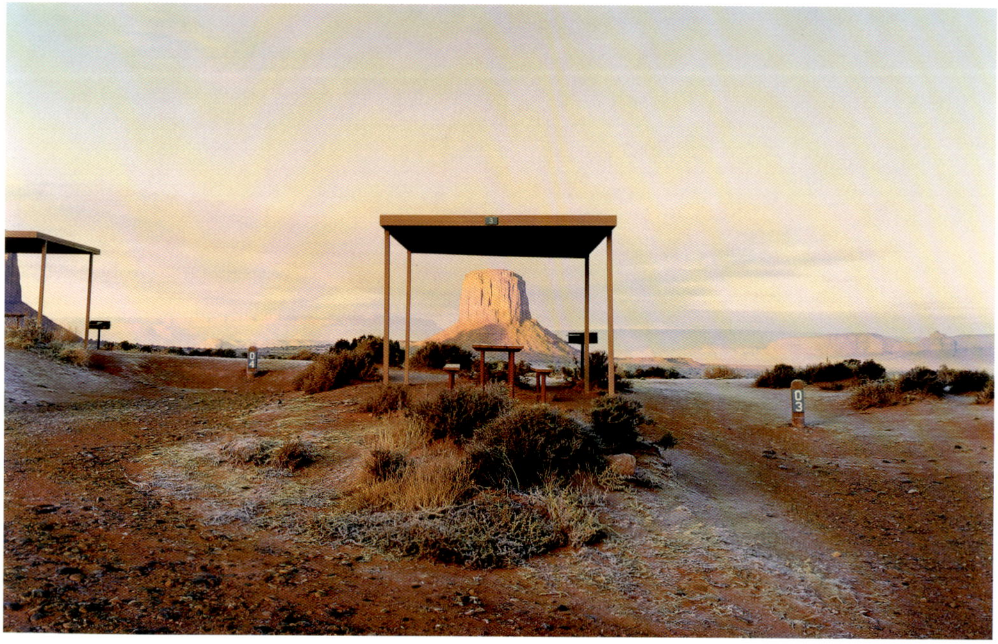

(Fig. 4) Terry Falke (b. 1950), *Mitchell Butte, Arizona/Utah Border*, dye coupler print (Fujicolor), 1995, Amon Carter Museum, Fort Worth, Texas, © 1995, Terry Falke, Gift of Dominic Lam, P1999.20

African-American way of life during the post-Civil War period.

Following the turn of the twentieth century, as communities in Texas grew, a sense of civic pride and yearning for cultural, spiritual, and intellectual fulfillment led to a desire for exposure to the visual arts. This led the way to the formation of today's major urban art museums in Dallas, Fort Worth, Houston, El Paso, and San Antonio. The cities of Dallas, in 1900, and Fort Worth, in 1901, opened Carnegie Public Libraries that housed special exhibition galleries for the display of original artwork. Support organizations for these activities were established with the formation of the Dallas Art Association in 1903 and the Fort Worth Art Association in 1910. Other cities were quick to follow; the core organizations for the Museum of Fine Arts, Houston, the El Paso Museum of Art, and the San Antonio Art Museum were all founded by 1912, and each of these institutions has loaned works to this exhibition.

Typically, these groups were headed by zealous women who, as others across the country did during the Progressive Era, campaigned to bring visual art to their communities through acquisition and exhibition.[1] The culturally minded women of Texas diligently sought to rectify what they perceived to be the absence of fine art in their state. A member of the El Paso Woman's Club, seeking the loan of a work in 1912, stated: "We have never had a great picture here and I am sure there are many who never saw one. . . ."[2] Despite a universal lack of funds, the scarcity of appropriate venues for showing art, and slow acceptance by the general public, each of these Texas organizations possessed grand aspirations and refused to be deterred. In 1904 Dallas and Fort Worth each acquired their first paintings: in Dallas, Childe Hassam's *September Morning* (1900); in Fort Worth, by public subscription, George Inness' 1875 masterpiece *The Approaching Storm* (pp. 42–43).

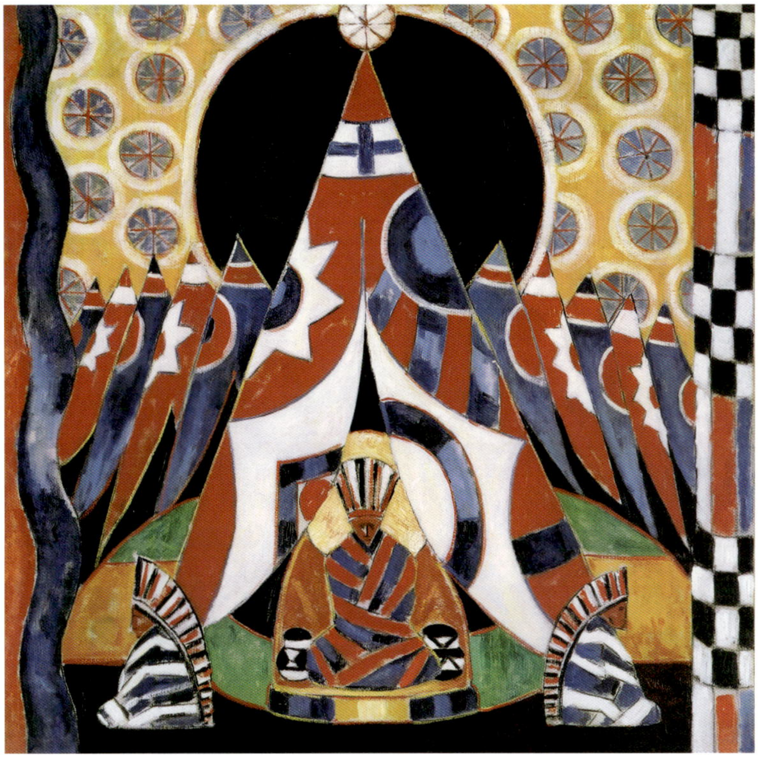

(Fig. 5) Marsden Hartley (1877–1943), *American Indian Symbols*, oil on canvas, 1914, Amon Carter Museum, 1999.8

In 1909 Fort Worth set a decisive example for the rest of the state when the art community's enterprising mastermind, Jennie Scott Scheuber (1860–1944), persuaded the newly formed American Federation of Arts (AFA)—a national organization established by an act of Congress that year for the purpose of encouraging an appreciation of the arts around the country—to send their first traveling exhibition to Fort Worth. The exhibition, which included works by contemporary American artists Childe Hassam, Irving Couse, and Robert Henri, traveled to a part of the country that in the minds of some fell into the category of the "hinterlands," as expressed by Secretary of State Elihu Root in his opening address at AFA's founding.[3] The first of many national tours organized by the AFA, this exhibition initiated nearly thirty years of AFA tours in Texas, with Scheuber arranging the statewide circuit on their behalf and encouraging other cities to participate, including San Antonio, Houston, Austin, Waco, and Galveston. Loans from such prestigious institutions as the Detroit Art Museum (now the Detroit Institute of Arts), the National Arts Club in New York City, and the Albright Gallery in Buffalo (now the Albright-Knox Art Gallery) exposed Texas audiences to many fine masterworks. Paintings from commercial galleries were also included, offering the tantalizing possibility of purchasing works, a practice fully endorsed by the AFA. This in turn led to significant acquisitions by the fledgling art institutions, an activity that caused one writer for Washington, D.C.'s *Evening Star* to assert in 1913 that "There is more vital interest shown in art and proportionately more pictures bought in Texas today than in many of the eastern states."[4]

These tours fostered a positive reception for the arts, which then led to prescient acquisitions of long-term benefit. For example, in 1925 the Friends of Art, a supporting group attached to the Fort Worth Art Association, acquired Thomas Eakins' masterpiece *Swimming*, now owned by the Amon Carter Museum (fig. 7). Clarence Cranmer (1874?–after 1952), a Philadelphia sportswriter who had been a friend of Eakins and to whom Mrs. Eakins had turned in the early twenties for help in selling her husband's work, brokered the sale. He later recalled this transaction, his first on Mrs. Eakins' behalf, as the "turning point" for the distribution of Eakins' art, which had generally fallen from favor in the wake of the artist's death. Within a few years of *Swimming*'s sale, Cranmer had successfully placed Eakins' work both with leading private collectors of the day and major art repositories, including the Metropolitan Museum of Art, the Cleveland Museum of Art, the Museum of Fine Arts, Boston, and the Detroit Institute of Arts.[5]

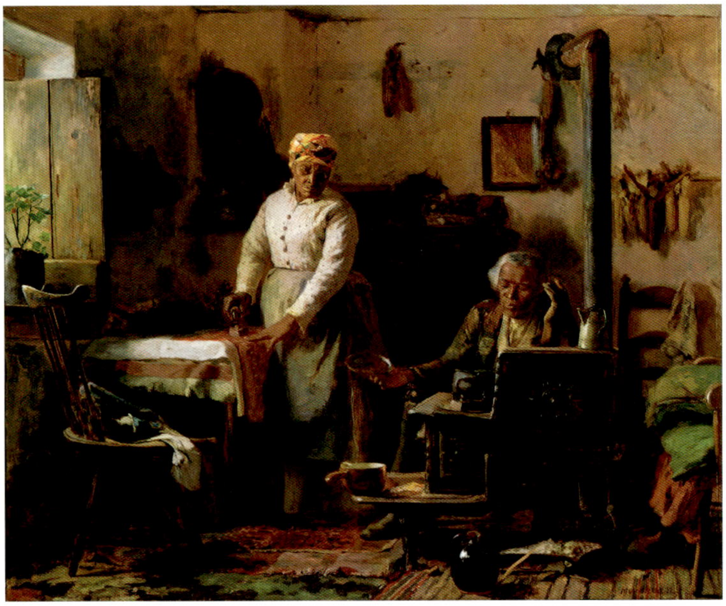

(Fig. 6) Thomas Hovenden (1840–1895), *Chloe and Sam*, 1882, oil on canvas, Purchase with funds provided by the Council of the Amon Carter Museum, 1992.3

In addition to fostering acquisitions, these early traveling exhibitions exposed Texans to new art styles and eventually led to more aggressive collection development in different areas of the state. The Museum of Fine Arts, Houston, began presenting annual exhibitions of Texas photographers in 1926, and in 1930 it introduced the modernist photographs of Edward Weston to the region. In the 1940s, traveling exhibitions of contemporary figure painting and nonobjective art from the Guggenheim Foundation exposed Texas viewers to the much-disputed aspects of unconventional artistic experimentation. The works made a significant and lasting impression, evident most recently in the construction of the new Modern Art Museum of Fort Worth, designed by Tadao Ando and scheduled to open in late 2002 with 53,000 square feet of gallery space. This institution, the oldest museum in the state, was founded as the Fort Worth Public Library and Art Gallery in 1892.

Fort Worth's Kimbell Art Museum, which opened in 1972, also benefited greatly from the legacy of these early traveling exhibitions. Velma Fuller Kimbell (1887–1982), influenced in part by the works she had seen in these tours, began collecting British portraits in 1935. The collecting tradition established by Kimbell and her husband, Kay (1886–1964), continues today through the world-renowned museum itself, whose painting by Benjamin West, *The Death of the Earl of Chatham* (pp. 30–31), is a

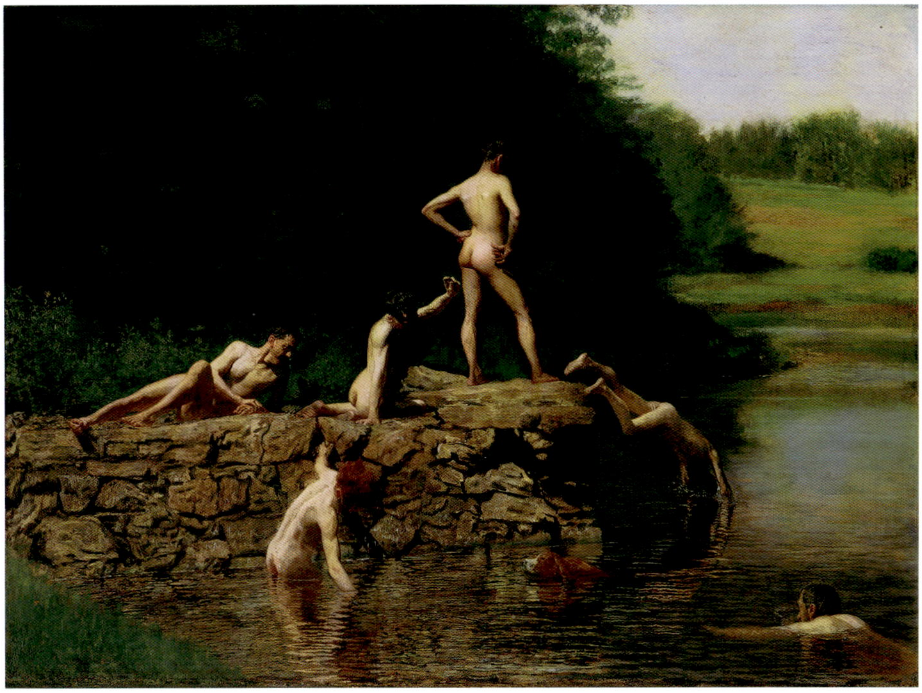

(Fig. 7) Thomas Eakins (1844–1916), *Swimming*, 1885, oil on canvas, Purchased by the Friends of Art, Fort Worth Art Association, 1925; acquired by the Amon Carter Museum, 1990, from the Modern Art Museum of Fort Worth through grants and donations from the Amon G. Carter Foundation, the Sid W. Richardson Foundation, the Anne Burnett and Charles Tandy Foundation, Capital Cities / ABC Foundation, *Fort Worth Star-Telegram*, the R. D. and Joan Dale Hubbard Foundation, and the people of Fort Worth, 1990.19.1

superlative example of the influence exerted on early American artists by English painting traditions.

Specialized collections in Texas, evolving from this instilled atmosphere for the appreciation for the fine arts, naturally reflected a preference for the art of the American West. A number of such collections were assembled by entrepreneurs who were born in the nineteenth century and made their fortunes in the twentieth. Five men in particular assembled western collections of such depth and caliber that they now form the nuclei of major public institutions. These pioneering collectors were Amon G. Carter Sr. (1879–1955), William C. Hogg (1875–1930), Sid W. Richardson (1891–1959), C. R. Smith (1899–1990), and H. J. Lutcher Stark (1887–1965). With the exception of Stark, whose broad-based collection developed into the Stark Museum of Art in Orange, Texas, these collectors focused their acquisitive energies, to varying degrees, on works by Charles M. Russell (fig. 8) and Frederic Remington (fig. 9), the two greatest artists of the American West. Carter's collection now resides in the Amon Carter Museum; Hogg's collection is housed in the Museum of Fine Arts, Houston; Richardson's collection is now the Sid Richardson Collection of Western Art,

Fort Worth; and Smith's collection is in the Jack S. Blanton Museum of Art in Austin. These men sought to surround themselves with imagery that depicted the world of their pioneer predecessors, stalwart individualists who had similarly availed themselves of the region's endless possibilities and formidable challenges. The art of Remington and Russell, with its evocations of raw courage, frontier humor, and hard-won triumphs, reinforced the lifestyles and aspirations of these collectors, who were among the most influential leaders of their time.

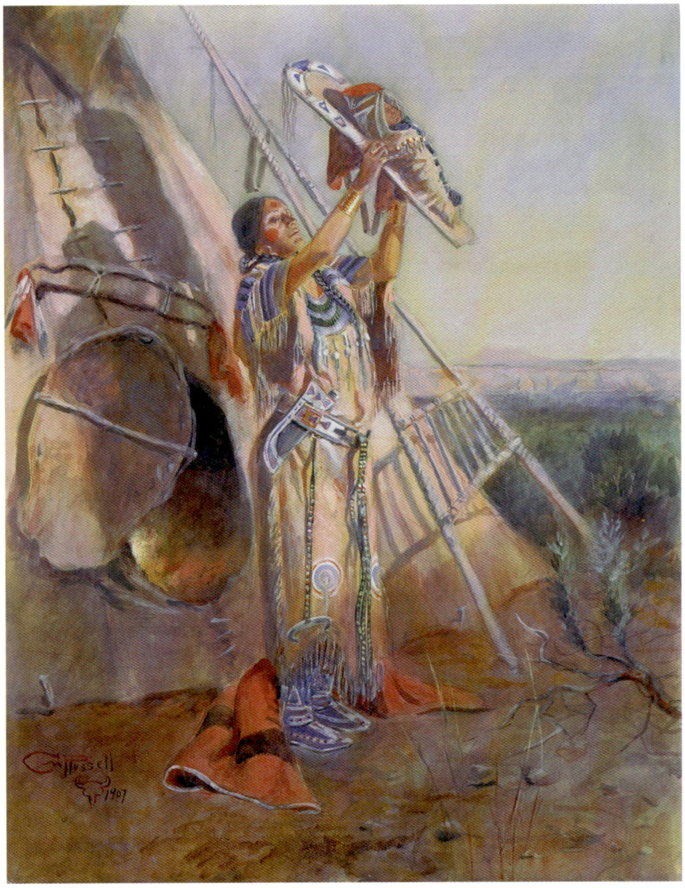

(Fig. 8) Charles M. Russell (1864–1926), *Sun Worship in Montana*, 1907, Opaque and transparent watercolor over graphite underdrawing on paper, Amon Carter Museum, 1961.150

Beyond their appreciation for fine art, these five collectors were dedicated philanthropists. Their generosity emanated from their gratitude to Texas, which they expressed through a desire to give back to the communities that had nurtured their careers. As Carter wrote in his last will and testament, "[The] pioneer spirit that peopled the wide spaces and laid the foundations of a happy future comes down to me in the strain of the blood, and I wish to share it with others who would make Texas their home and their inspiration."[6] Such a legacy underscores these remarkable collections of traditional western art and illuminates an area that recently has only begun to receive scholarly attention.

Beyond the arena of western art, a number of other individual Texas collectors amassed collections of such consummate quality and depth that they boasted some of the finest works produced during the twentieth century. As a young woman, Ohio native Marion Koogler McNay (1883–1950) saw two of this country's formative modernist exhibitions: the Armory Show at its Chicago venue in 1913, and the Forum Exhibition in New York City in 1916. In 1925 she moved to San Antonio, bringing with her a discerning appreciation for modern art. Four years later she completed the house where the Marion Koogler McNay Museum is located today. In addition to works by European masters Vincent van Gogh, Paul Gauguin, and Pablo Picasso, McNay also acquired works by American artists. This example is followed today by the museum she established, which

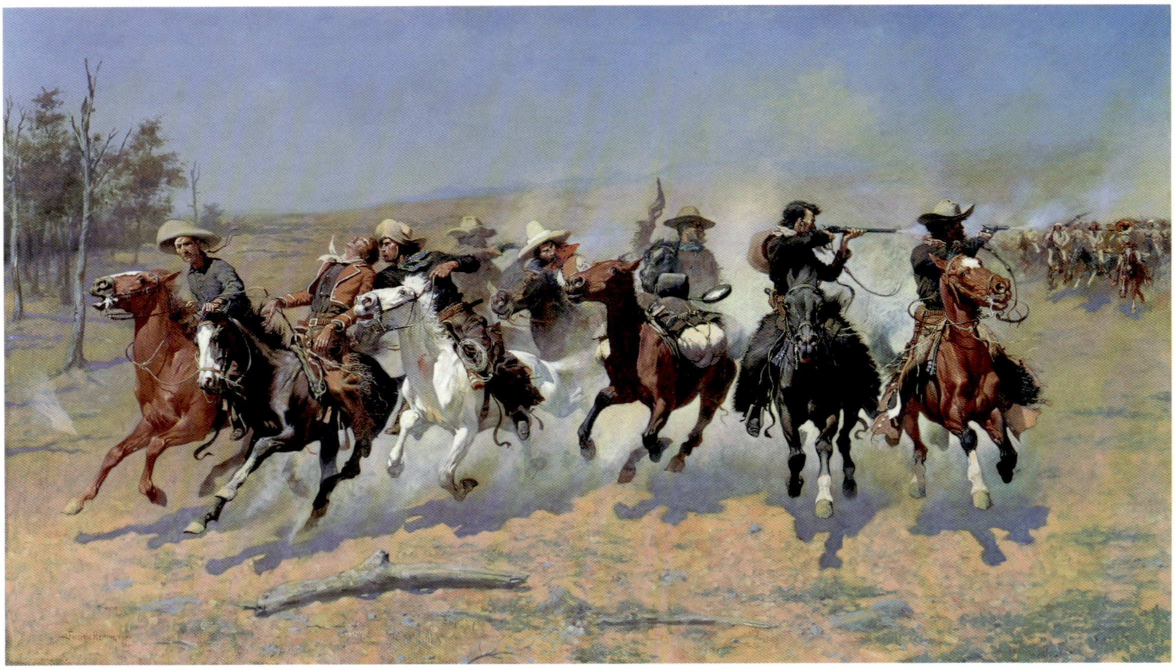

(Fig. 9) Frederic Remington (1861–1909), *A Dash for the Timber*, 1889, oil on canvas, Amon Carter Museum, 1961.381

opened to the public in 1954 and now houses more than 14,000 objects.

Bill Bomar (1919–1991), a native of Fort Worth and himself an artist, began collecting in 1936. He was greatly influenced by the early traveling exhibitions on display at the Carnegie Public Library in Fort Worth. Eventually dividing his time between New York City and Fort Worth, he became an important conduit in an active and ongoing dialogue between the art scenes in those two cities. Bomar owned examples of American modernism, satisfying a particular affinity for works that display an abstracted figurative style, such as Charles Demuth's *Sailors and Girl* (pp. 80–81). Bomar helped further the efforts of a discerning group of collectors and artists in the community who shared his penchant for a modernist sensibility. His collection joined that of his cousin, Reilly Nail, when the Old Jail Art Center in the small town of Albany, Texas, opened in 1980. Twenty-two years later, the collection there houses 1,500 objects and includes works by such luminaries of American art as Thomas Hart Benton, John Marin, and Grant Wood.

Dominique (1908–1997) and John de Menil (1904–1973) began to collect actively after settling in Houston in 1941, the year World War II drove them from their native France. Their wide-ranging cultural interests resulted in one of the most important privately assembled collections of art in the twentieth century. This collection of more than 15,000 objects was made available to the public in 1987, when the renowned Menil Collection opened in Houston. Works from antiquity, world tribal cultures, and twentieth-century European and American modernism are represented in the museum's holdings, as well as masterworks of American photography such as Walker Evans' now classic image, *Floyd Burroughs' Bedroom* (p. 110–111).

Dallas collector Raymond D. Nasher and his late wife, Patsy (1928–1988), brought their premier collection of twentieth-century sculpture to a broad audience as early as 1965, when Nasher developed a shopping center and office complex in Dallas as a showcase for major works from their holdings. Considered the world's most important private collection of modern sculpture, the Nasher Collection ranges from the innovative work of Paul Gauguin and Auguste Rodin at the end of the nineteenth century to works by Alexander Calder, David Smith (pp. 124–125), Claus Oldenberg, and Jonathan Borofsky. Nasher will soon realize a culmination of his ongoing desire to make sculpture a rich experience for the public with the creation of the Nasher Sculpture Center, which is scheduled to open in Dallas in 2003.

Apart from these large and diverse collections, a broad range of masterworks are held privately in Texas as either singular examples of American art or as part of a focused interest. The anonymous lender of Georgia O'Keeffe's *Open Clam Shell* and *Closed Clam Shell* (pp. 88–89) came to know the artist personally and purchased these works from her in 1967. Similarly, Adelaide Fuller (1915–1985), supported by her husband, William (1914–1992), developed an appreciation for the work of Maurice Prendergast, whose work she collected in depth after building a new home in Fort Worth in 1952.[7] The Fullers met and befriended Eugenie Prendergast (1894–1994), the artist's sister-in-law, who shared with them her intimate knowledge of the artist's work and from whom the Fullers acquired the adroitly painted watercolor, *Along the Shore–St. Malo* (pp. 62–63).

It was a sense of personal heritage that influenced the collecting direction of Dr. and Mrs. Harmon Kelley. While visiting a traveling exhibition at the San Antonio Museum of Art in 1986, they discovered the rich scope of African-American art. This had a profound and life-changing impact on them, leading them to establish the Harmon and Harriet Kelley Foundation for the Arts, whose holdings now number over 150 works and include Edmonia Lewis' lovely sculpture *Bust of a Woman* (pp. 38–39). The foundation seeks to redress the absence of African-American art in mainstream institutions and publications by avidly collecting works that convey the spiritual vitality, fortitude, and artistic achievements of African-Americans in the nineteenth and twentieth centuries.

In addition to Texas' extensive record of collecting efforts by individuals, the state's corporate forbears long ago recognized the benefits of commissioning and using artworks to publicize their services. The Great Northern Railway Company's campaign to lure visitors to their lodges in Glacier National Park led to the patronage of artists like Winold Reiss (pp. 108–109), whose imagery proved indispensable to their promotional campaign. Rail giant Burlington Northern Santa Fe, the present-day descendant of Great Northern and now headquartered in Fort Worth, is the steward of a large number of Reiss' beautiful pastels depicting various members of the Blackfoot tribe.

The California Gold Rush led to the establishment of freighting and banking companies like Wells Fargo & Co., which in 1852 began providing dependable financial services as well as reliable transportation of money, information, and goods across the frontier. Today, their corporate collection in Houston comprises an excellent survey of American art and history. Their support of the arts is further evidenced by their generous underwriting of this exhibition.

Corporate collecting expanded in the late twentieth century, encouraged by initiatives such as the nonprofit Business Committee for the Arts (BCA), which was founded in 1967 by David Rockefeller to bring business and the arts together by supporting corporate arts programs. Through BCA initiatives, SBC Communications in San Antonio began collecting in 1985, extending its mission beyond telecommunication to explore art as visual communication. It chose to acquire twentieth-century American art to reflect the changing cultural environment during which the company evolved and thrived. Through its diverse holdings of American art by such masters as Alfred Stieglitz (pp. 68, 70–71), the company endeavors to enrich the lives of both its corporate family and the communities it serves.

Other catalysts began to result in the formation of significant collections in Texas, and scholarship was not the least among them. In 1957, Galveston native Harry Huntt Ransom (1908–1976), University of Texas at Austin's vice president and provost from 1957 to 1961, established the Humanities Research Center at that university. Later renamed the Harry Ransom Humanities Research Center, the center began with the combination of several large rare book and manuscript holdings. Although primarily a collection of works by nineteenth- and twentieth-century American, British, and French writers, the center's mission rapidly expanded to encompass a broader humanities focus. In 1963 the center acquired the collection of Helmut (1913–1995) and Alison Gernsheim (1911–1969), then the largest private collection of historical photography in the world. The Ransom Center was initially interested in the collection as a supplement to its holdings of Victorian manuscripts, primarily because it included a large group of photographs by English photographers like Charles Lutwidge Dodgson, better known as Lewis Carroll. The Gernsheims' interests were broad enough, however, that the collection also included works by major American photographers like Carleton E. Watkins, Edward Weston, and Paul Strand (pp. 40–41, 98–99, and 104–105 respectively). The collection's importance eventually led the Ransom Center to create a separate department for photography, and the growing appreciation for the medium encouraged its continued expansion. Today, the collection contains approximately five million objects.

The stature of the Ransom Center's holdings so impressed Mari Michener (1920–1994), the wife of writer James A. Michener (1907–1997), that it became a deciding factor in the couple's subsequent donation of their large collection of American paintings to the University of Texas' Archer M. Huntington Art Gallery (now the Jack S. Blanton Museum of Art). Originally collectors of Japanese prints, the Micheners changed their focus and eventually amassed hundreds of examples of American regionalist and contemporary art. James, who was fascinated by the parallels between the creative

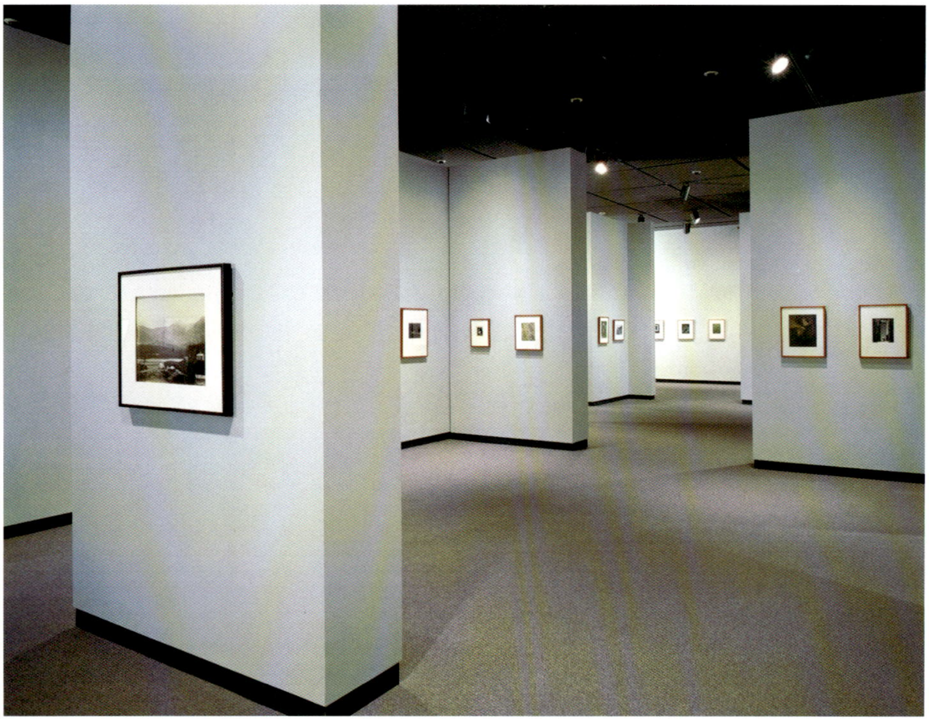

(Fig. 10) Given in memory of Amon G. Carter Jr., the Carter's expanded photography galleries comprise nearly 4,000 square feet.

processes of writing and painting, felt a personal kinship with works that evoked his memories of the Great Depression, which he found aptly reflected in the figurative works of Thomas Hart Benton (pp. 102–103). Although regionalist art was out of fashion when he purchased the paintings, Michener believed the work of Benton and others embodied core American ideals: "It would be difficult for me to describe the impact these men had on me when I was young and grappling with the depression; they gave meaning to what I was experiencing. . . ."[8]

In a similar way, the recently founded Wittliff Gallery of Southwestern and Mexican Photography, located in the Alkek Library of Southwest Texas State University in San Marcos, grew out of a private collection built on scholarship. Screenwriter, photographer, and publisher Bill Wittliff—the founding donor—assembled the collection through his own interest in the photographic culture of the region. This resulted in the creation of the gallery and, because of Wittliff's desire to encourage research, an ongoing series of publications. To further promote such scholarly research, whenever the gallery acquires a photographer's work it also seeks to acquire a large number of images in order to represent the artist's lifework. As an example, the Russell Lee Collection of 366 photographs, which includes the photographer's image of tenant farmers Mr. and Mrs. John Landers (pp. 114–115), came to the gallery through donation by both Wittliff and Lee's widow, Jean.

Considering the attention that is currently given to photography auctions, print fairs, and festivals, it is perhaps surprising to realize that the collecting of photographs in general has developed only over the past thirty years (fig. 10). At the national level, this activity grew during the 1970s in tandem with the rise in popularity of the medium. Photography magazines and monographic publications were established to feed a new public appetite. Universities added photography courses to their programs, and photographers throughout the country began to teach workshops to eager audiences. In Texas, groups of photographers organized "artist spaces," such as the Allen Street Gallery in Dallas in 1975 and the Houston Center for Photography in 1981. Regional camera clubs and associations, like the Texas Photographic Society, were established to serve the need for a sense of community among the growing ranks of photography enthusiasts.

The presence of major photographers teaching at Texas universities served to fuel this growing interest in photography throughout the state. After working for the Farm Security Administration documenting the Great Depression and for the Standard Oil documentary project during World War II, photographer Russell Lee settled in Austin. Lee established the photography program at the University of Texas in 1965, teaching there until his retirement in 1973. He remained an important catalyst to the growth of photography by continuing to serve as a mentor to many young artists in the community until his death in 1986. The photographer Garry Winogrand succeeded Lee at the University of Texas at Austin (1973–78). His photographs of contemporary American life redefined "street photography," or the practice of taking candid photographs of everyday life in the street (pp. 140–141). Like Lee, Winogrand greatly influenced numerous photography students, who then went out to document contemporary society. By instilling in their students a love of the medium, both Lee and Winogrand left a photographic legacy that resonates in Texas today. Though many of these students did not become photographers in their own right, they had learned to appreciate the power of the photographic image so much that they ardently began to collect.

The Texas African American Photography Archive in Dallas, like a number of other institutions in the state, developed its collecting strategy and mission out of a keen perception that some facets of American art were being neglected. Alan Govenar, co-director of the archive, was researching Texas blues for a project commissioned by the Dallas Museum of Art when he realized that the public institutions in the state did not have the kind of photographic documentation he sought. Through further investigation he discovered that while African-American photographers had documented their communities, these bodies of work were scattered and in danger of being lost. He subsequently organized the archive to provide a broad overview of Texas through the eyes of African-American photographers, acquiring most of the collection through donations from the artists and their families. Beyond this, Govenar began acquiring singular works by major African-American photographers in order to provide a national context for the state's photographers. The archives today

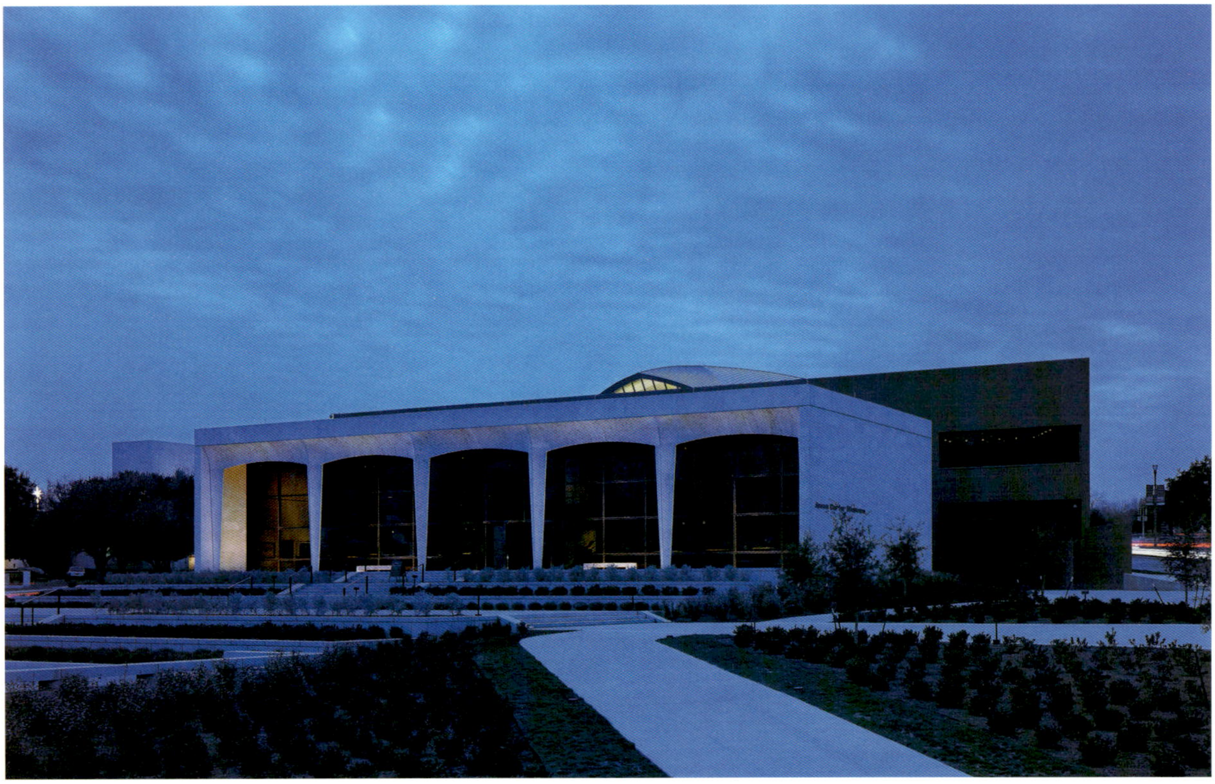

(Fig. 11) The Amon Carter Museum at dusk, 2002.

are home to more than 30,000 photographic negatives and prints, dating from the 1870s to the present, and include J. P. Ball's early daguerreoptype *[David and Mary Wardell with daughter Amelia]* (pp. 32–33).

Ansel Adams, arguably the most well-known photographer of the twentieth century, fed the public's appetite for photography by conducting regular workshops. He taught annual workshops in the Yosemite National Park from 1955 to 1981. He also was instrumental in organizing the Friends of Photography in Carmel in 1967, which became the largest nonprofit photography organization in the world, offering regular workshops to enthusiasts. While several Texas photography collectors met Adams through his workshops and acquired individual works by him in remembrance of those occasions, he figured even more prominently in one collector's acquisition, which grew out of a business relationship. As Adams' ophthalmologist during the 1970s, Joseph W. Gray, the lender of *Aspens, Northern New Mexico* (pp. 130–131), acquired each of the photographer's portfolios directly from him.

Many photography collectors in Texas acknowledge that they learned the history of the medium—and focused their own collecting interests—through regular visits to local galleries. The Afterimage

Gallery in Dallas was among the first galleries to specialize in photography; founded in 1971, it is the oldest continually operating photography gallery in the nation. In the last ten years, numerous galleries devoted to fine art photography have sprung up in the major urban centers of Texas. In 1988 Fotofest, a nonprofit international arts organization located in Houston, presented its first International Month of Photography. This biennial event, during which galleries throughout the city present photographic exhibitions and programs, draws curators, dealers, and photographers from around the world.

Texas is a relatively young state, but from the beginning its citizens have made it a center for the collecting of American art. For 100 years individuals, organizations, and institutions in Texas have shared their passion and knowledge in a mutually beneficial relationship that has served communities throughout the state. Texans are known for their independent spirit and their willingness to take risks. A sense of adventure inspired their love of the pursuit; good instincts and a sharp eye for quality ensured the acquisition of superlative examples. Above all, most had the perspicacity to look beyond their own time in order to bestow their collections on future generations. The individual works in those collections prevail, each embodying the personalities of the maker, the collector, and the times in which they lived.

The old arteries of western expansion are today transcontinental thoroughfares, and the industry of fine art sales is global, conducted from the major urban hubs of the world. In the years to come, as treasures of American art become available, the Amon Carter Museum (fig. 11) will carry on its tradition of acquiring the finest examples from among them and, like the Bowens' portraits, bringing them to Texas. With the same degree of commitment, the Carter will also continue in its mission to make these masterworks accessible to the public through ongoing exhibitions, publications, and an ever-expanding array of programs devoted to the study of American art.

Jane Myers, *Chief Curator*

Barbara McCandless, *Curator of Photographs*

August 2002

1 See Karen J. Blair, *The Torchbearers: Women and Their Amateur Arts Associations in America, 1890–1930* (Indianapolis: Indiana University Press, 1994).
2 Resa C. Oglesby, "History of the Fort Worth Art Association" (master's thesis, Denton: Texas State College for Women, 1950), 191.
3 Elihu Root, quoted in Suzanne Ramljak, "A Brief History of the American Federation of Arts," May 6, 2002, www.afaweb.org/news/history.asp.
4 Oglesby, "History," 32.
5 Clarence Cranmer in a letter to Mrs. Charles Scheuber, June 6, 1936, Amon Carter Museum object file.
6 The last will and final testament of Amon G. Carter, Article XIII, p. 33, Amon Carter Museum Archives.
7 Carol Clark, *American Impressionist and Realist Paintings from the William Fuller Collection* (Fort Worth: Amon Carter Museum, 1978), 5.
8 From the Preface by Earl A. Powell III, in *The James A. Michener Collection: Twentieth Century American Painting* (Austin: University Art Museum, University of Texas at Austin, 1977), xvi.

A Note on the Catalogue

This catalogue is chronologically organized. Photographs are sequenced according to the year when the photographic image was made rather than when it was printed. A work assigned an approximate date (e.g., "ca. 1918") follows one known to have been completed that year; two or more works produced during the same year are alphabetically ordered by artist name. (An exception to this chronological arrangement occurs with the placement of Dennis Miller Bunker's *Portrait of Kenneth Cranford* [1884] before an essay in which two photographs are addressed, one by William Henry Jackson [1881] and the other by Laton Alton Huffman [1884]. Bunker would otherwise have followed Jackson.)

Height precedes width in measurements for paintings, works on paper, and photographs; for works of sculpture, height is provided. The lender information in the cataloguing data appears as stipulated on the lender agreement forms.

Authors' names are abbreviated as follows:

Patricia Junker	PJ
Rebecca E. Lawton	REL
Barbara McCandless	BMC
Jane Myers	JM
Shirley Reece-Hughes	SRH
Rick Stewart	RS

JOHN SINGLETON COPLEY

(Boston 1738–1815 London)

Jabez Bowen, ca. 1771–74
Oil on canvas (29 13/16 x 24 7/8 in.)
Private Collection

Sarah Brown Bowen, ca. 1771–74
Oil on canvas (29 13/16 x 24 7/8 in.)
Mr. and Mrs. Frank A. Ladd

SELF-TAUGHT, COPLEY BECAME THE PREEMINENT PORTRAIT PAINTER of colonial Boston within two decades of beginning his career in the mid-1750s. Born into the working poor, by the time of his departure for England in June 1774 he had become the richest artist in pre–Revolutionary Boston, having painted over 300 portraits in oil and pastel for an elite clientele.

When Copley painted Jabez Bowen's (1739–1815) portrait, his sitter was a prominent attorney in Providence, both politically powerful and well connected. With his marriage in 1762 to the daughter of the shipping magnate Obadiah Brown, Bowen became closely associated with that city's wealthy mercantile class. Copley shows Bowen with one arm draped over a chair back and his other hand tucked into the waistcoat, a gesture that eighteenth-century etiquette books recommended as expressive of "Decency and genteel Behaviour."[1] Here, as in similar portraits, Copley combines a casual pose with a serious expression. He alludes to Bowen's status by placing him within an elegant, imaginary setting that includes a column with drapery. Bowen wears a wig and a suit of fine wool cloth with gold braiding and brass buttons on the vest, attire befitting a man of his profession. Although Bowen could have afforded a more elaborate costume, as a staunch Congregationalist he would have eschewed such ostentation.

In the years preceding the Revolution, Bowen became increasingly supportive of the colonies and eventually served as a colonel of the First Regiment of Providence County. As deputy governor of the colony from 1778 to 1786, he was deeply involved in the state's political and financial affairs. A strong supporter of the Constitution, he was active in securing its ratification. He also was instrumental in founding Rhode Island College (which would become Brown University) and served as its second chancellor from 1785 until his death in 1815.[2]

Like her husband's portrait, Sarah Bowen's (1742–1800) is modest in size but no less compelling than many of Copley's larger, more elaborately staged half-length compositions (p. 29). Her costume is a feast of finely painted, brightly colored fabrics of varying textures set against a somber background. She wears a loose, royal blue velvet gown—trimmed on the sleeve with embroidered gold braid and pearls—over a sheer, white, silk shift edged in fine lace. Billowing around her décolletage is a swath of

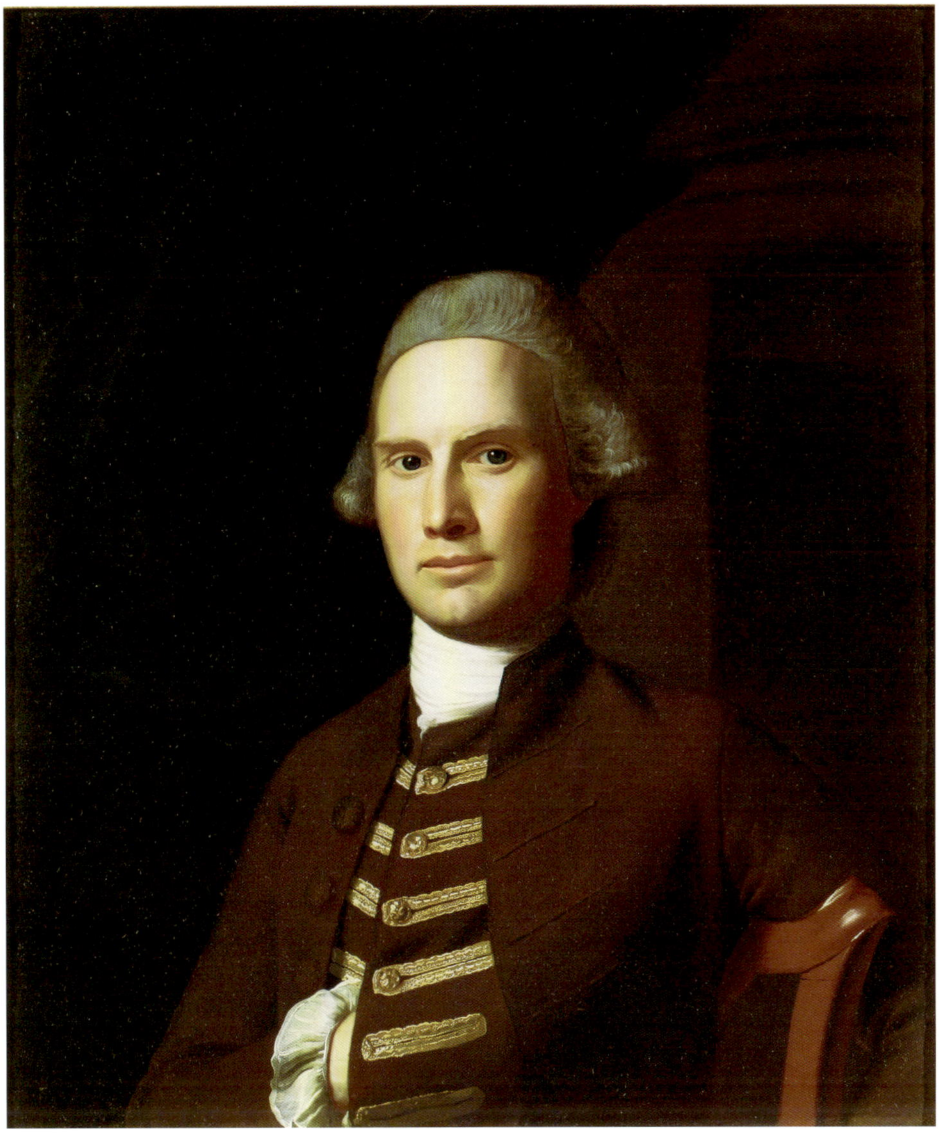

red satin drapery. Her hair is adorned with more pearls and a blue silk scarf that resembles a turban. Copley painted Mrs. Bowen's rather plain face, double chin, and rounded features with considerable care. Like her husband, she is also presented close to the picture plane, directly confronting the viewer. The fine brushwork that models her face helps to create the portrait's striking realism.

Copley may have included the red drapery at her bodice to add color and sculptural volume to her figure. The decision to do so was likely mutual, since he worked collaboratively with his sitters.[3] At the outset of a commission, Copley often engaged his clients by offering them a portfolio of mezzotints and engravings to help them decide how they wished to appear in their portraits. Mrs. Bowen's pose is similar to that of Mrs. Moses Gill in her Copley portrait (1773, Museum of Art, Rhode Island School of Design). It is highly possible that Mrs. Bowen saw Mrs. Gill's portrait in the artist's studio when she came to sit for him and requested to be portrayed in a similar fashion, with the Turkish-like head-dress and whorl of drapery. Like Mrs. Gill, Mrs. Bowen would never have appeared either in public or at home in turquerie, an affectation that established the sitter's affiliation with elite English culture.[4] For Mrs. Bowen, it may also have been a way of equating her status, as a member of Rhode Island's extremely prosperous Brown family, with that of one of Boston's wealthiest and most stylish women.

Although both Bowen portraits share similar compositions, Copley chose not to depict them in the customary eighteenth-century fashion in which the sitters face one another. As portraits, they work together as pendants while also functioning alone—a reflection, perhaps, of the Bowens themselves.

REL

1 Carrie Rebora, et al., *John Singleton Copley in America*, exh. cat. (New York: Metropolitan Museum of Art in association with Harry N. Abrams, Inc., 1995), 264.
2 For biographical information on Bowen, see Dorothy Twohig, ed., *The Papers of George Washington: Presidential Series* (Charlottesville: University of Virginia Press, 1987), 454.
3 Carrie Rebora, "Transforming Colonists into Goddesses and Sultans: John Singleton Copley, His Clients and Their Studio Collaboration," *The American Art Journal* 27, no. 1–2 (1995–96): 17.
4 Paul Staiti, "Character and Class," in Rebora, et al., 67–68.

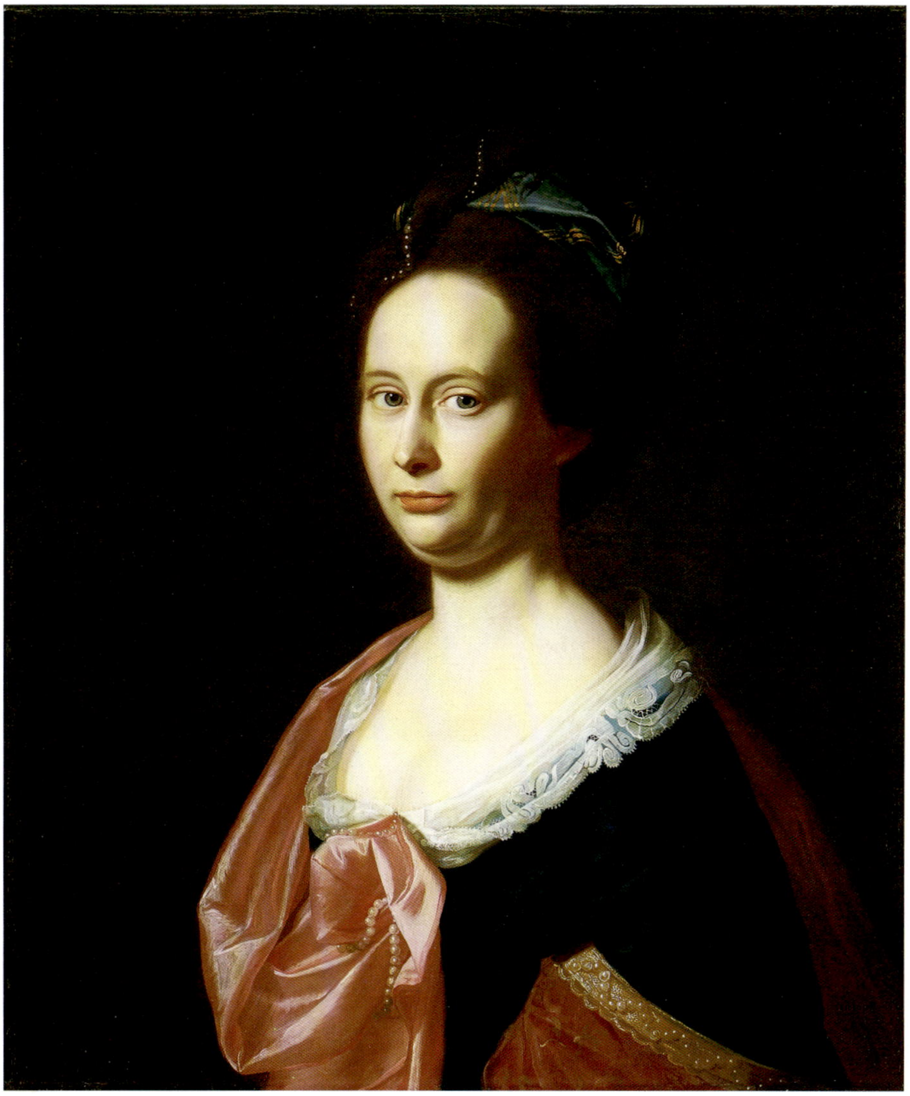

BENJAMIN WEST
(Swarthmore, PA 1738–1820 London)

The Death of the Earl of Chatham, 1778
Oil on canvas (28 1/8 x 36 1/4 in.)
Kimbell Art Museum, Fort Worth, Texas

ALTHOUGH HE WAS CONSIDERED A PAINTER OF DISTINCTION before leaving America in 1760, West's remarkable professional career took root in London, where he worked until his death. It was there that he achieved renown, first with his appointment in 1772 as historical painter to King George III and later, in 1792, as the second president of the Royal Academy.

West's *The Death of the Earl of Chatham* has a complex history.[1] The painting, first recorded by Horace Walpole in 1771 as "a small sketch," had disappeared from public view after its sale in 1829 from the artist's estate, but not before John Singleton Copley (1738–1815) had created a larger version of the same subject.[2] The two paintings are important landmarks in the development of eighteenth-century history painting and of great significance as contemporary documents of Britain's conflicted attitudes toward the American colonies at the height of the Revolutionary War.

This painting portrays a meeting, held on April 7, 1778, in the British House of Lords, during which the lords argued their positions concerning the rebellious colonies. Standing near the center of the composition is the Duke of Richmond, who had just made a speech calling for the king to withdraw his forces and grant the colonies their freedom. The painting's eponymous figure, William Pitt the Elder, Earl of Chatham (1708–1778), is shown collapsed in a chair and surrounded by his son, close friends, and members of his Whig party. Pitt, the architect of Britain's imperial expansion, was known as the "Great Commoner." He was much admired in Britain for his moderate views, and he was popular in the American colonies for his military leadership against the French during the Seven Years War (1756–63). As the elder statesman of the opposition party, he was the king's chief adversary.

West depicts the ailing Chatham moments after he had asserted his belief that for England to sever all ties with the colonies would be a tragedy for the nation and lead eventually to her decline as a world power. The painting's title is slightly misleading, since West did not portray Chatham at the actual moment of death—which occurred about a month after the incident—but rather at his most courageous hour. The painting is a tribute to him, for West shared Chatham's unswerving sympathy for America, as well as his views against its complete independence.

West's treatment of a contemporary political incident was innovative. In this work, the artist presented contemporary life as history painting—a lesson in civic responsibility, moral duty, and honor—without the cloak of antiquity to disguise it. REL

1 Object file, Kimbell Art Museum, Fort Worth, Texas. This essay draws freely from Doreen Bolger Burke, "Benjamin West's *Death of Chatham*," unpublished lecture, Kimbell Art Museum, April 27, 1991.
2 Copley's *The Death of the Earl of Chatham* (1779–81) is in the collection of the Tate Gallery, London, and is on long-term loan to the National Portrait Gallery, London.

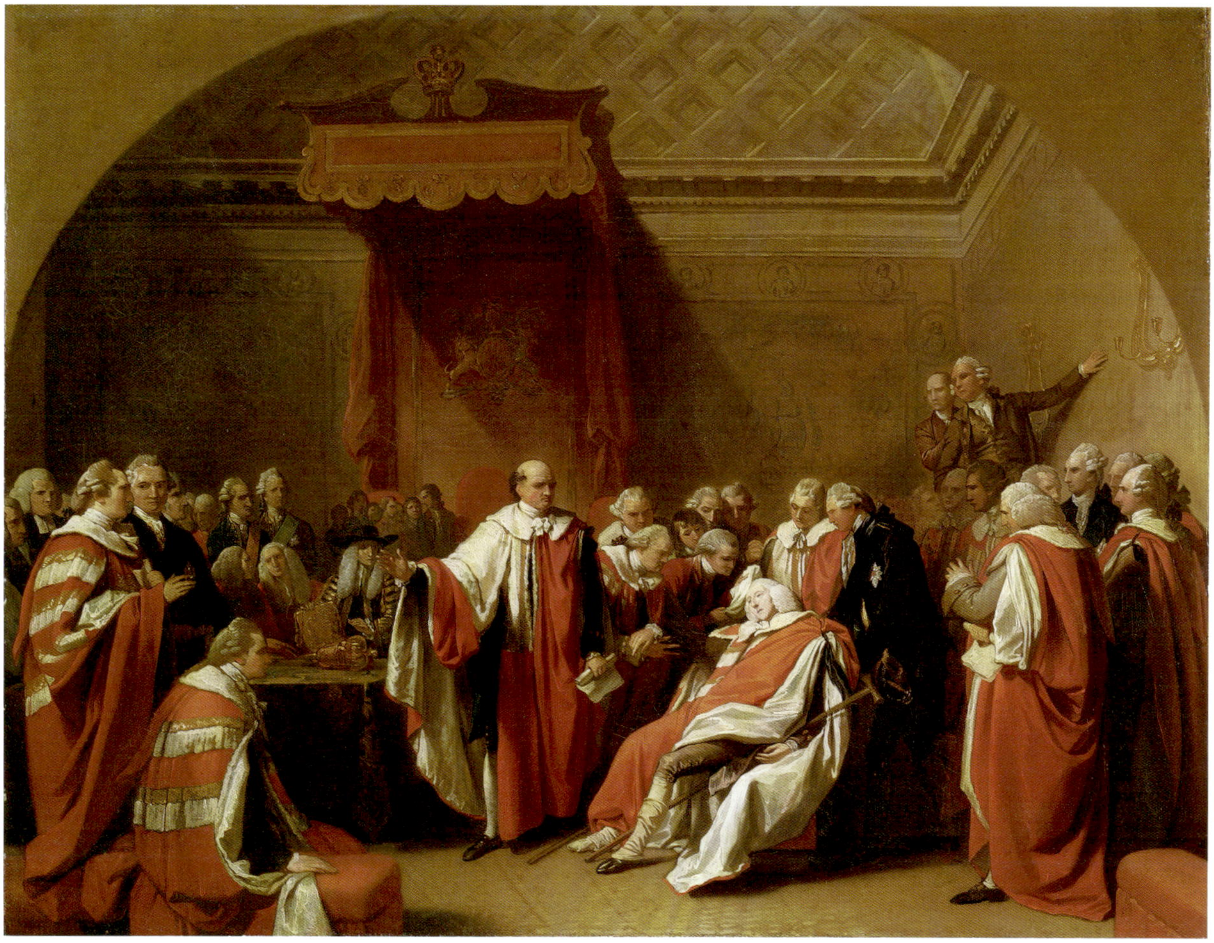

JAMES PRESLEY BALL

(state of Virginia 1825–1904 Portland, OR)

[David and Mary Wardell with daughter Amelia], 1855
Daguerreotype, quarter plate (3 1/4 x 2 3/4 in.)
Texas African American Photography Archive, Dallas, Texas

SITUATED ON THE OHIO RIVER, just north of the Mason-Dixon Line, Cincinnati was simultaneously an important center of trade and abolitionist activity in the 1850s. During this same period, the most elaborate photographic studio in the city was owned and managed by Ball, a freeborn African-American. Choosing to patronize Ball's studio over the fifty other studios in the city was not only a political statement regarding slavery but also the wisest choice in terms of quality.

Ball was born in Virginia and, like many young entrepreneurs of the time, decided to take up the newly developed photographic process as a career. After learning how to make daguerreotypes—the earliest practical form of photography—he moved to Cincinnati in 1847 to open a studio. Although the city was a center for the "free black" population and offered a receptive environment for a young African-American businessman, Ball was unsuccessful at finding clients. He traveled as an itinerant daguerreotypist for two years and then returned to Cincinnati in 1849 to open a second gallery, which became enormously successful.

James P. Ball's Great Daguerrian [*sic*] Gallery of the West was located on Fourth Street between Main and Walnut, a fashionable thoroughfare of the time that was also home to a fairly prosperous free-black community. Ball used this gallery to display nearly 200 examples of his best work, including portraits of celebrities like Jenny Lind and P. T. Barnum, to help attract customers. Also on display were six landscape paintings by Robert S. Duncanson (1821–1872), an African-American artist referred to in the press at the time as the best landscape painter in the West.

Ball's gallery was so successful that the local press also recommended it as the best in the city and reported that its patrons included the area's best families, both white and black. Additionally, reports claimed that "Few go to Cincinnati without paying the daguerrean [*sic*] gallery of Mr. Ball a visit."[1] Although this young family is identified, their names do not appear in city directories of the time. They may well have been traveling through on their way west. BMC

1 Martin Robison Delany, *The Condition, Elevation, Emigration, and Destiny of the Colored People of the United States* (Philadelphia: self-published, 1852; reprint, New York: Arno Press and the *New York Times*, 1968), 118.

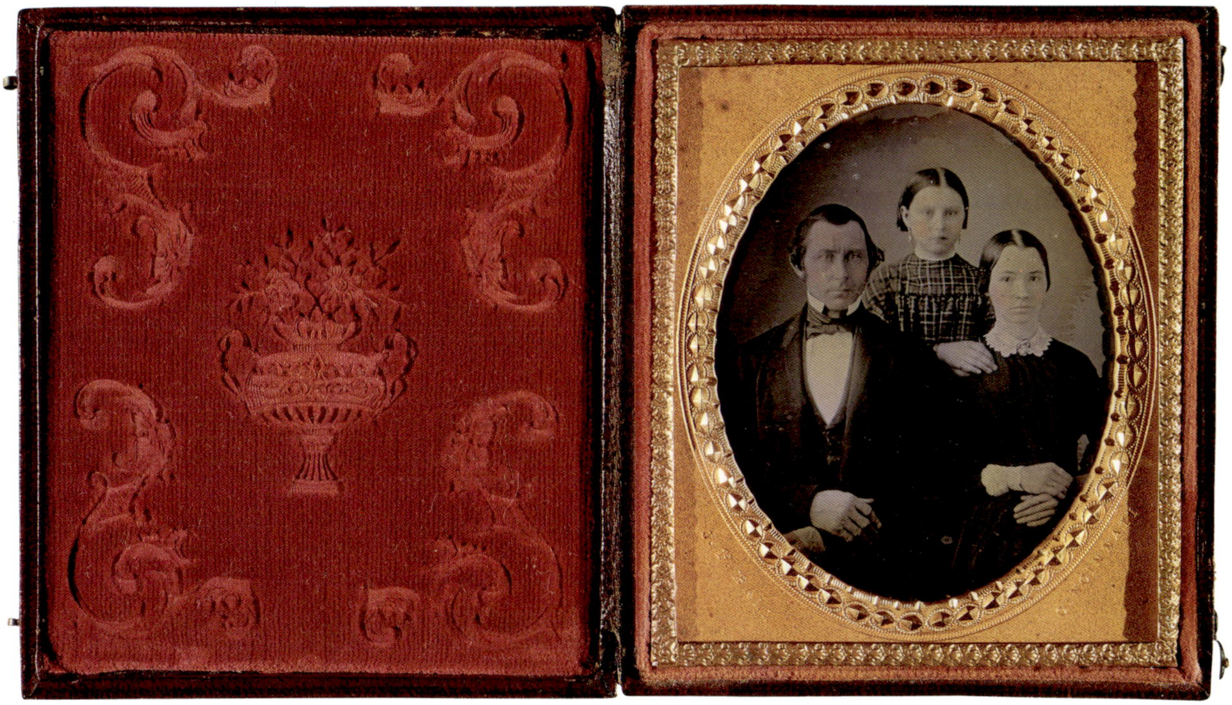

RANDOLPH ROGERS
(Waterloo, NY 1825–1892 Rome)

Nydia, the Blind Flower Girl of Pompeii, modeled 1855–56
Marble (36 in. high)
Signed on capital: *Randolph Rogers / Rome*
Steve and Katherine Hardee

AT THE TIME OF ITS DEBUT IN 1856, *Nydia, the Blind Flower Girl of Pompeii* was one of the most critically and publicly acclaimed neoclassical sculptures of its day. It secured the reputation of Rogers, an American expatriate who had been studying and working in Rome since 1851. Having absorbed the lessons of ancient Greek and Roman statuary, he created striking sculptures, based on literary heroines, that received notable praise. But it was his powerful interpretation of Nydia, a character derived from Edward Bulwer-Lytton's historical romance *The Last Days of Pompeii* (1834), that became Rogers' greatest success.[1]

The sensation of the work was not only a testament to the sculptor's gifts but reflected the popularity of the novel and of Pompeii itself, destroyed by Mount Vesuvius in 79 AD. The volcano's eruption left nearly twenty feet of ash covering the city, the remains of which were partially uncovered in eighteenth- and early-nineteenth-century excavations. In 1833 Bulwer-Lytton toured the ruins and was inspired to create the character of Nydia after his guide commented that it would have been easier for a blind person, rather than a sighted one, to find her way through the dense volcanic ash. *The Last Days of Pompeii* tells how Nydia, a slave girl, saved her beloved Glaucus, whose true affections belonged to the beautiful Ione. When Vesuvius erupted, Nydia led them all through the rubble and darkness but eventually became separated from her companions.

Rogers chose to depict Nydia at this climactic moment. With one hand cupped to her ear and the other on her walking staff, Nydia strains to hear her friends' voices above the din. Rogers eloquently communicates her distress through her concentrated facial expressions, while he conveys her position in mid-stride through the slight tilt of her back foot. As Pompeii crumbles to the ground, represented by the broken Corinthian capital, Nydia courageously advances to find her lover. The modeling of her dress in cursive waves signifies the volcano's heavy winds.

In Bulwer-Lytton's novel, Nydia eventually found her friends and led them to safety. But the next morning, realizing her love for Glaucus would never be returned, she killed herself. Through this subtle yet compelling modeling in white marble, however, Rogers again tells her story, and the frail heroine lives.

SRH

1 For biographical information on Rogers, see Millard F. Rogers, *Randolph Rogers: American Sculptor in Rome* (Amherst: University of Massachusetts Press, 1971).

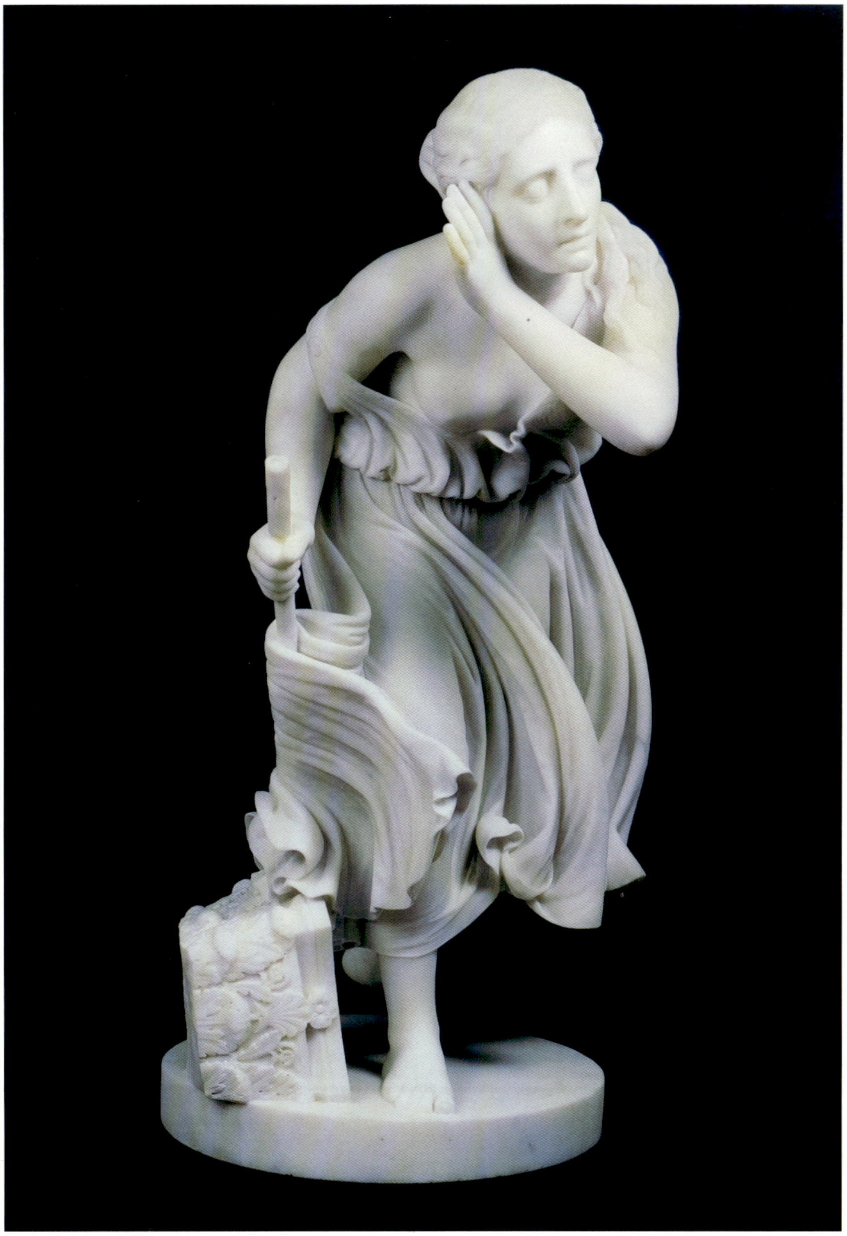

FITZ HUGH LANE

(Gloucester, MA 1804–1865 Gloucester, MA)

Sunset at Gloucester Harbor, 1858
Oil on canvas (30 x 50 1/8 in.)
Signed and dated lower right: *F. H. Lane, / Gloucester, Mass. / 1858*
Private Collection

THE HARBOR VIEWS LANE PRODUCED in the decade preceding the Civil War are distinguished not only for their historical importance as emblems of New England's maritime tradition but also for their stylistic significance as hallmarks of mid-nineteenth-century luminism. Before resettling in his native Gloucester, Massachusetts, in 1849, Lane had painted picturesque views of Boston's North Shore. His depictions of Cape Ann's industrious harbors and rock-strewn inlets reflect his interest in topography and background in lithography, as well as his familiarity with the work of marine painters such as Robert Salmon (1775–after 1858). Evident in these canvases are the themes and formal attributes of traditional maritime subjects, which Lane increasingly refined throughout the 1850s. As his aesthetic concerns evolved, his paintings exhibited greater clarity and balance. By the end of the decade, his personal vision had coalesced into a number of eloquent masterpieces, including *Sunset at Gloucester Harbor*, one of the largest and most sophisticated of all his harbor views.[1]

In its pictorial structure, this painting is among the sparest of Lane's works from the late 1850s. The scene is more general in location than in most of his paintings portraying the transitional hours of the day. Here, two distinct and vastly different types of watercraft—a small workboat and a full-rigged merchant ship—figure prominently in the middle ground, while the foreground is empty and only a trace of the distant shoreline is visible. An assortment of other vessels is present, but here they punctuate the composition as subtle notes of color, rather than provide anecdotal detail. The sky, occupying fully two-thirds of the canvas, is composed of thinly painted layers of carefully nuanced pink and lavender tints through which a vivid yellow sun descends toward the horizon.

As in all Lane's paintings, his exacting knowledge of ship architecture is registered in his deft handling of the three-masted ship and the small fishing boat. Sailors on both vessels can be observed, yet their actions seem insignificant, for here the artist's remarkable articulation of light and orchestration of color stand as the painting's major elements. While Lane has ostensibly presented a scene in which sailors make ready for the evening tides, his overarching subject is the sheer radiance and utterly compelling beauty of an ephemeral moment. REL

1 For biographical information on Lane, see John Wilmerding, *Paintings by Fitz Hugh Lane* (Washington, D.C.: National Gallery of Art in association with Harry N. Abrams, Inc., New York, 1988).

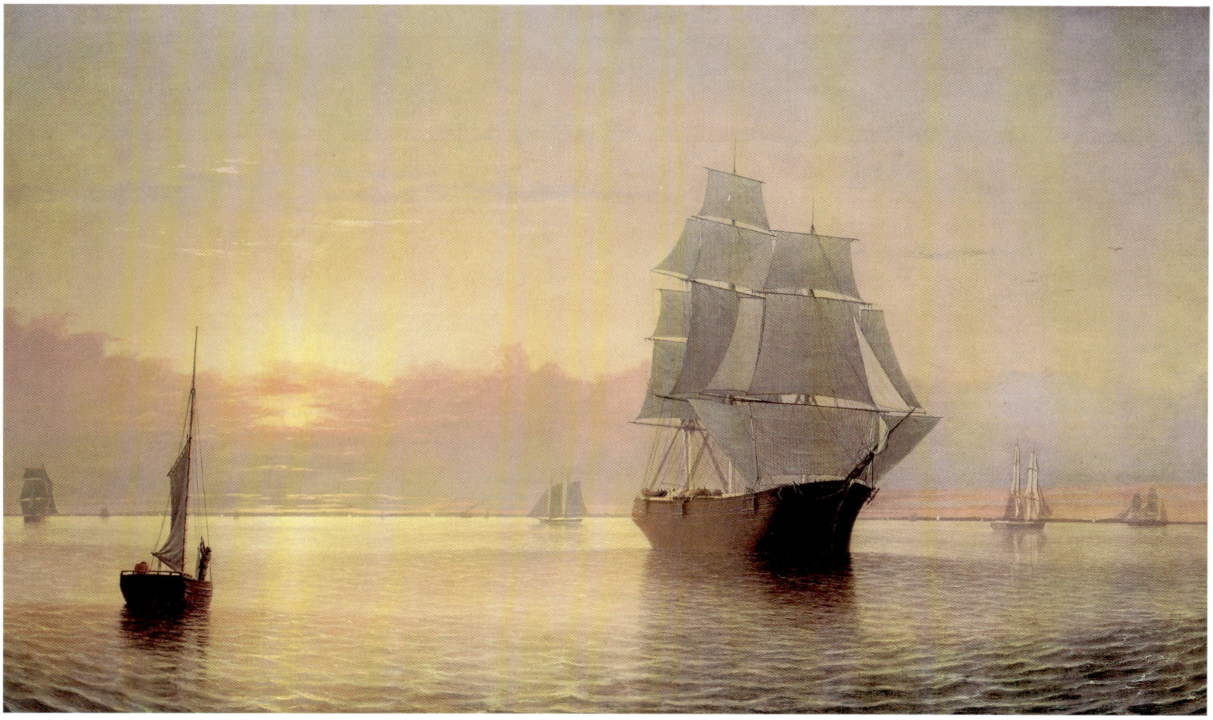

EDMONIA LEWIS

(Greenbush, NY ca. 1840–after 1909 unknown)

Bust of a Woman, 1867
Marble (27 in. high)
Signed on base, reverse: *EDMONIA LEWIS / F[ecit à Roma] 1867*
The Harmon and Harriet Kelley Foundation for the Arts

AMERICA'S FIRST PROMINENT AFRICAN-AMERICAN SCULPTOR, Lewis arrived in Boston in 1863, the year the Emancipation Proclamation was signed by President Abraham Lincoln. Moving from Ohio, where she had attended Oberlin College—an institution that welcomed black students and was the first American college to admit women—she came bearing an introduction to William Lloyd Garrison (1805–1879), one of the country's most vocal opponents of slavery. Boston's importance as a center for abolitionist activity made it a likely destination for Lewis. Garrison's influential antislavery newspaper, *The Liberator,* had been published in Boston since 1831. Black citizens enjoyed the right to vote there, and, contrary to Victorian custom, female abolitionists were encouraged to play active political roles outside the home.

Without the benefit of formal training, Lewis learned the sculptor's craft, producing portraits, relief medallions, and busts. She deliberately selected subjects among prominent white Bostonians, including Colonel Robert Gould Shaw, killed in 1863 while leading his African-American 54th Massachusetts Regiment in an assault on a Confederate stronghold near Charleston, South Carolina. Among the area's abolitionist sympathizers was a circle of white women who warmly received Lewis' work, having taken it upon themselves to assuage the difficulties encountered by blacks by supporting their educational and creative pursuits. The unidentified sitter of this bust is likely one of those women.[1]

The inscription on this work indicates the figure was carved after Lewis' 1865 move to Rome, the destination for other expatriate American sculptors of the era. Lewis carved the sitter's soft features, elegant coiffure, and gracefully arranged drapery to achieve a somewhat generalized treatment that both idealizes and ennobles the figure. These attributes characterized the neoclassical style that prevailed throughout the mid-nineteenth century, particularly in Boston, where its reference to ancient classical models was popular with collectors who sought to convey their endorsement of democratic principles, advanced education, and genteel taste. Such benefactors were also drawn to Lewis' narrative figural sculptures, which typically addressed the emancipation of the slaves and themes from Henry Wadsworth Longfellow's epic poem *The Song of Hiawatha* (1855). Although the popularity of neoclassical sculpture declined during the 1870s and Lewis' later years are cast in shadow, the Catholic Church, to which Lewis had converted following her move to Italy, helped the artist continue her vocation through commissions for religious sculpture.

JM

1 I am grateful to Marilyn Richardson for information on Lewis' life and work. See Richardson's "Taken from Life: Edward M. Bannister, Edmonia Lewis and the Memorialization of the 54th Massachusetts Regiment," in Martin H. Blatt, et al., *Hope & Glory: Essays on the Legacy of the 54th Massachusetts Regiment* (Amherst: University of Massachusetts Press in association with Massachusetts Historical Society, 2001).

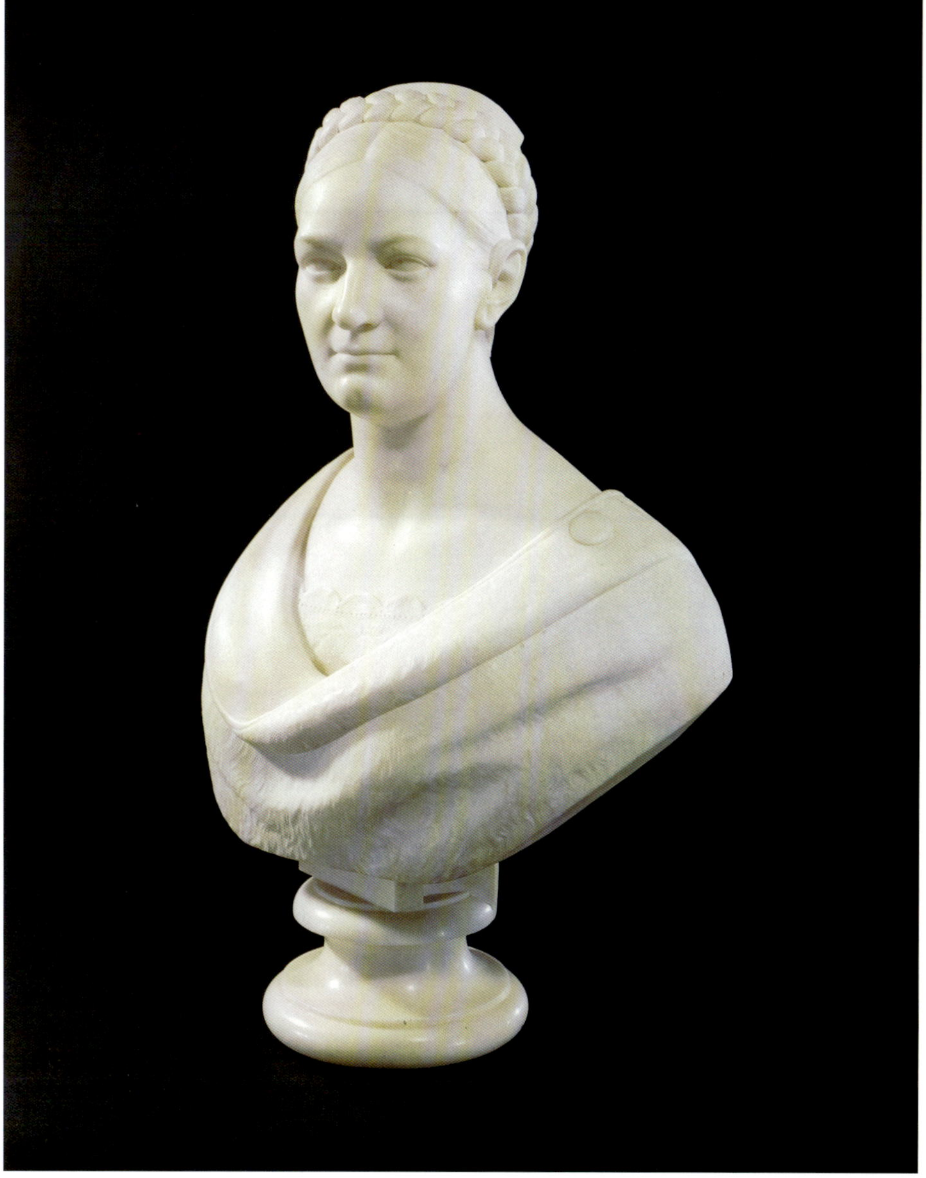

CARLETON E. WATKINS
(Oneonta, NY 1829–1916 Imola, CA)

Mount Hood from The Dalles Oregon, 1867
Albumen silver print (15 5/8 x 20 9/16 in.)
Inscribed on mount at bottom: *Mount Hood from the* [*sic*] *Dalles Oregon*
Gernsheim Collection, Harry Ransom Humanities Research Center, The University of Texas at Austin

IN THE YEARS FOLLOWING THE CIVIL WAR, PHOTOGRAPHERS set out to record the breadth and wonders of the nation. Watkins made his reputation with large-scale landscapes of the Yosemite Valley area in 1861, and in the years following he achieved great prominence for his skill and artistic eye. Wishing to expand his stock of both mammoth-plate views like this one and smaller stereographic views, he made his first photographic trip outside of central California in 1867 to depict the area along the Columbia River.[1] Since the river was navigable for several hundred miles, it was an important economic component of the Northwest. The Oregon Steam Navigation Company held a transportation monopoly on both riverboats and portage railways around the rapids. Watkins may have received some sponsorship from this company since most of his photographs were made along the river and rail routes.

Arriving in Portland, Oregon, in mid-July, Watkins began a four-month stay in the region. By late September, after traveling upstream by steamboat, the photographer arrived at The Dalles, a longtime trading center on the Columbia River where a recently completed, thirteen-mile railroad provided a portage route around the treacherous waters between there and Celilo Falls. He made this photograph looking southwest toward Mt. Hood, the highest peak in Oregon. The strong lines of the horizon and the diagonals of the railroad tracks and the dark basalt cliff on the left create a simple triangular composition that emphasizes the vast empty space of the West. Only the central focal detail of the white house hints at the impending arrival of settlement and expansion.

Although Watkins usually traveled and photographed alone, there is evidence in this image that suggests he may have used an assistant. The collodion negative process Watkins employed for these mammoth-plate landscapes required an exposure of up to half an hour. Thus, anything in motion would not be recorded. Here, however, barely visible below the house, there is a ghost image of a man walking on the tracks. He must have stopped for a time while Watkins exposed the image. Since the stereographs Watkins produced in this area were made from a lower elevation, it is possible that while he produced this large view, an assistant was making small views and had momentarily stopped far below in the valley to take directions from Watkins. BMC

1 For biographical information on Watkins and his work in the Columbia River region, see James Alinder, ed., *Carleton E. Watkins: Photographs of the Columbia River and Oregon* (San Francisco: Friends of Photography, Inc., 1979).

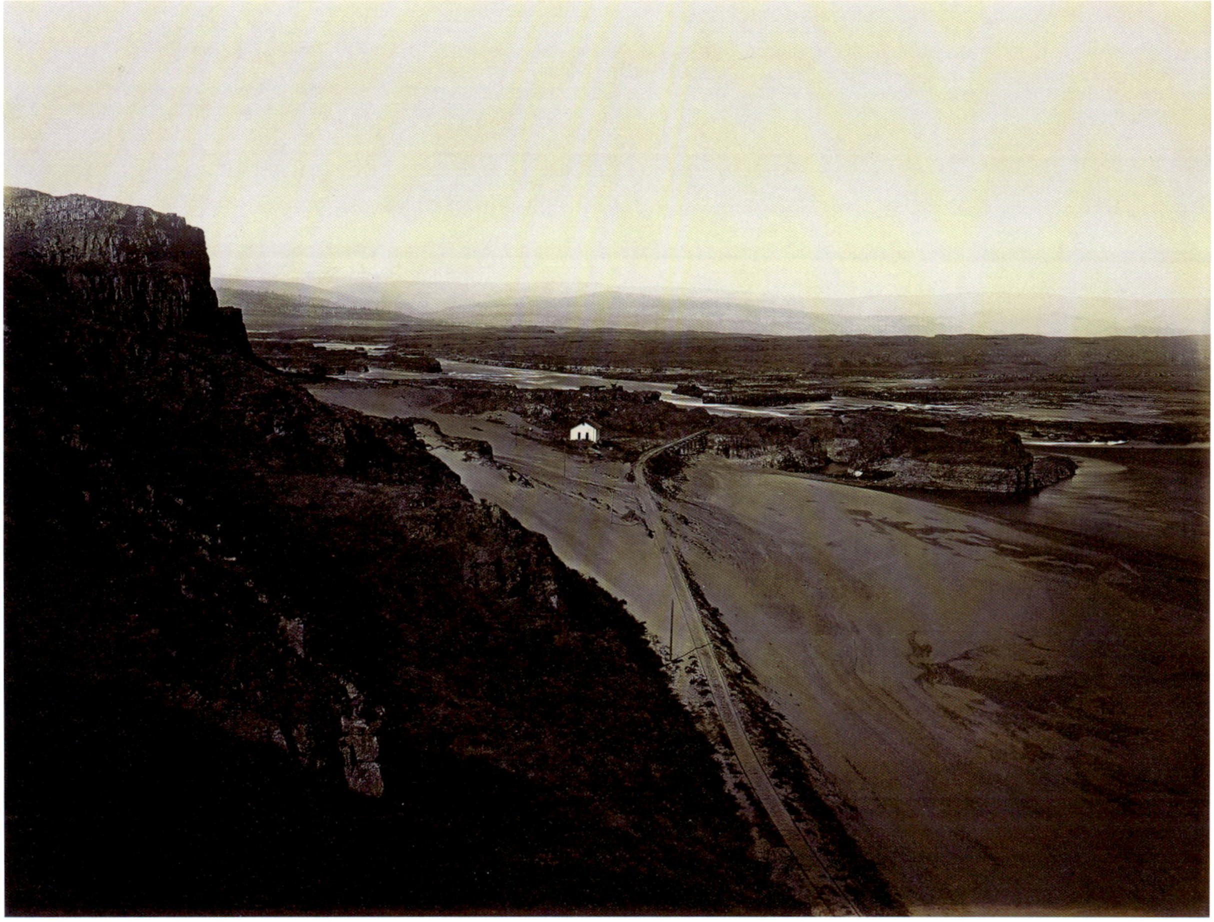

GEORGE INNESS

(Newburgh, NY 1825–1894 Bridge of Allan, Scotland)

The Approaching Storm, 1875
Oil on canvas (19 1/2 x 29 1/2 in.)
Signed and dated lower right: *G. Inness 1875*
Modern Art Museum of Fort Worth, Purchase by public subscription in 1904

In June 1875 Inness joined a long line of artists who had been sketching the spectacular scenery of the White Mountains since the early nineteenth century. *The Approaching Storm* is a view of the eastern slope of Moat Mountain from the Intervale at North Conway, New Hampshire, with the Saco River at right. One of at least twenty-five identified White Mountain subjects Inness developed at North Conway, this work captures the elusive moments of climatic change.[1] In marked contrast to the pictorial conventions of landscape painting that portray the area as an agrarian paradise, Inness presents it here as a place dominated by climate and weather. His greatest concern in this painting was not to describe a specific place, but to use color and brushwork to recreate visual phenomena. His primary interest was in the artistic effects he could achieve to convey light's effect on the landscape.

Inness posited the proto-modern idea that the role of the artist was not to mimic nature but to manipulate it in order to evoke emotions. The verdant plains of the Intervale, with its conjunction of fields, streams, and mountains, as well as its fugitive weather, offered the artist an ideal location to reinterpret nature in a modern way. By incorporating the vignette of the artist sitting at his easel, Inness engaged the trope of the artist in nature. Yet here, Inness presents himself at work *with* nature, almost tucked into it, oblivious to the threatening sky and most likely unaware of the woman approaching him. One scholar has commented that Inness' White Mountain landscapes appear "as though nature was not merely observed, but internalized and artistically reconstituted."[2] This canvas may be the painting described in *Appleton's Journal* in September 1875 in which there appear "great masses of cloud and vapors that precede the mountain storms, which, descending the upper ridges of the mountain, settle down toward the valley below, and wrap its huge shoulders in obscurity and gloom."[3]

As the first painting purchased by the people of Fort Worth for what was then the Carnegie Public Library, *The Approaching Storm* is a landmark in Texas' cultural history. The painting debuted in the city on loan from a Boston dealer as part of an exhibition held in April 1904 to raise book funds.[4] Although the library included an art gallery, it lacked both a collection and an organization to administer it. The purchase of Inness' painting inaugurated the gallery and initiated the Fort Worth Art Association, the precursor of what is today the Modern Art Museum of Fort Worth. REL

1 Leroy Ireland, *The Works of George Inness: Illustrated Catalogue Raisonné* (Austin: University of Texas Press, 1965), 175–193.
2 Nicolai Cikovsky Jr., *George Inness* (New York: Harry N. Abrams, Inc., in association with the National Museum of American Art, Smithsonian Institution, 1993), 79.
3 "The Arts," *Appleton's Journal* 14 (September 18, 1875), 376; quoted in Nicolai Cikovsky Jr. and Michael Quick, *George Inness*, exh. cat. (Los Angeles: Los Angeles County Museum of Art, 1985): 132.
4 Fourth Annual Report 1904–05, Carnegie Public Library, Fort Worth Public Library Files. Photocopy in object record, Modern Art Museum of Fort Worth.

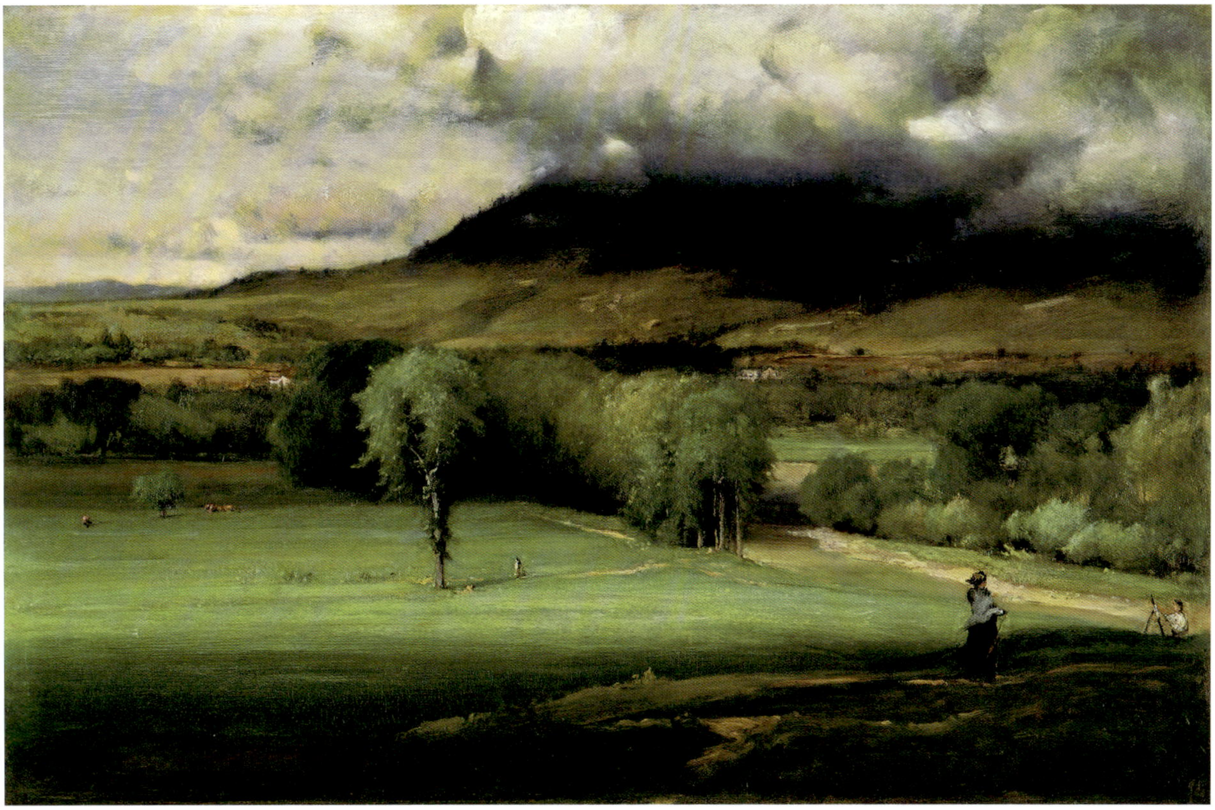

JOHN K. HILLERS

(Hanover, Germany 1843–1925 Washington, D.C.)

"Wolpi," One of Moqui Towns, 1876
Albumen silver print (10 x 13 in.)
Melba and Ted Whatley

HILLERS FIRST LEARNED PHOTOGRAPHY IN 1871 WHILE WORKING as a boatman on one of the four great United States geological surveys, John Wesley Powell's Exploration of the Colorado River. After serving as an assistant for chief photographers E. O. Beaman and James Fennemore, Hillers became chief photographer for the August 1872 excursion. It was during this survey that he made a side trip from the Grand Canyon to photograph Hopi villages in what is now northeast Arizona, returning to photograph them again that winter and in the summer of 1875.

At the time Hillers visited the area, there were seven villages built on top of three mesas. The Hopi had originally settled at the base of the mesas during droughts in the thirteenth century because springs along the escarpment made it possible to farm the land at the base. However, following the 1680 Pueblo revolt against the Spanish, they moved their villages to the tops of the mesas to avoid attacks. The easternmost mesa, called First Mesa, held three villages. The first was the Tewa village Hano, which was followed by the two Hopi villages of Sichomovi and Walpi (often spelled "Wolpi" in the nineteenth century) at the mesa's tip.

After returning to Washington, D.C., in the fall of 1875, Hillers began to prepare a display of the Powell Survey photographs for the Centennial Exposition, held in Philadelphia the following year. However, he realized that he did not have enough views of the Hopi pueblos, so he returned to the West with a survey team in January 1876. It was on this trip that he took this view of the sheep pens on the terraces below the mesa.

The exhibition of Hillers' survey images, along with others made by photographer William Henry Jackson (1843–1942) during the Hayden Survey of the Western Territories, appeared in the Government Building at the exposition, along with an original copy of the Declaration of Independence. The display brought wide recognition to both artists, establishing them as the leading photographers of both Native Americans and the West.[1] BMC

1 For biographical information on Hillers, see Don Fowler, *The Western Photographs of John K. Hillers: "Myself in the Water"* (Washington, D.C.: Smithsonian Institution Press, 1989).

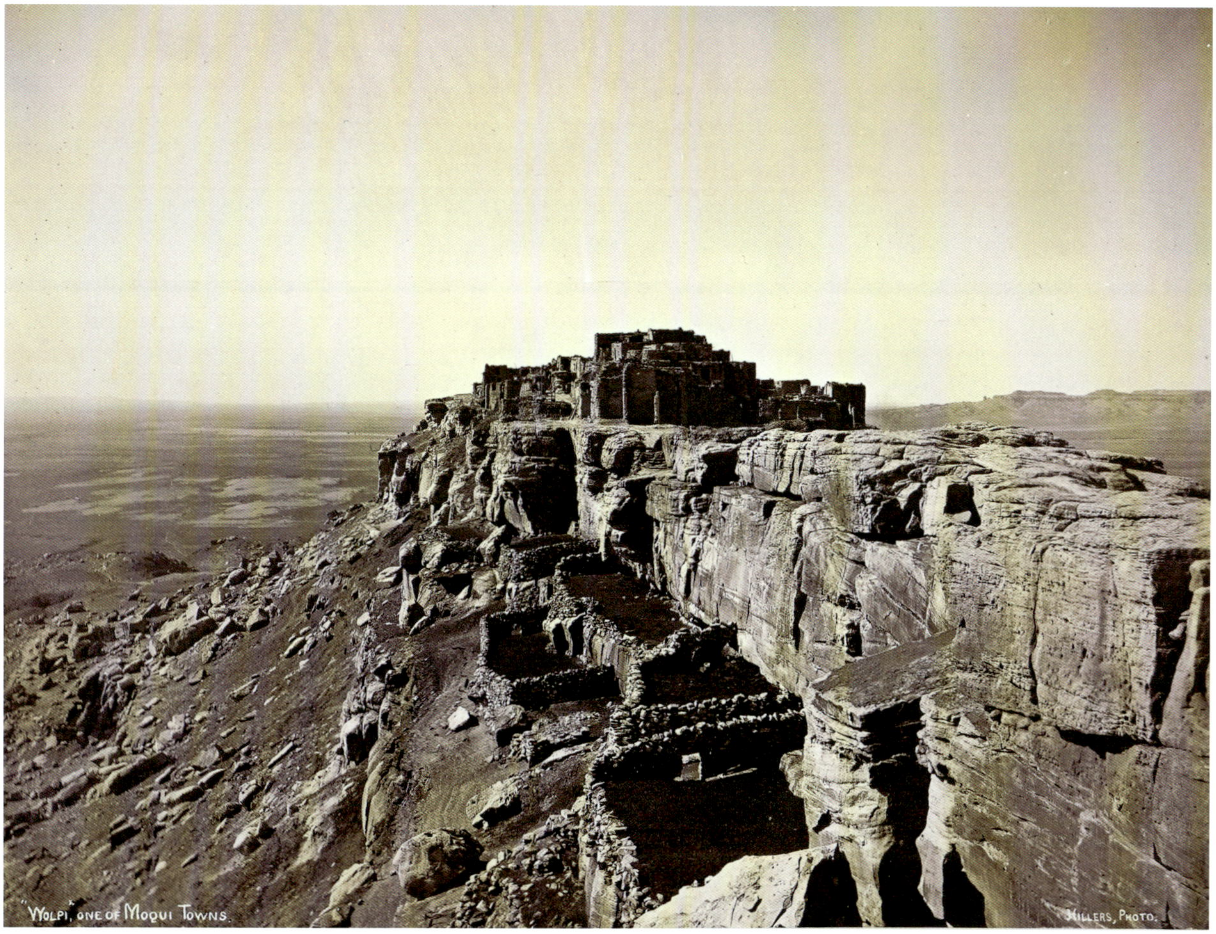
"WOLPI," ONE OF MOQUI TOWNS.
HILLERS, PHOTO.

JOHN SINGER SARGENT

(Florence 1856–1925 London)

Young Man in Reverie, probably 1880
Oil on canvas (30 x 24 in.)
Signed and dated lower right: *John S. Sargent / 1876*
The Hevrdejs Collection

SARGENT MAY HAVE ERRED, AS HE DID ON OCCASION, when he dated this canvas before it left his London studio. His biographer, Charles Merrill Mount, recorded the picture as *Study of a Man,* dated 1880.[1] One scholar, discerning Sargent's interest in the *plein-air* effects of outdoor painting, assigns the picture to 1878, executed during a summer holiday in Naples and Capri.[2] The date 1880, however, seems more plausible given the similarities between this painting and Sargent's exquisite masterpiece of 1880, *Fumée d'ambre gris* (Sterling and Francine Clark Art Institute).

Young Man in Reverie exudes a sensuous, dreamy quality without being overtly romantic. The painting is a magnificent drama of light and shadow. When viewed from a distance, the illusion of a vividly three-dimensional figure is made strikingly physical. The palette is overwhelmingly white, making the painting essentially a study of values and the effects of brilliant light upon a variety of tones and textures; in other words, it is less about the subject than about how the subject is *seen*.[3]

Here, a male model leans languorously against a white wall. His torso is plainly cloaked in a dark brown material that drapes over the right shoulder, leaving the left shoulder and arm exposed. To his right is a still life of three jugs. Sargent describes the earthenware pottery with nearly as much interest as he does the figure. The vessels enhance the play of white against white, sparkle with highlights, and add luminous notes of color to the composition. The attention he paid to these objects suggests Sargent's admiration for the Spanish master Diego Velázquez (1599–1660), who included such breathtaking vignettes within his genre paintings.

By the close of 1878, the twenty-two-year-old Sargent had passed the rigorous competition at the École des Beaux-Arts for the third time, achieving a second place, the highest rank yet awarded to an American. The following year, the spirited portrait of his teacher, *Carolus-Duran* (1879, Sterling and Francine Clark Art Institute), appeared at the Salon, where it won an honorable mention. The attention brought Sargent important portrait commissions, including three from the well-connected Pailleron family of Paris. Thus, with his years of arduous training behind him—and before him the promise of further income from portraiture—Sargent was free to travel in search of his own subject matter and poised to make what would become his masterful and indelible mark on the world of art.

REL

1 Charles Merrill Mount, *John Singer Sargent: A Biography* (New York: W. W. Norton & Co., Inc., 1955), 443.
2 Patricia Hills, *John Singer Sargent*, exh. cat. (New York: Whitney Museum of American Art in association with Harry N. Abrams, Inc., 1986), 29–31.
3 Marc Simpson, *Uncanny Spectacle: The Public Career of the Young John Singer Sargent*, exh. cat. (New Haven and London: Yale University Press, 1997), 79–80.

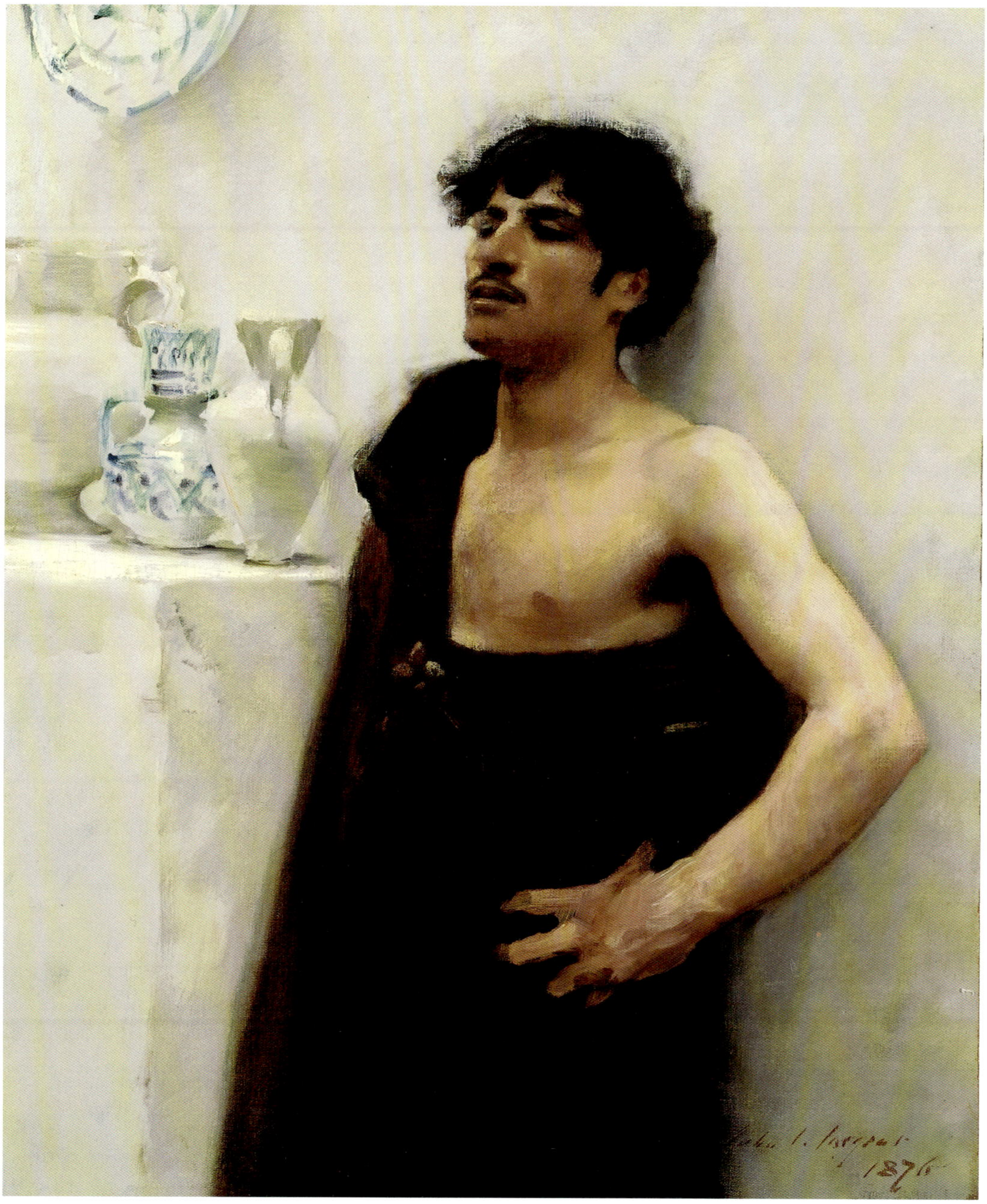

HELEN CORSON

(Philadelphia 1846–1935 Philadelphia)

Uncle Ned and His Pupil, 1881
Oil on canvas (20 1/4 x 26 1/2 in.)
Signed and dated lower right: *H Corson '81*
Wells Fargo

In 1881 Corson married painter Thomas Hovenden (1840–1895), whom she had met while living abroad in the American artists' colony of Pont-Aven on the Brittany coast of France. The two settled in the Corson family home in Plymouth Meeting, Pennsylvania.[1] The house had served as a stop on the underground railroad, and the two artists painted side-by-side in the studio they set up in the adjacent "abolition barn," where Corson's father had, decades earlier, led antislavery meetings of his fellow Quakers. Over the next year, both artists would create charming genre scenes that could have come right from the pages of Harriet Beecher Stowe's *Uncle Tom's Cabin, or Life among the Lowly* (1852).

Before their marriage in June 1881, Corson and Hovenden seem to have announced their personal and artistic bond when that March they entered closely related paintings into the spring exhibition of the National Academy of Design in New York. Hovenden exhibited *Dat Possum Smell Pow'ful Good*, a genre scene featuring old Sam Jones of Plymouth Meeting, an elderly black man who would become a favorite model over the next year.[2] Corson entered this painting, which she titled *Uncle Ned and His Pupil*, depicting another perennially favorite character made popular in a song by Stephen Foster (1826–1864). "Uncle Ned" was firmly established in the popular imagination as the old black slave, and the character appears in paintings of this period by Winslow Homer (1836–1910), Thomas Waterman Wood (1823–1903), and others. Decrepit after years of backbreaking labor and no longer able to see, Uncle Ned has had to lay down both his hoe and his banjo. Here, he listens intently while his young student plays. That the boy is white underscores the powerful, unifying nature of music, a common theme in American genre painting both before and after the Civil War.

As this canvas attests, Corson was as meticulous a realist as her better-known husband, who succeeded the great empirical painter Thomas Eakins (1844–1916) as painting instructor at the Pennsylvania Academy of the Fine Arts. She has rendered every detail carefully, describing each item's texture and character with brilliant clarity, thereby creating a palpable sense of place, time, and mood. The painting studio that Hovenden and Corson came to share in Plymouth Meeting was an elaborate set. In their quest for authenticity in their storytelling paintings, they recreated believable rustic interiors from a collection of props—country furniture, well-used pots and pans, an old banjo—and painted their models in carefully controlled light. PJ

1 Little is known about the life and career of Helen Corson, and biographical information is most easily found in sources on her husband, Thomas Hovenden. See especially Anne Gregory Terhune, Sylvia Yount, and Naurice Frank Woods Jr., *Thomas Hovenden (1840–1895): American Painter of Hearth and Homeland*, exh. cat. (Philadelphia: Woodmere Art Museum, 1995).
2 The painting is in the collection of the Robert Hull Fleming Museum, University of Vermont, Burlington.

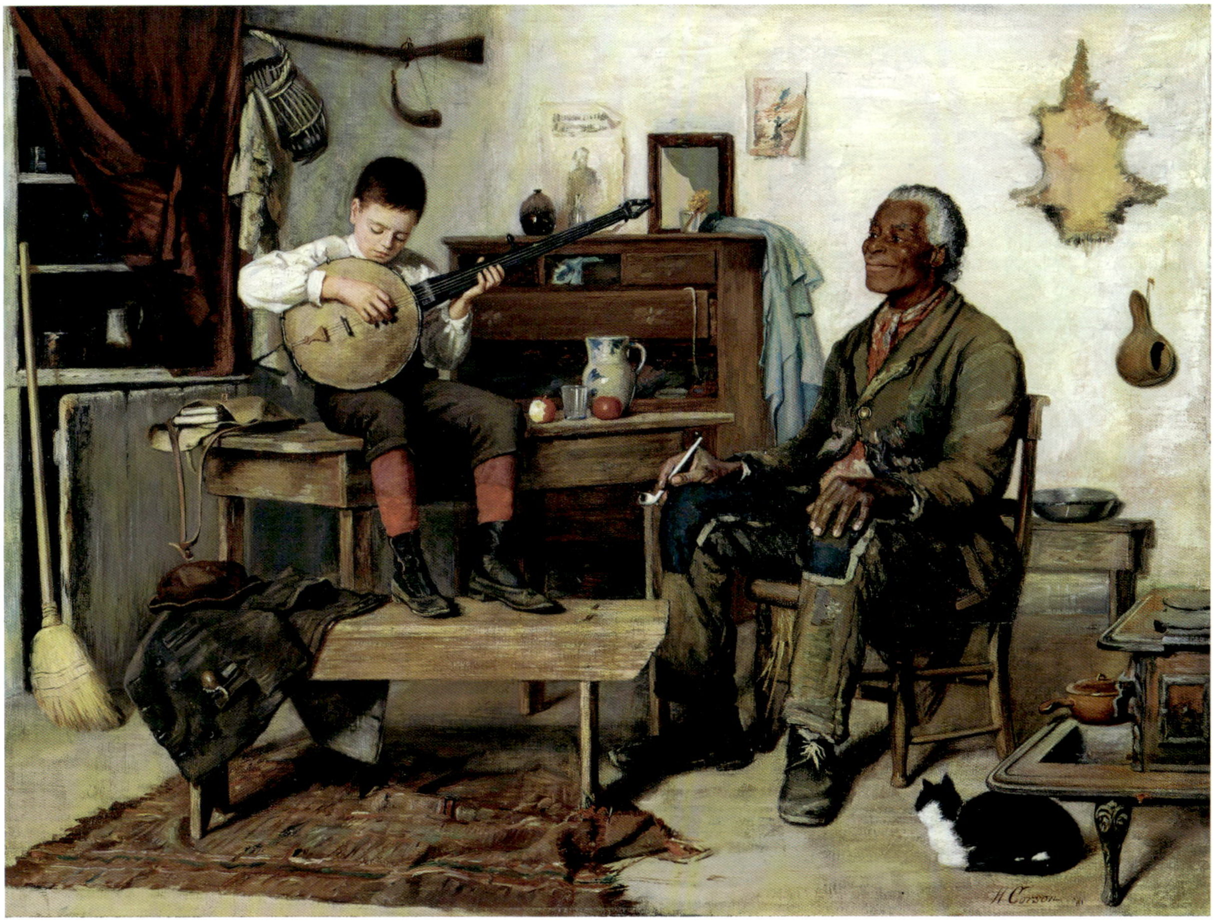

DENNIS MILLER BUNKER

(New York 1861–1890 Boston)

Portrait of Kenneth Cranford, 1884
Oil on canvas laid down on board (16 1/4 x 13 in.)
Signed, dated, and inscribed lower right: *A MON CHER AMI / KENNETH CRANFORD / DENNIS BUNKER / PARIS / 1884*
Graham D. Williford

IN HIS SHORT LIFETIME, BUNKER WAS BRIEFLY AT THE CENTER of America's artistic vanguard. His prodigious talent was admired by eminent teachers—William Merritt Chase (1849–1916) in New York and Jean-Léon Gérôme (1824–1904) in Paris—and a close circle of painter friends, which included the great John Singer Sargent (1856–1925). Sargent's admiration for Bunker's innate talent was surpassed only by his deep affection for the charming and gifted man.

Close bonds that Bunker developed with a group of young artists in the early 1880s greatly affected his art for the decade that he painted; he died at age twenty-nine from spinal meningitis. These friendships inspired sensitive portraits, such as this one of painter Kenneth Cranford (1857–1930), and this "brotherhood of the brush" fostered a spirit of adventure and mutual support that made bold experimentation in painting possible.[1] In the 1880s, Bunker was both a brilliant figure painter in the classical tradition and an early, innovative impressionist.

Bunker befriended Cranford when the two were art students in New York, where Bunker was studying at the National Academy of Design and the newly founded Art Students League. Cranford's departure for Paris in 1882 fed Bunker's increasing desire to study abroad, and he followed his friend to France later that year, enrolling in the École des Beaux-Arts. Their painting forays into the countryside soon tempered Bunker's severe academic style with a freer, looser brushwork and a feeling for light and color that came from painting in the open air.

A breakthrough work in closely harmonized dark color tones, this penetrating portrait was considered by Bunker, at this formative stage in his career, to be "the best thing I've painted."[2] Bunker shows Cranford at ease in his studio, holding his painter's mahlstick in his hand. At upper left is a small oil sketch, one similar to the studies Cranford and Bunker had produced on their painting holidays along the River Oise. It is a sweet tribute to a friend—"A MON CHER AMI," Bunker has inscribed it. It is also a touching display of a remarkable young man's artistic ambitions left largely unrealized.

PJ

1 Erica E. Hirshler, *Dennis Miller Bunker, American Impressionist* (Boston: Museum of Fine Arts, 1994), 30.
2 Bunker in a letter to his friend Joe Evans, November 24–25, 1885, quoted in Hirshler, 30.

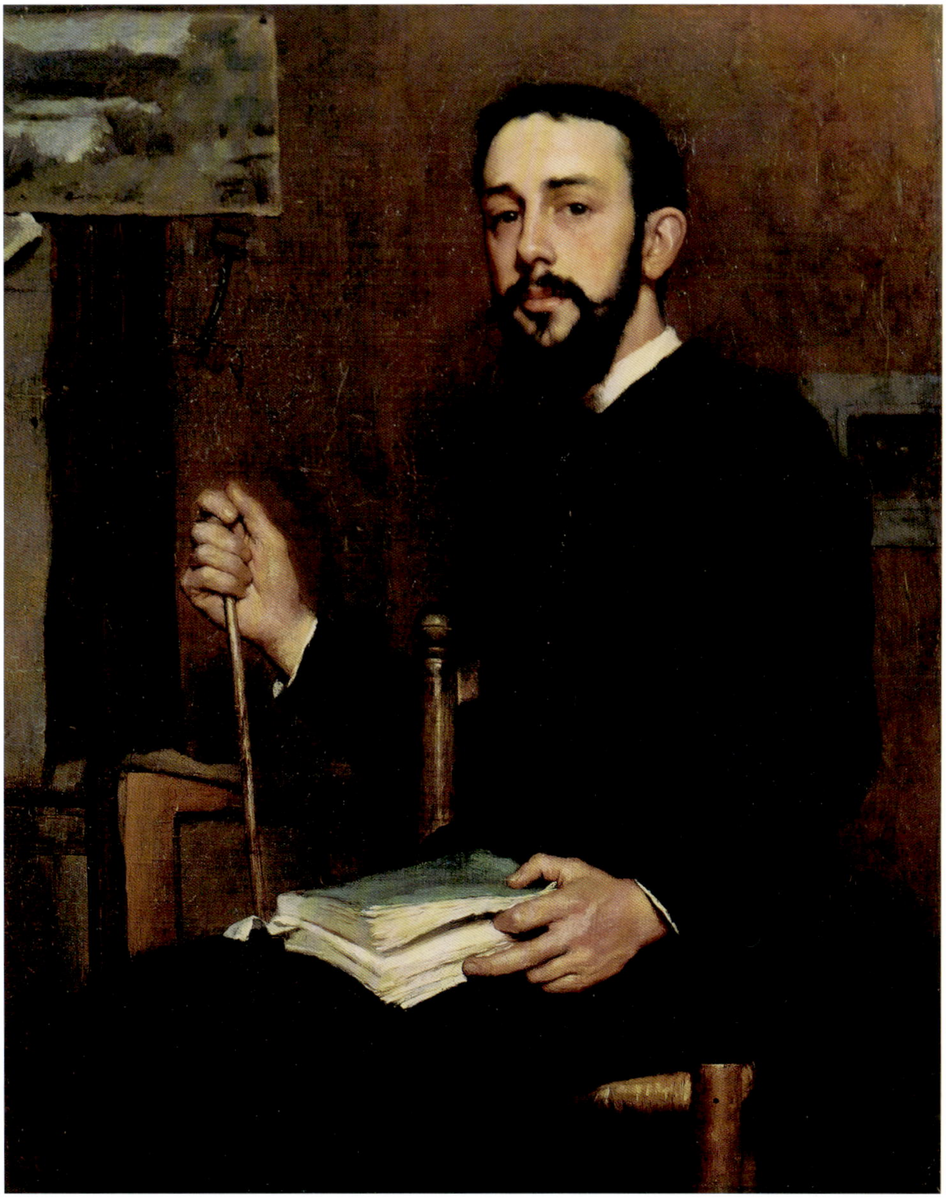

WILLIAM HENRY JACKSON

(Keeseville, NY 1843–1942 New York)

Clear Creek Canon, Colorado, 1881, printed ca. 1899
Photochrom (21 x 17 in.)
Michael H. Marvins

LATON ALTON HUFFMAN

(Castalia, IA 1854–1931 Billings, MT)

Hot Sheep in the Powder River Badlands near Broadus, Montana, 1884, printed 1907
Photogravure (19 3/8 x 25 3/8 in.)
Michael H. Marvins

By the last two decades of the nineteenth century, the West had become relatively tame. Photographers expecting a great adventure instead ended up recording the passing of the wild frontier. In subsequent years, they recast the Old West in nostalgic terms and celebrated the civilized nature of living and traveling in the region.

After working for Ferdinand V. Hayden's United States Geological and Geographic Survey of the Western Territories (from 1870 to 1879), Jackson secured lucrative assignments with railroad companies that wanted to use his scenic views to stimulate travel along their recently completed lines. He moved from Washington, D.C., to Denver, and such work became his specialty. Traveling in a private railcar provided by the Denver and Rio Grande Railway, Jackson could easily capture picturesque views that celebrated the land as a pleasure ground for tourists.

In 1881, on one of the earliest railroad lines cut into the mountains, Jackson made the original negative for this print of Clear Creek Canyon, west of Denver. Ten years earlier, the Colorado Central Railroad—the first railroad corporation in Colorado—laid a single, three-foot, narrow-gauge line up the first thirteen miles of the canyon to the Forks of Clear Creek. In the mid-1870s, two lines were extended west from the Forks, up the North Creek to Central City and up the South Creek to Georgetown. Tracks were laid at the base of a narrow gorge where the granite mountains rise over 2,000 feet on each side, and the stream is compressed to a rapid torrent. The space between the cliffs was just enough for the creek and roadbed. In 1881, when Jackson exposed the negative for this image, every foot of the creek bed in this area had already been scoured by miners in search of gold, though some stragglers remained, still going over the claims.

In 1898 Jackson became a partner in the Detroit Publishing Company and continued to market his earlier images. The company was the only American firm to license the Photochrom process, which produced continuous-tone color renditions of black-and-white images through multiple impressions

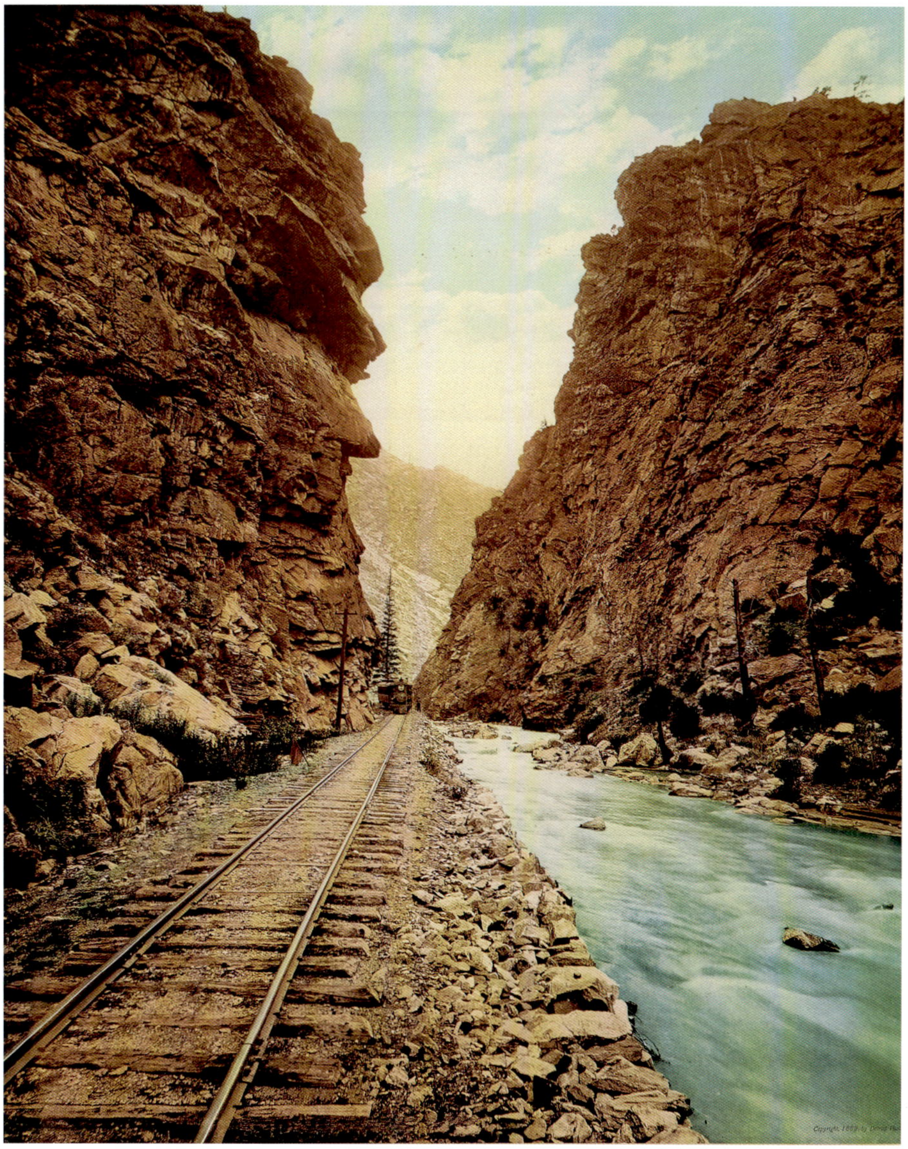

of lithographic stones. A company brochure claimed that "the results combine the truthfulness of a photograph with the color and richness of an oil painting or the delicate tinting of the most exquisite watercolor."[1] By translating his 1881 image into a romantic color scene in 1889, Jackson softened the land's ruggedness and presented it as a playground for railway travelers.

Like Jackson, Huffman first arrived in the West when it was still Indian Territory. He lived well into the twentieth century, marketing his views as documents of an earlier time. Arriving at the Fort Keogh military post in 1878, Huffman became its civilian photographer in 1880 and documented the transition of the southeastern Montana region into Anglo-settled ranching territory. After the railroad arrived in 1881, Huffman established a studio in nearby Miles City, where arriving settlers and adventurous travelers provided sufficient clients to make a photographic establishment viable.

Huffman was not content with remaining in the studio, however, and photographed on the open range whenever possible. In 1884 he began using a single-lens camera that he built himself from a kit ordered from the Eastman Kodak Company. It weighed fifty pounds and used 6 ½-by-8 ½-inch dry-plate negatives. Although the camera was somewhat cumbersome, Huffman was able to use it without a tripod and photograph from horseback, storing the glass negatives in his saddle bags.

Both cattle and sheep ranching had become the primary livelihood of the region by 1884. Huffman owned his own ranch, so he knew the difficulties faced by the ranchers and thus documented specific activities from an insider's perspective. The words "hot sheep" in the title allude to a sheep's reluctance to move in hot weather. "There was an old saying in those days," Huffman wrote, ". . . when natives wanted to compliment a faithful man in any endeavor they would say. . . 'There is a man who can get along with hot sheep.' Hot sheep won't move but each ducked his head under his neighbor and the wise herder would not dog them under those conditions."[2]

After 1905 Huffman ceased making new images and concentrated on producing and selling prints from his stockpile of glass negatives. Like Jackson, he looked for opportunities to update the images, sometimes hand-tinting them and even introducing hand-drawn elements he felt improved the compositions. He translated them into multiple formats, from postcards and packaged sets of smaller views to oversized enlargements, and utilized a variety of print processes to publish larger quantities, including mechanical reproductions like collotypes and photogravures. BMC

1 Jim Hughes, *The Birth of a Century: Early Color Photographs of America* (London and New York: Tauris Parke Books, 1994), 8.
2 Mark H. Brown and W. R. Felton, *Before Barbed Wire: L. A. Huffman, Photographer on Horseback* (New York: Henry Holt and Co., 1956), 217.

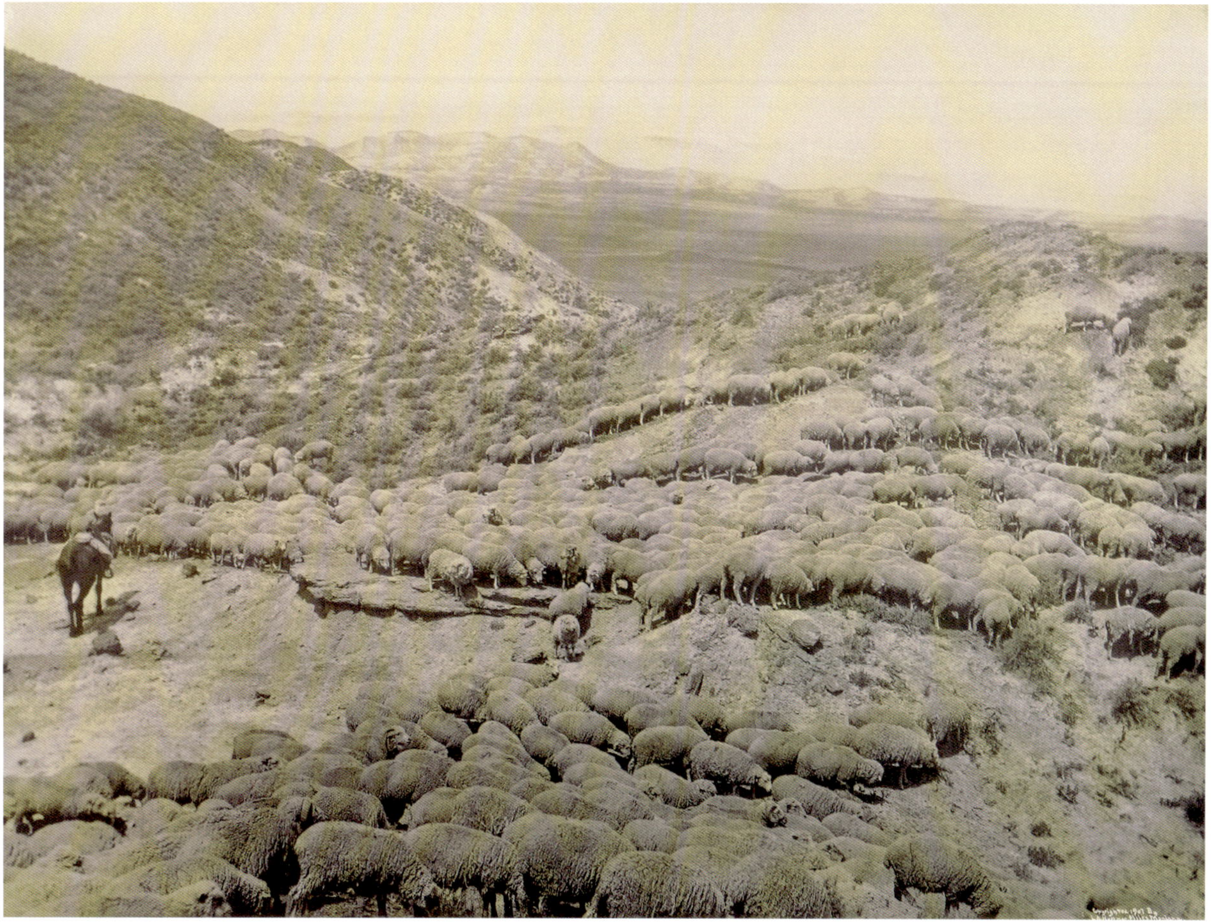
Copyrighted 1907 By

MARTIN JOHNSON HEADE

(Lumberville, PA 1819–1904 St. Augustine, FL)

Passion Flowers with Three Hummingbirds, ca. 1885–1904
Oil on canvas (17 1/4 x 22 1/8 in.)
Signed lower left: *M. J. H*
Courtesy of the San Antonio Museum of Art, purchased with funds provided by the
Robert J. and Helen C. Kleberg Foundation, 82.77

THE STILL-LIFE PAINTINGS HEADE PRODUCED after his third and final trip to Latin America in 1870 are brilliant examples of his innovative approach to the genre. They offer a striking departure from the conventional format for floral pieces by presenting tropical flora in a natural setting, rather than as a static table-top arrangement of cut flowers in a vase.

After returning from Latin America, Heade began a series of works of flowers and hummingbirds that occupied him for the rest of his life. He concentrated on images that combined orchids and hummingbirds, painting only ten known examples that included passion flowers.[1] The Christian symbolism of the passion flower would not have escaped either Heade or his contemporary audience, for the plants were widely cultivated in the nineteenth century and their significance recorded in literature. This painting is particularly unusual in that it features three, rather than two, hummingbirds.[2]

Heade offers a vivid picture of the tropics in this work. The atmosphere is hot and humid, redolent of both decay and sweetness, and the colors set against the verdant foliage are spectacular. His composition expresses the lively interactions of tropical species, highlighting the correspondences between the plants and animals, giving equal weight to each. Heade is at his best when he portrays elements in terms of dualities. He creates dramatic tension by dividing the canvas into two vertical components: the hummingbirds at left and the two large passion flowers at right. He strategically placed the brilliant red-hued flowers along a serpentine vine that twists in a V-shape in the foreground. The beaks of the two hummingbirds on the top branches nearly touch, and the upper bird's wings are in motion as it arcs toward the lower bird. As if echoing the action of the hummingbirds, the two large blossoms follow suit, one curling forward or the other arching back. Heade set his vibrant tableau against a lush, dramatic background in which a passing rain shower descends over a broad sweep of densely forested mountains. The storm reinforces Heade's conceit of presenting nature as transitory.

Heade's images of flowers and hummingbirds express an extraordinary sense of wonder and recreate the experience of discovery for armchair explorers. As Theodore Stebbins has noted, these paintings "seem perfectly private, as if one had stumbled on a privileged sight of breathtaking beauty in an impossibly remote location."[3]

REL

1 Karen E. Quinn, "Passion Flowers," in Theodore E. Stebbins Jr., et al., *Martin Johnson Heade*, exh. cat. (New Haven and London: Yale University Press in association with Museum of Fine Arts, Boston, 1999), 99.

2 Theordore E. Stebbins Jr. has identified the three hummingbirds as follows: the purple bird at left is a purple-backed thornbill (*Ramphomicron microrhynchum*), an Andean species not native to Brazil; to its right is a rufous-crested coquette (*Lophornis delattrei*), also a non-Brazilian species; below them is a ruby-topaz hummingbird (*Chrysolampis mosquitus*), native to Brazil, in *The Life and Work of Martin Johnson Heade: A Critical Analysis and Catalogue Raisonné* (New Haven and London: Yale University Press, 2000), 348.

3 Ibid., 92.

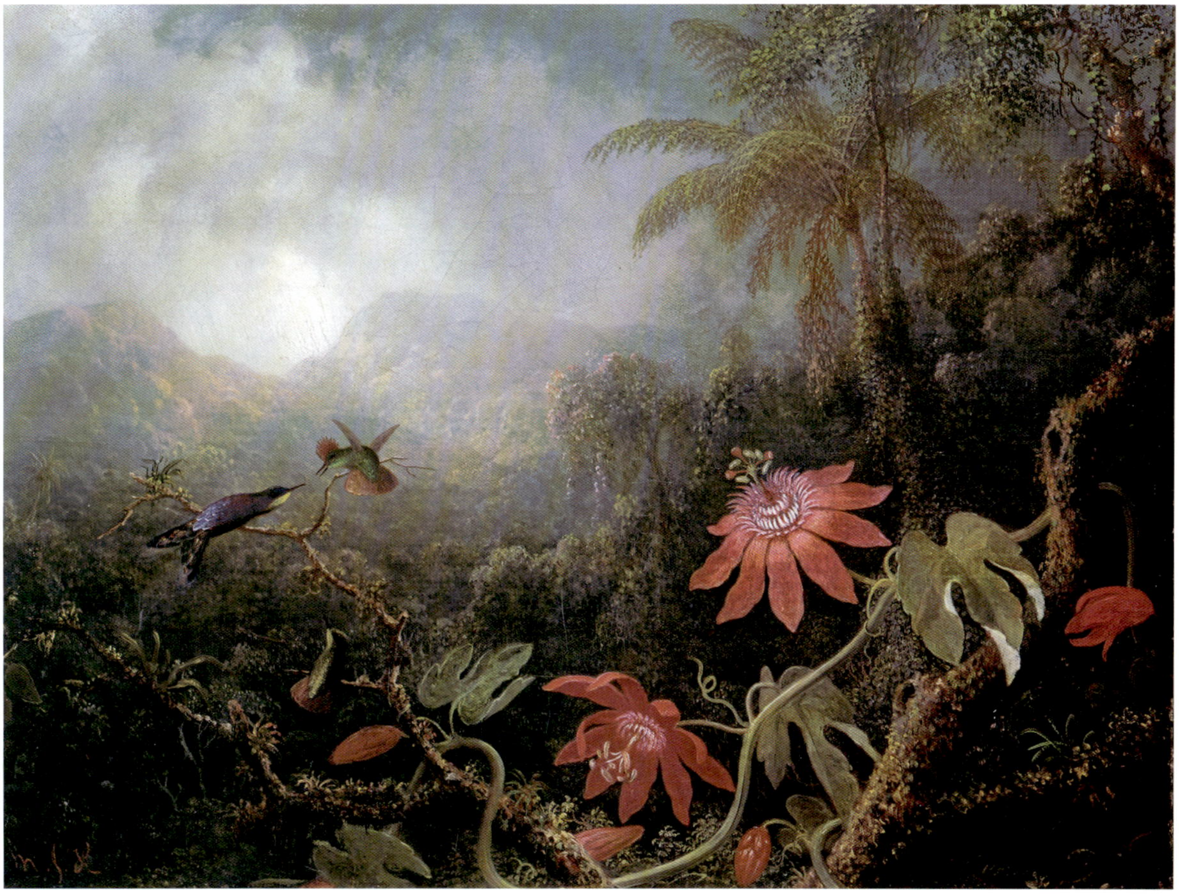

JOHN LA FARGE

(New York 1835–1910 Providence)

Peonies in a Breeze, 1890
Watercolor and graphite on paper mounted on canvas (37 3/8 x 20 1/2 in.)
Signed and dated lower left: *La Farge 1890*
Private Collection

PAINTER, MURALIST, STAINED GLASS ARTIST, AND WATERCOLORIST, La Farge was one of the most adventuresome American artists of the late nineteenth century. He epitomized the very spirit of the aesthetic movement, with its emphasis on the integration of the fine arts with the decorative arts, architecture, and design. His wide-ranging interests and versatility are impressive enough, but La Farge is also recognized as a master of every medium he embraced.

Around 1876, according to his friend Russell Sturgis, La Farge's interests in the decoration of architectural interiors "led him to the careful observation of ancient stained glass, with a view to providing the modern world with something that might be to it what the windows of Reims Cathedral and Fairford Church were to the Middle Ages."[1] La Farge pushed the art of stained glass to an unprecedented level of complexity and compositional fluidity. "Impressionistic" would seem an unlikely description of any work created by artisans in rigidly structured, segmented, almost cloisonné-like glass, but the term aptly sums up La Farge's most experimental window designs. *Peonies in a Breeze*, a window for which this large watercolor is a preparatory design, represents the height of his achievement in stained glass.

In his compulsion to create "light by colors," La Farge was drawn to painting in transparent watercolor.[2] He understandably used watercolor to plan his window designs, painting in brilliant hues with color washes applied thinly onto the white paper to create the effect of light shining through colored glass. This large and elaborate watercolor was probably a presentation piece La Farge made for his client, longtime friend John Hay, who desired a La Farge window for his townhouse in Washington, D.C.[3] La Farge obviously loved the challenge of translating such a fluid conceit as wind-blown peonies into rigid stained glass, and this study relates closely to an earlier masterwork, a magnificent peony-pattern window La Farge created in 1886 for the studio of English painter Sir Lawrence Alma-Tadema.[4] So fresh and brilliant, the painting testifies to La Farge's color sense; crimson, white, and the subtlest pink peonies stand out against a backdrop of watery aquamarine, ultramarine, and violet. The watercolor, an intricate pattern of delicate, animated, intertwining leaves and flower petals, is all the more extraordinary for its large size, a brilliant display of control over the fluid medium. PJ

1 Russell Sturgis, "John La Farge," *Scribner's Magazine* 26, no. 1 (July 1890): 9.
2 John La Farge, *The Higher Life in Art* (New York: McClure Co., 1908), 138; quoted in Kathleen A. Foster, "John La Farge and the American Watercolor Movement: Art for the 'Decorative Age,'" in Henry Adams, et al., *John La Farge* (New York: Abbeville Press, 1987), 150.
3 The Hay window, *Peonies in the Wind with Kakemono Borders*, was completed circa 1893 and is now in the collection of the Smithsonian American Art Museum, Washington, D.C.
4 *Peonies in the Wind* (1886) is now in the collection of the Museum of Fine Arts, Boston.

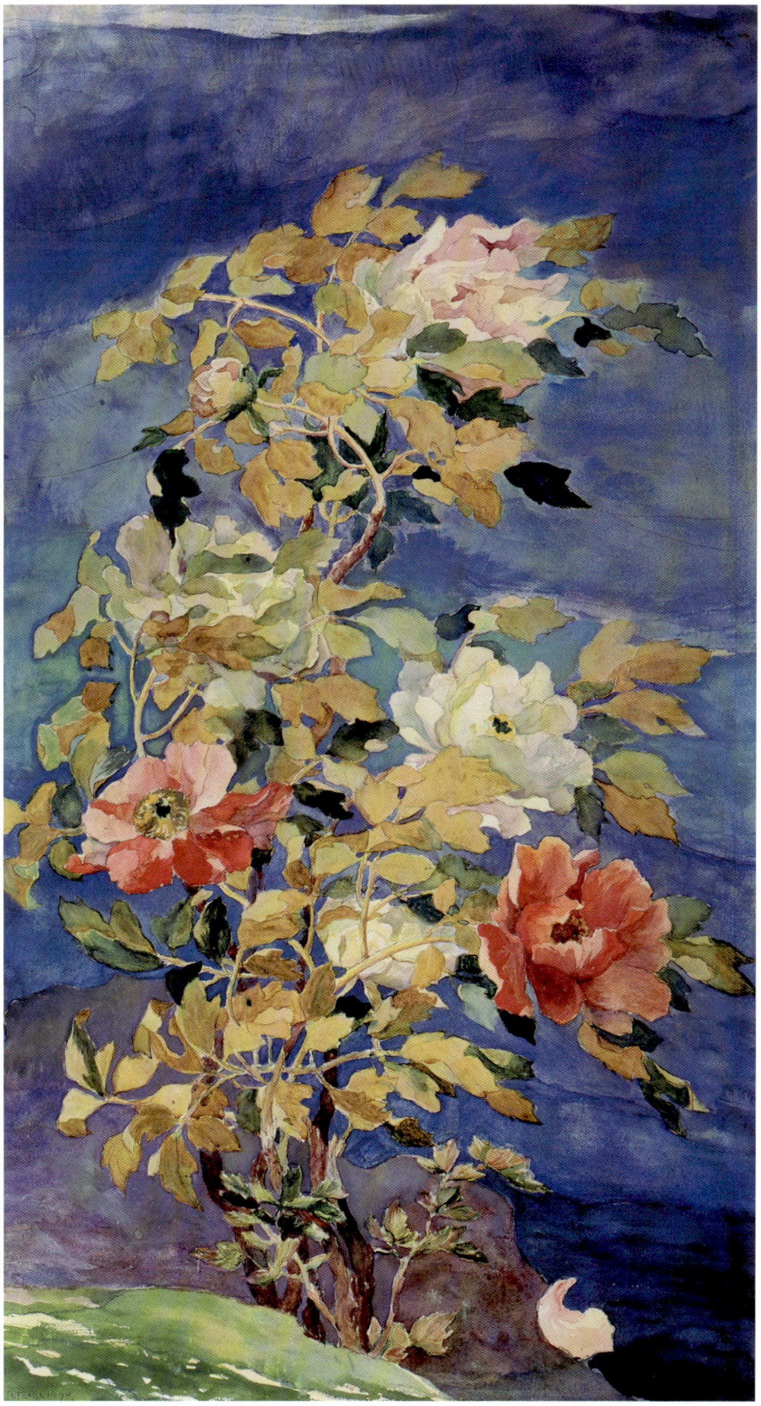

WINSLOW HOMER

(Boston 1836–1910 Prout's Neck, ME)

The Woodcutter, 1891
Watercolor and graphite on paper (13 3/4 x 19 7/8 in.)
Signed and dated lower left: *HOMER 1891*
Collection of Fayez Sarofim

HOMER DISCOVERED THE ADIRONDACKS REGION of northern New York around 1870. He painted there throughout his life but even more so after 1888, when he was elected to membership in the newly founded Adirondack Preserve Association, a private club for anglers and hunters. For Homer, the place was defined by the types who used these woods: sportsmen, yes, but also, and most importantly, the local guides.[1]

These denizens of the wilderness fascinated Homer. He saw them as noble subjects for a modern heroic art, and they dominated the artist's Adirondack subjects. Sometimes the guides appeared alone on the trout ponds, studying the surface of the water as they anticipated a fish rising or casting silently into a deep pool where the big trout prowled the depths. Expert in the ways of the woods, they used dogs, as Homer occasionally showed us, to drive deer to the water where hunters waited. The artist also allowed glimpses of them in moments of quiet contemplation of the mountain peaks, towering pines, and mirror lakes. Through these woodsmen, Homer conveyed the spirit of the wilderness, where encounters with wild nature were rapturous, sometimes brutal and terrifying, yet always ennobling.

Homer went to the Adirondacks as an angler, and his view of the place was most often from the small lakes of the North Woods Club, as the association came to be known. But at times he went up the mountain trails and placed his guides on high hillcrests, where they could be seen surveying the seemingly endless miles of dark mountains. A man alone in such a vast wilderness was, for Homer, the very idea of the heroic. Here, the solitary guide is a young man, but one already versed in the ways of the woods. He pauses on his climb, leaning easily upon his axe, which he always carries as he makes his way through the dense forests. Homer painted him in delicate watercolor and with a graceful elegance, posing him in a kind of classical *contrapposto* that underscores the young man's strength, confidence, and ease in his surroundings. Although the young guide's axe carries associations with death and destruction, he seems not to be an intruder in this realm of nature. He appears at home here, a part of the fabric of the place, a part of the natural pattern of life and death that is intensely felt in these woods. In Homer's eyes, this man is as majestic as America itself. PJ

1 For biographical information on Homer, see David Tatham, *Winslow Homer in the Adirondacks* (Syracuse, N.Y.: Syracuse University Press, 1996).

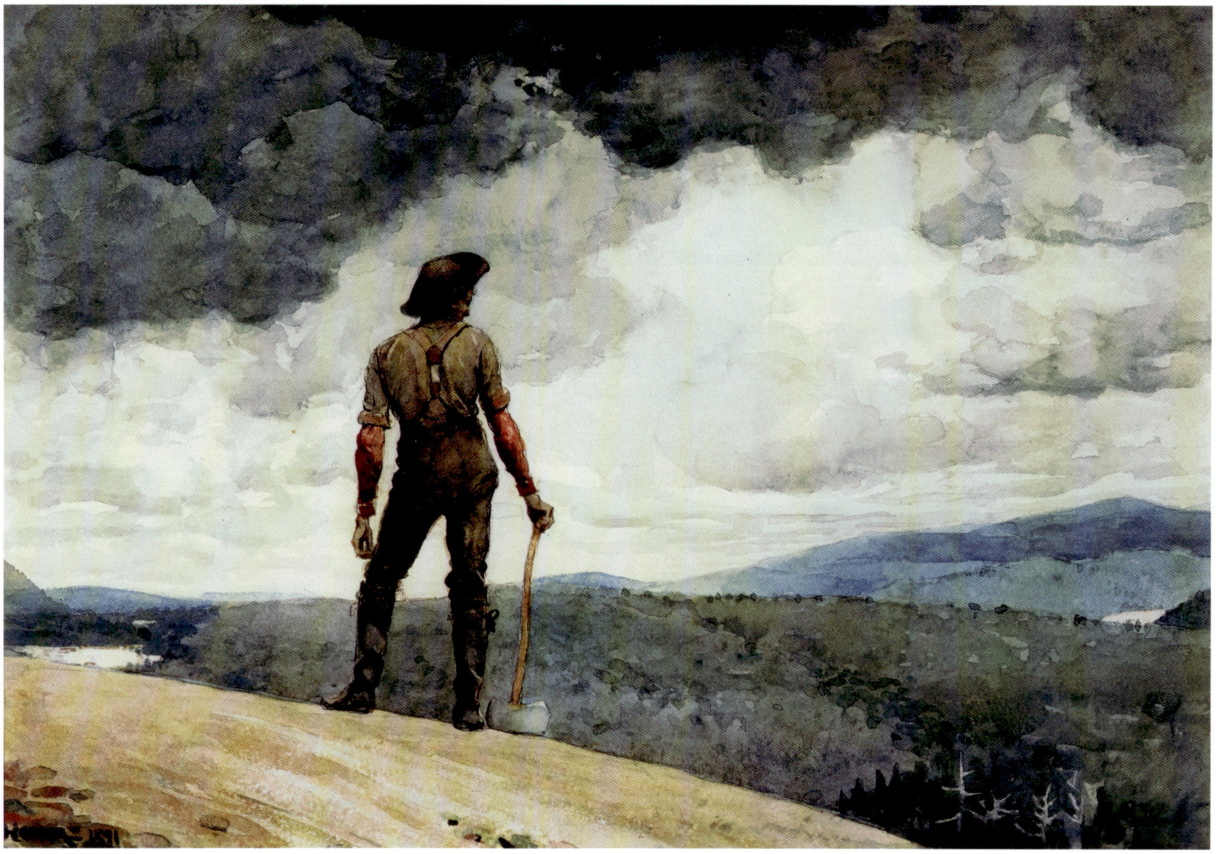

MAURICE PRENDERGAST

(St. John's, Newfoundland 1858–1924 New York)

Along the Shore–St. Malo, ca. 1898–99
Watercolor and graphite on paper (11 1/8 x 15 3/4 in.)
Signed lower left: *Maurice Prendergast*
Mr. and Mrs. L. R. French Jr.

IN 1898 PRENDERGAST, A CONSUMMATE MASTER of the watercolor medium, traveled to Italy, where he created a series of works that gave rise to his first artistic recognition in the United States. The third of six journeys taken abroad over the course of the artist's career, this trip may have been financed by Sarah Choate Sears (1858–1935), a wealthy arts patron and artist who, like Prendergast, moved within Boston art circles. Prendergast spent the majority of his eighteen-month sojourn in Venice, producing radiant watercolors of that city's magnificent and colorful outdoor spaces. During the winter, however, the artist traveled to Rome, Naples, and Capri, the island near the southern entrance to the Bay of Naples. It was here—despite the "St. Malo" of the title long associated with this work—that *Along the Shore* likely was set.[1]

By the late nineteenth century, the scenic cliff-lined island had become a popular tourist destination. Myriad striped rowboats plied the choppy swells near the Marina Grande, the primary embarkation point on the island. For a negotiated fee, the boatmen would transport tourists to popular sites, such as the famed Blue Grotto, a cave that was accessible only by boat. The area's choppy waters challenged all but the hardiest travelers, which included those few, like Prendergast, who braved the off-season between November and April when the north winds blew the hardest.

In this work Prendergast carefully positioned the bobbing vessels, each containing one or two figures dressed warmly against the stiff breezes of a crisp winter's day, in a zigzagging caravan receding into the distance. The presence of a large ship, its trailing smoke echoing the composition's dominant horizontal elements of sea and sky, establishes their proximity to the Mediterranean Sea. Employing a limited palette of red, blue, and green, Prendergast utilized pale, transparent washes in such areas as the forms of the boats, while he punctuated the image with passages of saturated pigment to denote the oarsmen's caps and the boats' unfurled flags. Loosely, yet with a sure hand, the artist described the churning water in the foreground through washes of delicate pigments in variegated blues, which, as they recede toward the high horizon line, fuse to mimic the sea's distant, richer hues. By leaving areas of the white paper untouched in the foreground and around the primary figural elements, Prendergast created the overall sensation of dancing highlights, thus imparting a remarkable sense of movement and light within extremely intimate dimensions. JM

1 Carol Clark, Nancy Mowll Mathews, and Gwendolyn Owens, *Maurice Brazil Prendergast, Charles Prendergast: A Catalogue Raisonné* (Munich: Prestel-Verlag, 1990), 402.

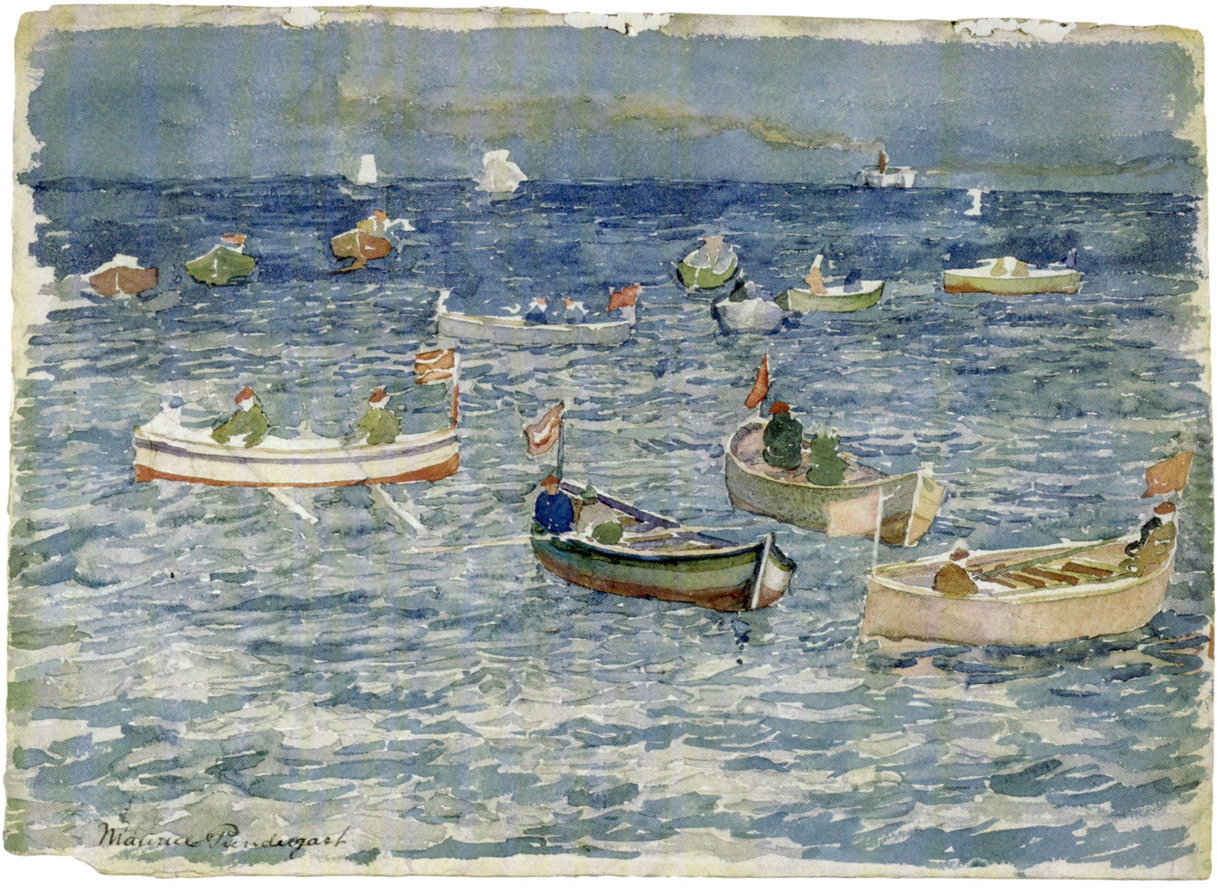
Maurice Prendergast

FREDERIC REMINGTON
(Canton, NY 1861–1909 Ridgefield, CT)

The Norther, 1900
Bronze (22 in. high)
Signed and inscribed on top of base: *Frederic Remington*; on side of base: *CIRE PERDUE CAST / ROMAN BRONZE WKS*; on underside of base: *EG cast*
Private Collection

REMINGTON IS UNIQUE AMONG AMERICAN ARTISTS for his brilliant achievements as a sculptor. He had no formal training in sculpture before he created his first bronze, *The Broncho Buster*, in 1895. An unerring observer of western life, Remington created sculptures that were highly imaginative and charged with energy. In his desire to create subjects that appeared to move through time and defy gravity, he pushed the bronze medium to technological limits never before attempted, let alone achieved. Initially, Remington used the rather staid and rigid sand-cast process to create his sculptures. However, within a few years he learned of the far more flexible lost-wax process and thus discovered the possibilities of "painting" with bronze.

In January 1891 Remington had experienced bitterly cold weather while riding with the Seventh Cavalry in South Dakota. At the time, he remarked that the men nearly froze to death on horseback while "the moon looked down on the frosty landscape and the cold wind from the north searched for the crevices in their blankets."[1] The same harsh conditions appear to be invoked in *The Norther*, a truly remarkable tour de force of artistic expression and vivid detail. Indeed, the lost-wax process allowed the artist, for the first time, to make changes and additions to the preparatory wax model of his subject before it was cast into bronze. In this instance, Remington described how he went to the foundry and was able to enjoy the "thrill of creative composition" by painting upon the surface of the model with a brush dipped in molten wax.[2] As can be seen in this example—one of only three that were cast—the result is an animated surface that perfectly evokes the cold, searching wind that the artist had described a decade earlier. Remington's careful eye for detail is everywhere apparent: the normally heavy wool chaps blow forward in the wind, and the cowboy's right hand is tucked under his body in a vain attempt to avoid frostbite. The rich surface of the bronze, with its variegated color and mixture of reflective surfaces, shimmers and scatters the light that strikes it. As he was working on *The Norther*, Remington told the noted illustrator Howard Pyle (1853–1911) that while knowledge of the elements of art was important, it was nothing compared to "Imagination."[3] In this unforgettable bronze, he underscored those beliefs.

RS

1 Frederic Remington, "The Sioux Outbreak in South Dakota," January 24, 1891, in Peggy and Harold Samuels, eds., *The Collected Writings of Frederic Remington* (New York: Castle Books, 1986), 69.
2 "Frederic Remington—Sculptor," *Collier's*, March 18, 1905, quoted in Michael D. Greenbaum, *Icons of the West: Frederic Remington's Sculpture* (Ogdensburg, N.Y.: Frederic Remington Art Museum, 1996), 85.
3 Remington in a letter to Howard Pyle, November 5, 1899, in Allen P. Splete and Marilyn D. Splete, eds., *Frederic Remington—Selected Letters* (New York: Abbeville Press, 1988), 291.

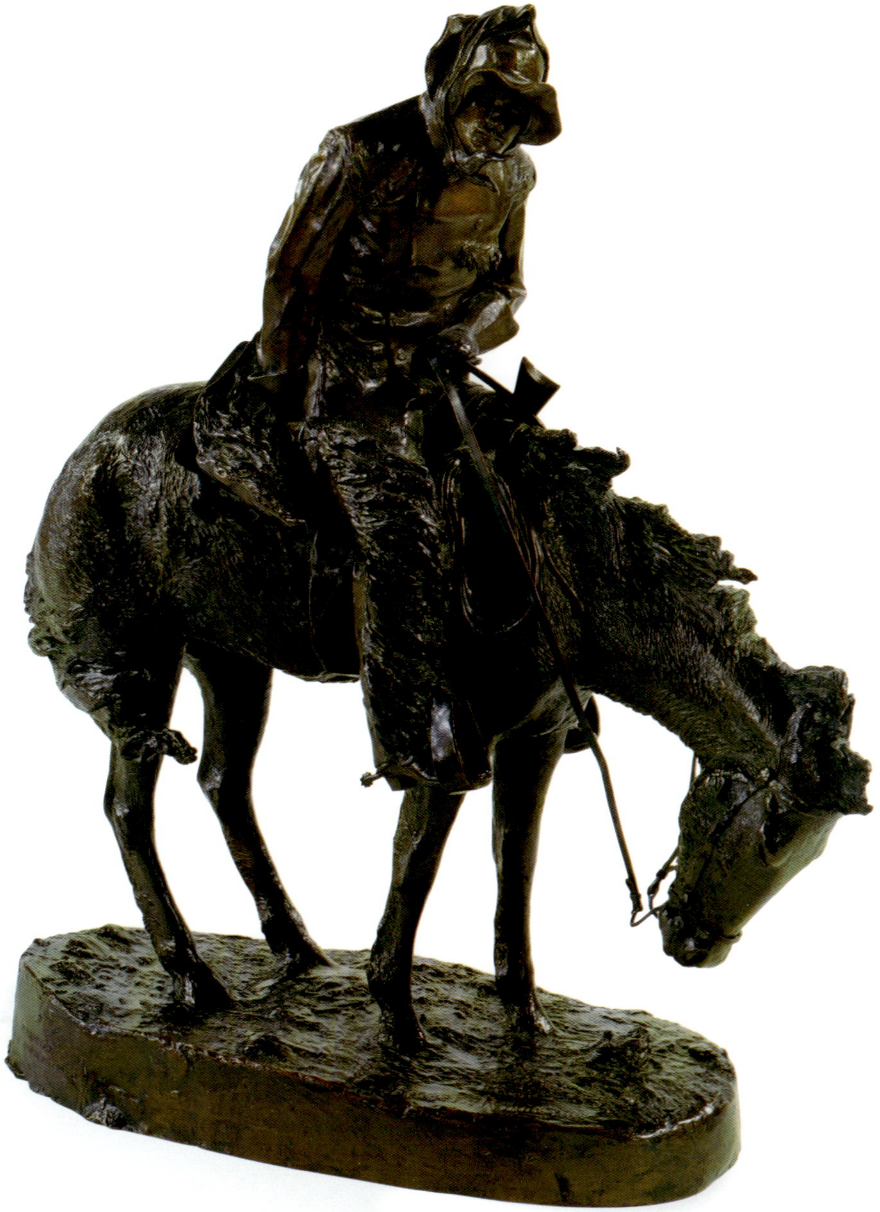

CHARLES M. RUSSELL

(St. Louis 1864–1926 Great Falls, MT)

Counting Coup [Medicine Whip], 1902
Oil on canvas (18 1/8 x 30 1/8 in.)
Signed and dated lower left: *C M Russell /* [skull] *1902*
Courtesy Sid Richardson Collection of Western Art, Fort Worth, Texas

ALTHOUGH RUSSELL WAS KNOWN IN HIS LIFETIME AS "the Cowboy Artist," his depictions of the Indians of the northern plains are equally noteworthy. As early as 1888, the artist visited Blackfoot encampments in Alberta to acquire firsthand knowledge of their culture, and he continued a lifelong habit of collecting stories and artifacts that he would use in his later paintings. In a letter written in 1902 describing the scene in this vivid painting of intertribal combat, Russell recounted that during his visit to Canada fourteen years earlier he had spoken with an old Blackfoot warrior of the Blood tribe named Medicine Whip, who told him the story of great personal valor that is recorded in this painting. The old man told how, many years earlier, he and other Blood warriors had pursued and caught a raiding band of Lakota (Sioux) and had killed the horse of their medicine man in a running fight. The Lakota gathered around their fallen leader and fought the Bloods to a standstill. A point was reached when the Bloods realized their own leader had fallen, and they were nearly out of arrows. When one of the Lakota warriors taunted and insulted Medicine Whip, he sprang into action, charging the bunched Lakota fighters.

Russell's painting depicts what happened next. Feinting with his lance, Medicine Whip downed the Lakota who had taunted him. Then he charged his pinto horse toward the Lakota medicine man, striking him across the face with his quirt in order to "count coup" on his hated adversary. At that point the other Lakota were upon him, several arrows pierced his body, and a tomahawk blow to the head knocked him unconscious. When he awoke, his fellow Bloods had triumphed, and all the Lakota lay dead. Medicine Whip lived to tell his story, and Russell described the scars on the old man's body that were a testament to youthful bravery.

Russell was one of the few western artists who took an active interest in portraying scenes of intertribal conflict, as he does here. He was later to refine the key elements of this story into a vivid subject in bronze, also titled *Counting Coup*.[1] In this painting, Russell shows the confusion and welter of a pitched battle. He may be forgiven if such a picture is not entirely accurate; for example, it is unlikely that the Lakota would have been wearing feather headdresses, or any other such finery, for battle. But Russell's intention here is to tell a story and convey the raw excitement and outright danger Medicine Whip and his fellow warriors experienced "in the moon of the painted leaves" so many years earlier.[2]

RS

1 A cast of this sculpture is now in the collection of the Amon Carter Museum.
2 For a recounting of Medicine Whip's story, see Rick Stewart, *Charles M. Russell, Sculptor* (Fort Worth: Amon Carter Museum in association with Harry N. Abrams, Inc., 1994), 147–49. A very good account of intertribal conflicts in Medicine Whip's time can be found in Anthony McGinnis, *Counting Coup and Cutting Horses: Intertribal Warfare on the Northern Plains, 1738–1889* (Evergreen, Colo.: Cordillera Press, Inc., 1990).

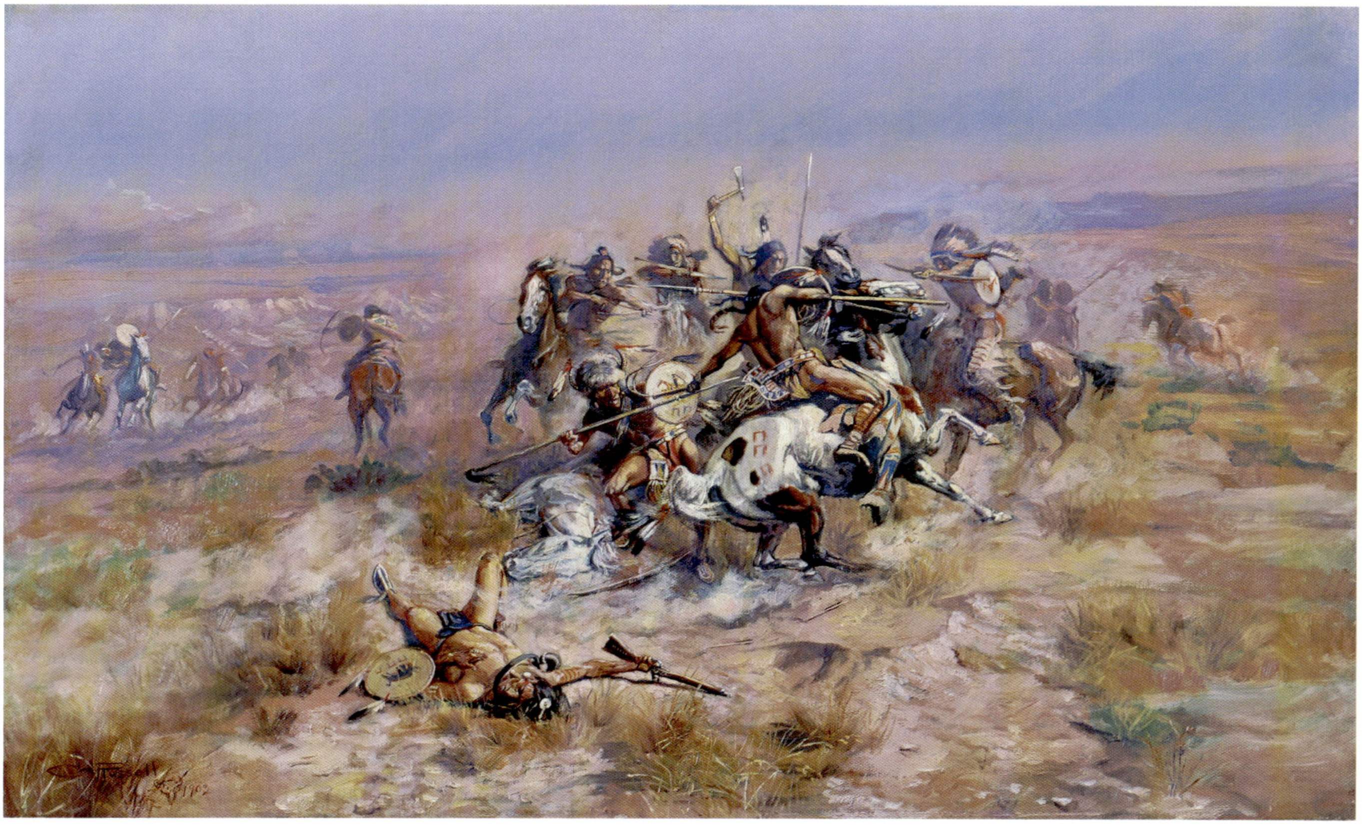

EDWARD STEICHEN

(Bivange, Luxembourg 1879–1973 West Redding, CT)

Rodin–Le Penseur, Paris, 1902, printed 1904
Photogravure (10 1/8 x 12 5/8 in.)
Signed and dated lower left: *STEICHEN MDCCCCII*
Reprinted with permission of Joanna T. Steichen
The Museum of Fine Arts, Houston; Museum purchase with funds provided by Harry M. Reasoner in honor of Joe Jamail and Harry H. Cullen at "One Great Night in November, 1998"

ALFRED STIEGLITZ

(Hoboken, NJ 1864–1946 New York)

The Steerage, 1907, printed 1915
Photogravure on Chinese tissue (12 1/4 x 10 in.)
Published as special supplement to no. 7–8 of *291*
Courtesy of SBC Communications Inc.

In 1902 a group of photographers led by Stieglitz and Steichen founded an organization called the Photo-Secession to further the recognition of photography as a fine art equal to other artistic media. While some of these photographers sometimes employed painterly techniques that added soft-focus, brushstrokes, and applied color, Stieglitz eventually maintained that the camera itself possessed unique qualities that could produce artistic results. To assist in the promotion of the aesthetic capabilities of the medium, Stieglitz—with Steichen's assistance—began the quarterly journal *Camera Work* in 1903 and opened a gallery, 291, in 1905. Although their approaches to the medium differed and they eventually went in completely different directions, their collaboration pushed photography in a radically new direction.

From 1900 to 1902, Steichen studied art in Paris. Immediately after arriving in the city, he went to the World's Fair to see the work of the master Auguste Rodin (1840–1917), whom the young photographer revered and hoped one day to meet. A year later he succeeded, and every Saturday for almost a year Steichen visited Rodin, who became the photographer's greatest mentor. After making many straightforward portraits of the sculptor, in 1902 Steichen finally conceived of the ideal way to depict him and formulated a plan to photograph him in his studio along with two of his greatest sculptures, *Le Penseur (The Thinker)* and his white marble statue of Victor Hugo. Unfortunately, the studio was crowded with artwork, and the photographer could not get the two sculptures close enough to have both in the photograph. He solved the problem by photographing Rodin in profile in front of the Hugo sculpture and then making a second exposure of *Le Penseur*. A master printer, Steichen then joined the two negatives into one image.[1]

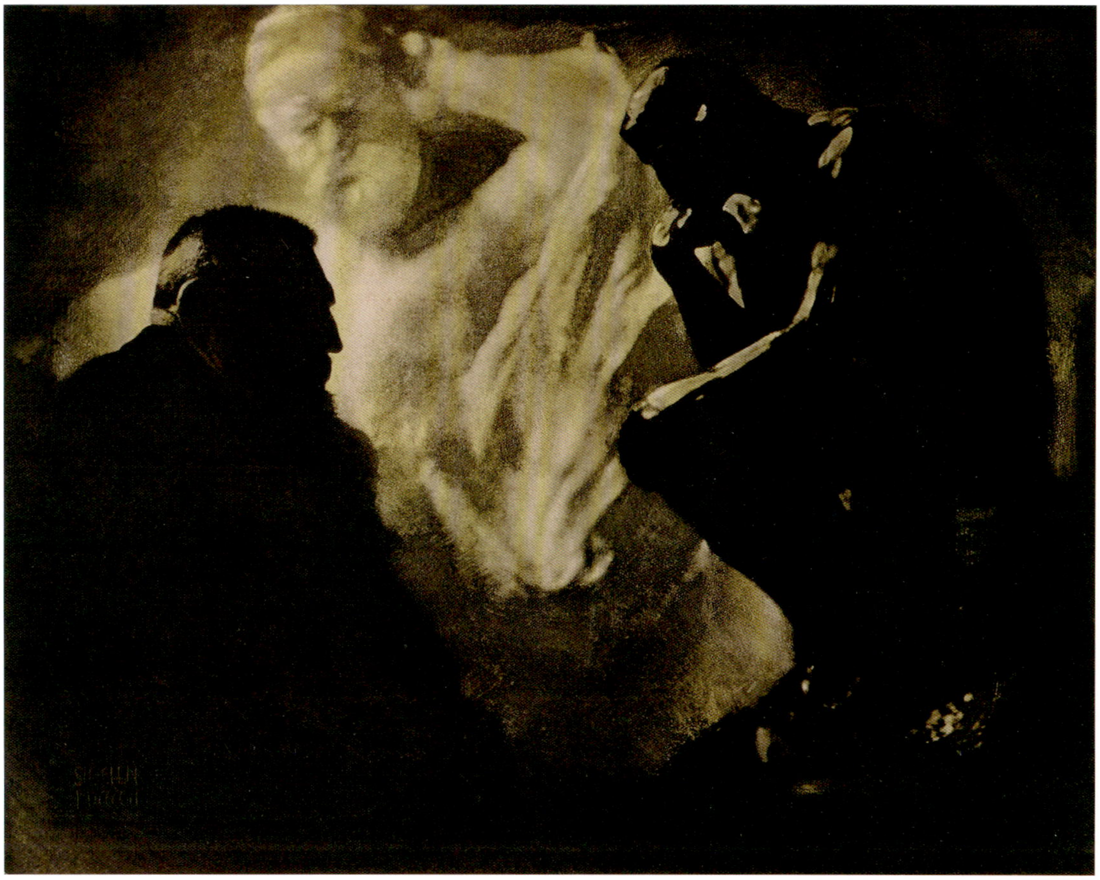

After Steichen returned to the United States, he immediately began to promote Rodin's work among New York collectors. He included a photogravure of this image in two issues of *Camera Work*, one in 1905 and another in 1906. Then in 1908, he assembled an exhibition of Rodin's drawings of female nudes for display in gallery 291 and organized a second exhibition in 1910. In a 1914 issue of *Camera Work*, a portfolio of drawings by Marius de Zayas (1880–1961) included one he did of Steichen and Rodin, signifying the cross-fertilization between the two artists and, by extension, the connections between photography, painting, and sculpture.

Stieglitz's *The Steerage*, on the other hand, is purely photographic. Believing that the handheld camera would revolutionize photography through its ability to instantly frame meaningful moments of life, the artist preferred to compose the image in the viewfinder, rather than relying upon darkroom cropping to manipulate the original scene. This image displays the full range of black-and-white tones and is sharply focused. Looking down from the top deck of the ship, Stieglitz was drawn to the compositional elements of the scene. He saw the white straw hat of the man looking down at the passengers in steerage as the central focal point of a complex arrangement of shapes. "I saw shapes related to one another—a picture of shapes, and underlying it, a new vision that held me: simple people, the feeling of the ship, ocean, sky. . . ."[2]

The white diagonal line of the catwalk separates the different sections of the image, with the dark tones on the top half and the white, flowing dresses on the bottom. This diagonal is the key to a political message as well, separating the different sections of the ship and referring to the economic divisions of society. The steerage area was for passengers who could not afford staterooms and held those undesirables who had been rejected by immigration officials and were being returned to Europe. The wealthier people on the observation deck could literally look down on them.

Stieglitz first published this image in *Camera Work* in 1911. In 1915 it appeared as a large-format photogravure in another art magazine he called *291* after his gallery. The image represented a major turning point for the artist, holding both its formal elements and its content in perfect balance.

BMC

1 Penelope Niven, *Steichen: A Biography* (New York: Clarkson Potter, 1997), 123–24.
2 Alfred Stieglitz, quoted in Dorothy Norman, *Alfred Stieglitz: An American Seer* (New York: Random House, 1973), 76.

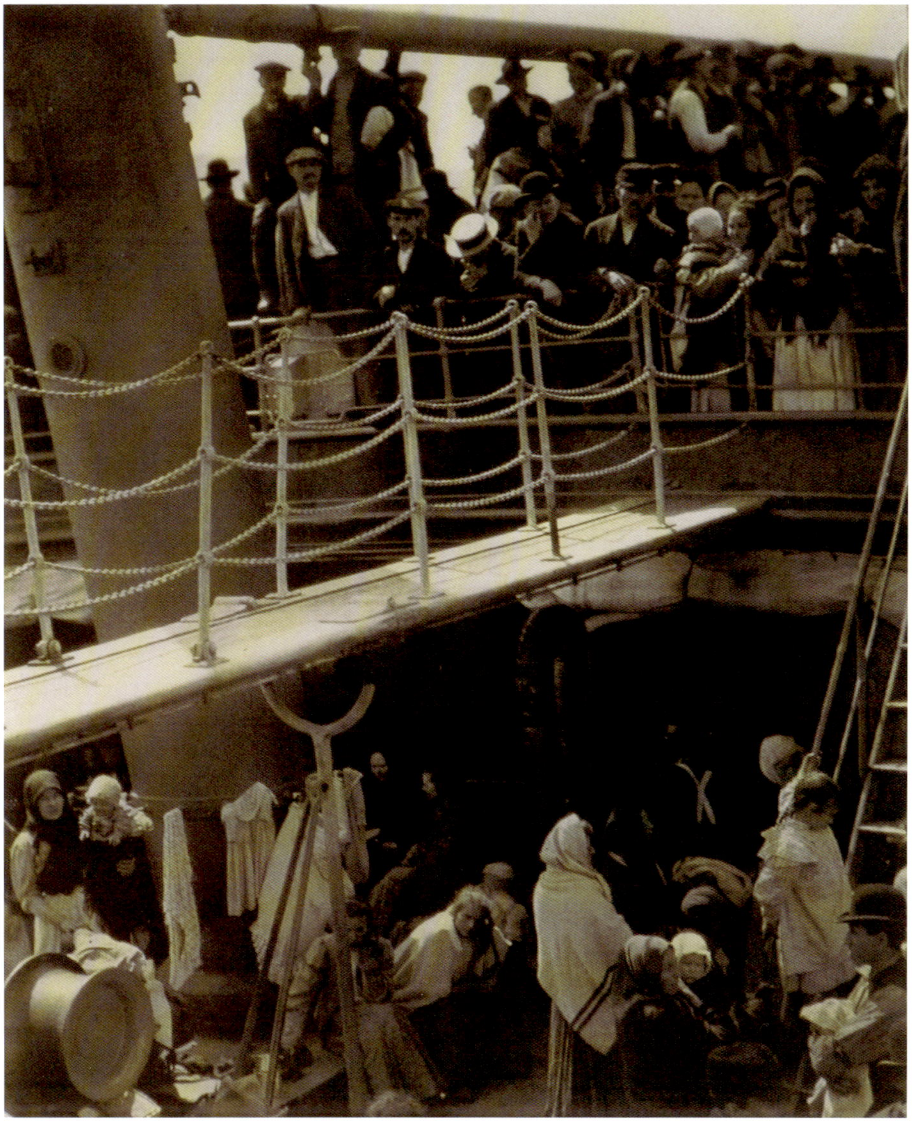

ANNE BRIGMAN

(Oahu, HI 1869–1950 El Monte, CA)

The Lone Pine, 1909
Gelatin silver print (7 3/4 x 9 3/4 in.)
Signed and dated lower right: *Anne Brigman*; on mount, lower left: *Anne Brigman, 1909*
Mr. and Mrs. Wallace S. Wilson

AT THE TURN OF THE TWENTIETH CENTURY, women turned to photography in increasing numbers, joining the field as both amateurs and professionals. Brigman had been photographing a mere two years when, in 1903, she became the only photographer west of the Mississippi to be made a Fellow of the Photo-Secession, a group founded by Alfred Stieglitz (1864–1946) and others to promote photography as an art form. The invitation created quite a stir among those veteran California photographers who had not been asked to join. Stieglitz likely was persuaded by Brigman's oath of loyalty to the organization's principles, a conviction she had made known to him immediately after seeing the inaugural issue of *Camera Work*, the pictorialist group's journal.

Among the artists represented in that first issue was Gertrude Käsebier (1852–1934), a co-founder of the organization and a photographer whose work revolved around themes of motherhood. The older artist's photographs inspired Brigman, though Brigman's free spirit infused her own work with a broader license, and her photographs of the female nude in the wilderness reflect her unconventional and bohemian tendencies. A self-proclaimed pagan, Brigman interpreted nature as the embodiment of the sacred—a tradition born of American transcendentalists Ralph Waldo Emerson and Henry David Thoreau—and took inspiration from the poetry and prose of Walt Whitman and the English mystic Edward Carpenter (1844–1929). Carpenter championed women's liberation, sexual freedom, and homosexual love, and Brigman equated her own goal of depicting the human figure as part of nature with a passage in Carpenter's multipart poem *Towards Democracy* (1883–1902): "How the human body bathed in the sheen / and wet, steeped in sun and air, / Moving near and nude among the elements. / Matches somehow and interprets the whole of nature."[1]

Brigman's photographs were admired both for their unconventional challenge to traditional Victorian mores and for their manner of incorporating a distinctly western landscape into metaphorical images. She camped in the High Sierras for months at a time, sometimes accompanied only by her dog and other times by companions who modeled for her photographs. Posed against the juniper and pine trees, the figure here curves her body to echo the sway of the branches, presenting a contiguous line that captures the mystical union of human and natural life. BMC

1 Edward Carpenter, quoted in Anne Brigman, "The Glory of the Open," *Camera Craft* 33 (April 1926): 161.

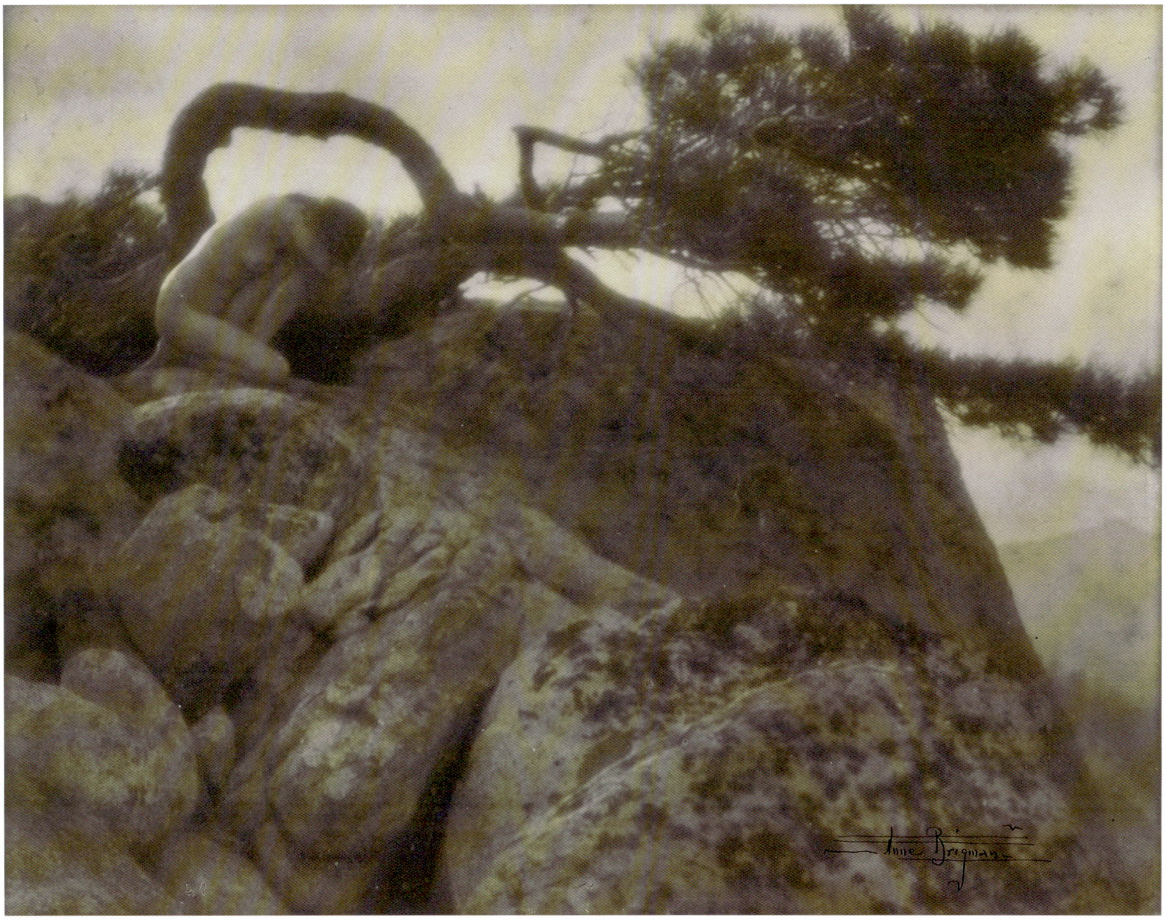
Anne Brigman

MARSDEN HARTLEY

(Lewiston, ME 1877–1943 Ellsworth, ME)

Portrait Arrangement, 1914
Oil on canvas (39 1/2 x 31 7/8 in.)
Collection of the McNay Art Museum, Museum purchase

LONG AFTER THE TRAGIC DEATH OF HIS MOTHER when he was only eight, Hartley recalled, "I was to know complete isolation from that moment onward."[1] His feelings of loneliness fueled a perpetual wanderlust that seemed temporarily assuaged, in 1913, when he traveled to Germany. There, he was inspired by Wassily Kandinsky (1866–1944), whose spiritual concepts of art validated Hartley's desire to paint directly from his emotions. He settled in Berlin near his close friends, the sculptor Arnold Rönnebeck (1885–1947) and Rönnebeck's cousin, Karl von Freyburg, both of whom were soldiers. The artist felt certain he had found his spiritual home, but then Germany declared war on Russia and France in August 1914.

Hartley initially responded to the armed crisis by idealizing the fate of the soldiers in such visionary paintings as *Portrait Arrangement*. While this diagrammatic picture of a fallen cavalryman's journey to heaven, rendered as a bucolic countryside, appears almost naïve, it was actually composed from a complex system of personal and somewhat elusive symbols. The work projects an overall message of transcendence, reflecting Hartley's study of mysticism. He forms the constellation of the Big Dipper with eight-pointed stars, which were part of the insignia on German helmets and could therefore refer to soldiers as well as the heavens. The billowing cloud—a motif derived from Bavarian votive painting—indicates that the mounted horseman is a celestial spirit. The artist had first seen such folk-art examples of votive paintings in Kandinsky's *Der Blaue Reiter* almanac.[2] Shortly thereafter, Hartley began collecting these religious objects, appreciating their pared-down styles, expressive use of color, and flat, simplified forms. He adopted similar hues and shapes to convey a spiritual message in this painting. His pure palette of primary colors probably symbolized his belief in the pureness of his subject: a German soldier's honorable and deserving journey to the afterlife.

Hartley's newfound ideals were shattered on October 7, 1914, when von Freyburg was killed in battle. The artist channeled his great despair into a moving elegy of symbolic portraits of his friend, and he remained in Berlin until the war forced him to return to New York in 1915. Although *Portrait Arrangement* and other works he created in Germany established Hartley as a pioneer of American modernism, his return home left him mired in alienation, and his frenzied traveling would eventually resume.

SRH

1 Bruce Robertson, *Marsden Hartley* (New York: Harry N. Abrams, Inc., in association with the National Museum of American Art, Smithsonian Institution, 1995), 12.
2 Barbara Haskell, *Marsden Hartley* (New York: Whitney Museum of American Art in association with New York University Press, 1980), 43.

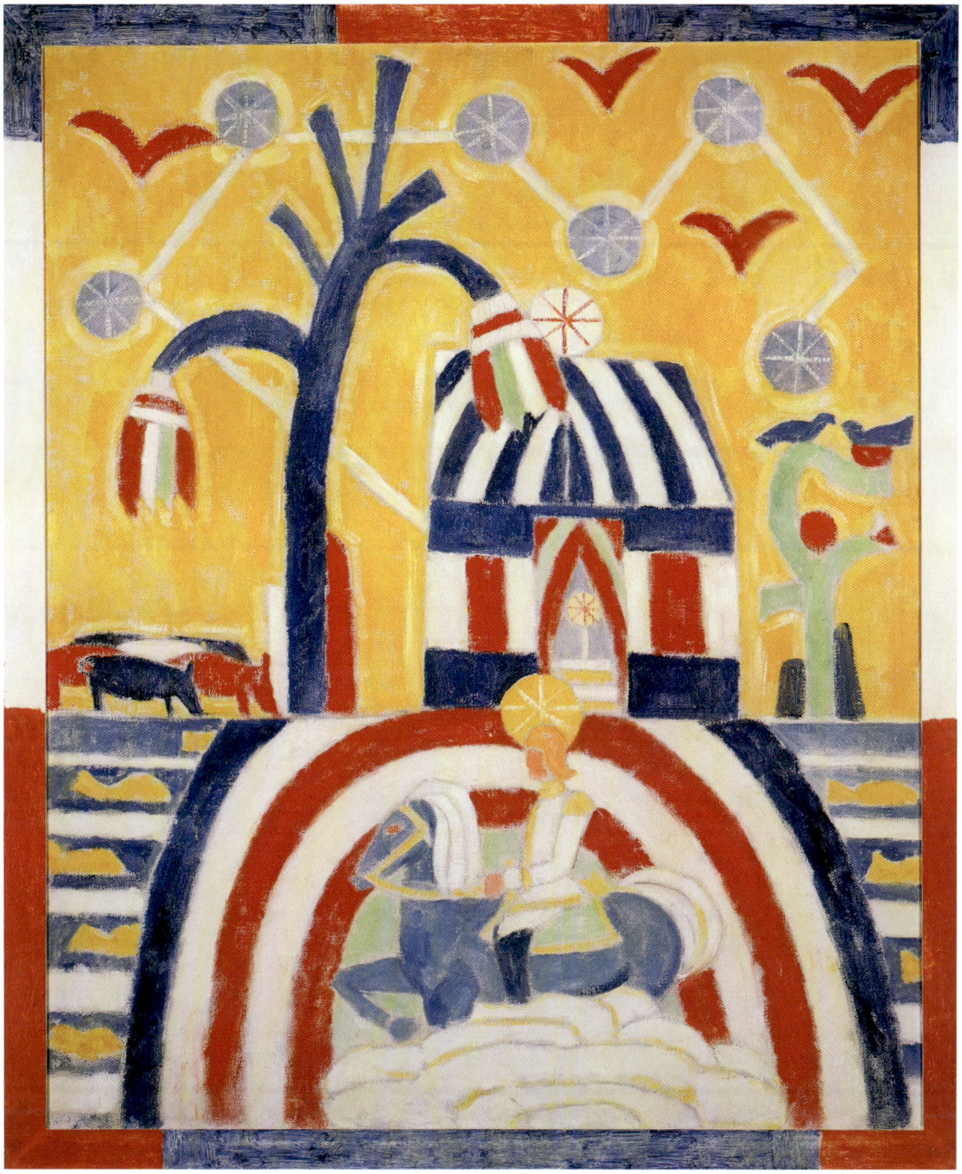

WILLIAM McGREGOR PAXTON

(Baltimore, MD 1869–1941 Newton, MA)

The Other Room, 1916
Oil on canvas (31 5/8 x 17 1/2 in.)
Signed lower right: *PAXTON*
El Paso Museum of Art: Museum Purchase with Funds Raised by the Members Guild of the El Paso Art Museum Association

ALTHOUGH AN ACCLAIMED TEACHER AND PORTRAITIST in Boston at the turn of the twentieth century, Paxton garnered fame through his elegant genre paintings of women. He specialized in depicting well-to-do ladies in the midst of leisurely pursuits, such as reading letters, drinking tea, or admiring precious objects.[1] The rise of immigration, industrialization, and feminism had by that time changed the patterns of American society forever, increasing female participation in the public sphere. Nostalgic for the seemingly simpler values of the nineteenth century, when women were the purveyors of manners and morals within the home, upper-crust patrons were drawn to Paxton's portrayals. His representations of females relaxing within illusory worlds of reverie and wealth not only preserved traditional notions of womanhood but provided a respite from the changing times.

The Other Room is an exquisite example of Paxton's approach, revealing his remarkable gifts in conveying both femininity and grace and in creating a sumptuous interior. He effortlessly translates this young woman into an ethereal vision on the canvas, likening her to an angelic figure. As she gently leans over the table to read a letter, the position of her hands indicates a sophisticated demeanor, while the slight tilt of her head imparts a contemplative mood. Quietude fills the room, as a soft diffusion of light glimmers upon the gold and silver objects.

The model was Lizzie Young, one of Paxton's favorite models, and she posed for him in his Boston studio. She was actually standing in a small side room—which perhaps explains the literal title of this work—where the artist kept the furniture and other accessories he repeatedly used in his pictures. The French secretary, Chinese vase, crimson chair, and chiffon gown Young wears all appear in other Paxton paintings. But while the artist most often rendered these props with a heightened degree of focus, in this picture only the gold-trimmed furniture and beading of the gown glisten with clarity. The objects in the room appear to dematerialize, as the model's gracious presence becomes the focal point of the composition. Set within this dreamlike atmosphere, her eloquent poise alludes to the nineteenth-century ideals of genteel womanhood that were quickly fading away. SRH

1 For biographical information on Paxton, see Ellen Wardwell Lee, *William McGregor Paxton, 1869–1941* (Indianapolis: Indianapolis Museum of Art, 1979).

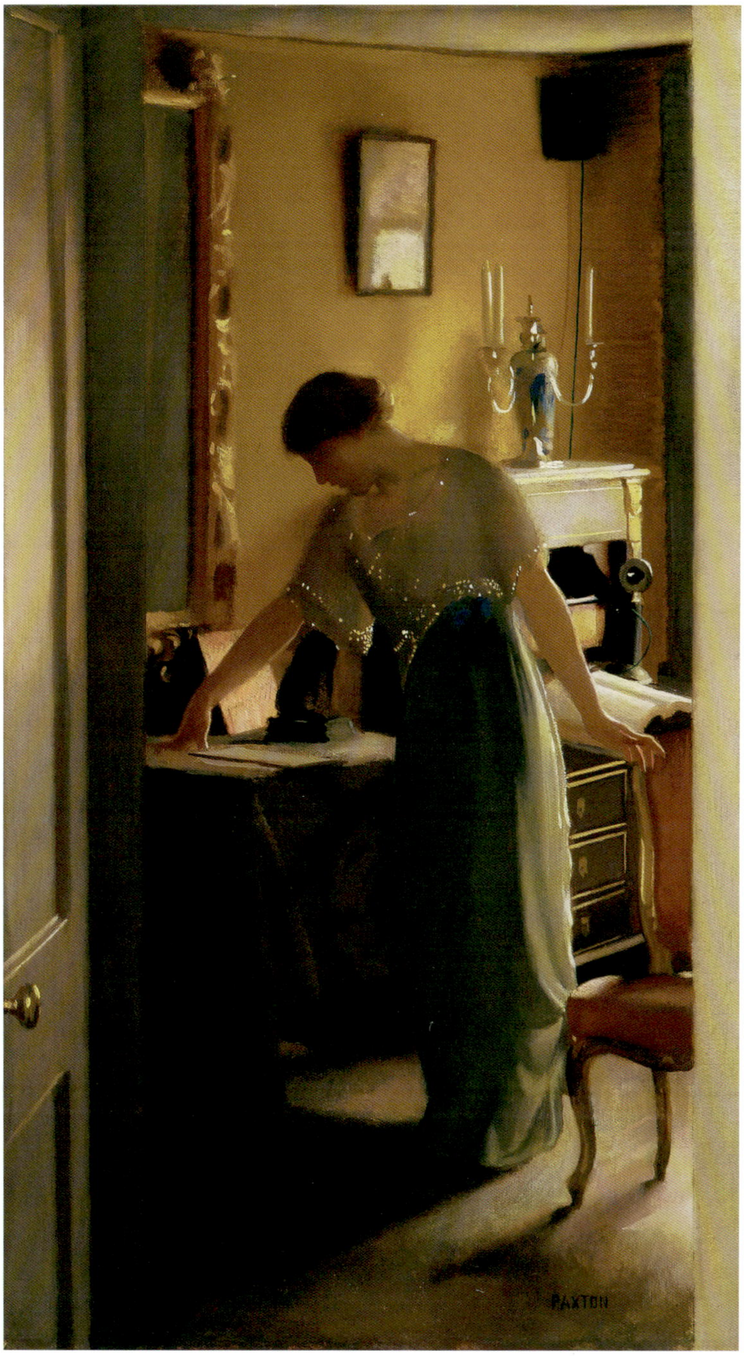
PAXTON

MAX WEBER

(Bialystok, Poland 1881–1961 Great Neck, NY)

Interior with Women, 1917
Oil on canvas (18 x 23 in.)
Mr. and Mrs. Meredith J. Long

After emigrating from Russia in 1891, Weber quickly became one of America's most important modern artists. He studied at Brooklyn's Pratt Institute with the innovative Arthur Wesley Dow (1857–1922), who prepared him for the advanced theories of European modernism. "When I got to Paris in 1905," Weber recalled decades later, "I was struck by the fact that Mr. Dow anticipated some of the aesthetic principles of art the Fauves had striven for only years later."[1] The Fauves, or "wild beasts" as a critic once referred to them, sought to rejuvenate painting through vibrant color; their leading exponent was Henri Matisse (1869–1954). While abroad, Weber studied directly under him and became acquainted with Pablo Picasso (1881–1973). On the eve of Weber's return to America in 1909, Picasso attended the artist's farewell party. The Spanish master's presence seemed to signify his blessing, and one year later Weber would become one of the pioneers of cubism in America.

In his search to find a style that conveyed the dynamism and spirit of the modern era, Weber early on adopted cubism, with its groundbreaking treatment of form and lack of traditional perspective. He first employed it in a 1910 series of female nudes, fragmenting their bodies into multifaceted planes. As *Interior with Women* reveals, by 1917 the artist was boldly applying the style to all aspects of a particular scene. Here, he fractured both the women and their surroundings—including the wallpaper, piano keys, balustrades, and wooden decor—into a kaleidoscopic cacophony of forms. In the upper third of the painting, he used intersecting planes to suggest heads and facial features, while the figure to the left possesses cones, or lamp shades, for eyes. Still, Weber adroitly conveyed the rounded femininity of the women's torsos; to integrate these disparate parts, he incorporated an overall palette of earthen colors, which harmonizes the composition.

The intimate subject of *Interior with Women* reflects Weber's introspection after his marriage in 1916. Before this event, he had concentrated on capturing the frenzied movement of New York City. Here, he also examines motion, but in the quieter, subtler subject of women interacting in a close environment. A few years after completing this painting, Weber abandoned cubism, deterred by unsympathetic critics. He returned to traditional figure painting, leaving behind the style for which he remains best known.

SRH

1 Weber in a letter to Mrs. Putman, October 30, 1958, Archives of American Art, "Arthur Wesley Dow Papers, 1858–1978," Smithsonian Institution, Washington, D.C.; microfilm reel 1034, frame 295.

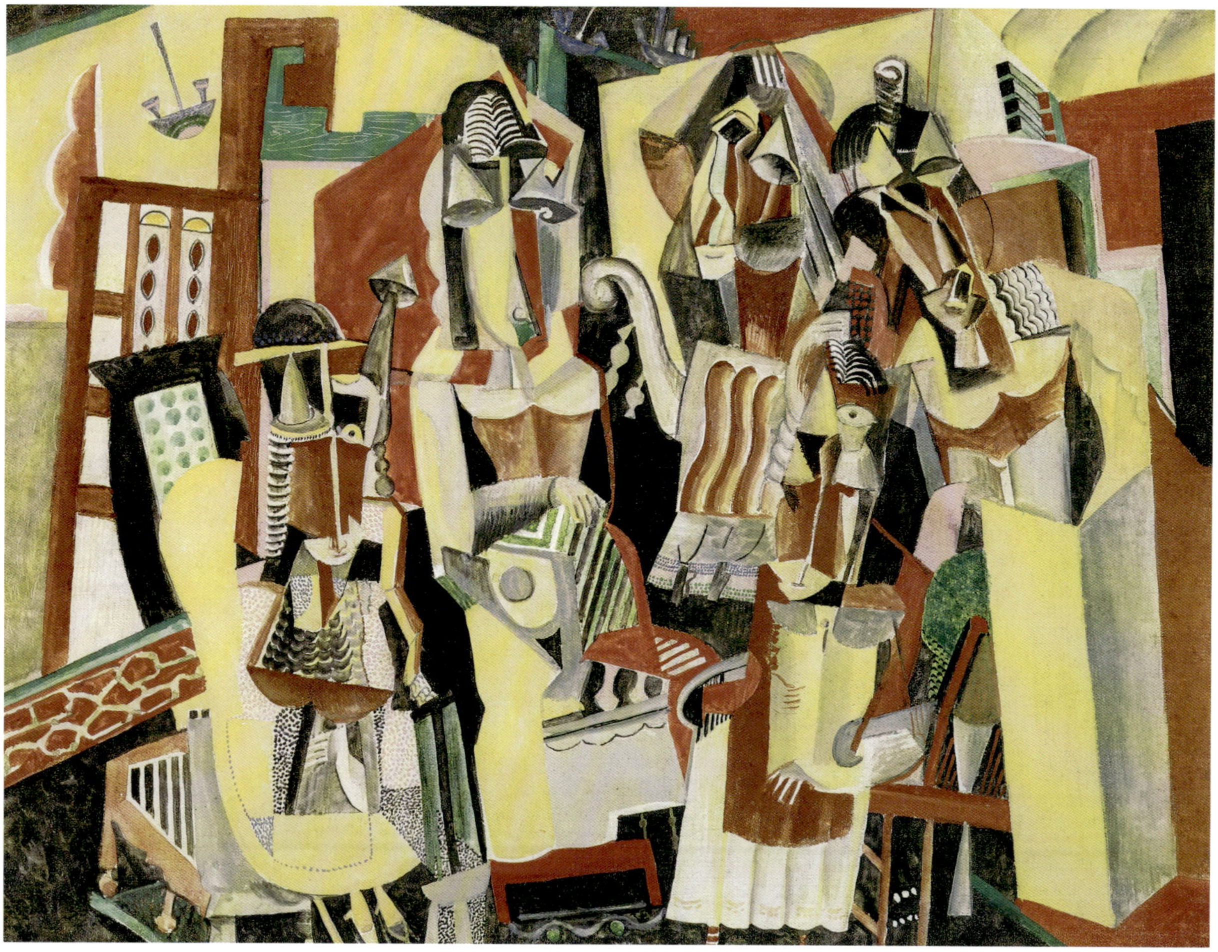

CHARLES DEMUTH

(Lancaster, PA 1883–1935 Lancaster, PA)

Sailors and Girl, ca. 1918
Watercolor and graphite on paper (18 x 12 in.)
The Old Jail Art Center, Albany, Texas, Gift of Bill Bomar

ISOLATED AS A CHILD BECAUSE OF ILLNESS, Demuth early on saw himself as an outsider, and art became his conduit to the world. Through drawings, paintings, short stories, and poetry, Demuth could explore experiences he felt relegated only to observe.[1] His detachment from life seemed to enhance his acuity, and many of his works have a striking sensitivity and directness, which is evident in *Sailors and Girl*.

Although Demuth spent much of his life in his hometown of Lancaster, Pennsylvania, he rendered this work during a visit to New York after extensive travels abroad. In the years surrounding World War I, the artist was known to patronize Greenwich Village dives and underground nightclubs, where off-duty military personnel often spent their free time. The atmosphere of promiscuity in those haunts undoubtedly inspired the subject matter of this particular work. The artist has portrayed three men surrounding a woman as if she is merely an object for the taking. As one sailor clutches her arm, another seems to flex his muscles in a display of masculine bravado. The forceful presence of the men overwhelms the woman, who appears slightly off balance. Demuth evocatively captures the coarseness of this encounter, conveying with minimal details the men's sexual aggressiveness.

Like other early American modernists, Demuth had learned to succinctly express himself through the suggestive power of color, line, shape, and form. In this example he captured his subject with watercolor, which allowed for quick renderings and thus made it his favored medium. He first sketched the figures in graphite, animating their presence with only a few lines. Then he filled in their silhouettes and the backdrop with color, employing the blotting technique, which involves applying color to the paper, then wiping some of it away before it dries. Through this method, Demuth varied the saturation of blues to suggest a shadowy, murky atmosphere. The floating, evanescent stains of color enhance the transient mood of the piece—this sordid encounter but a fleeting moment captured by the artist's watchful eye.

SRH

1 For biographical information on Demuth, see Barbara Haskell, *Charles Demuth* (New York: Whitney Museum of American Art in association with Harry N. Abrams, Inc., 1987).

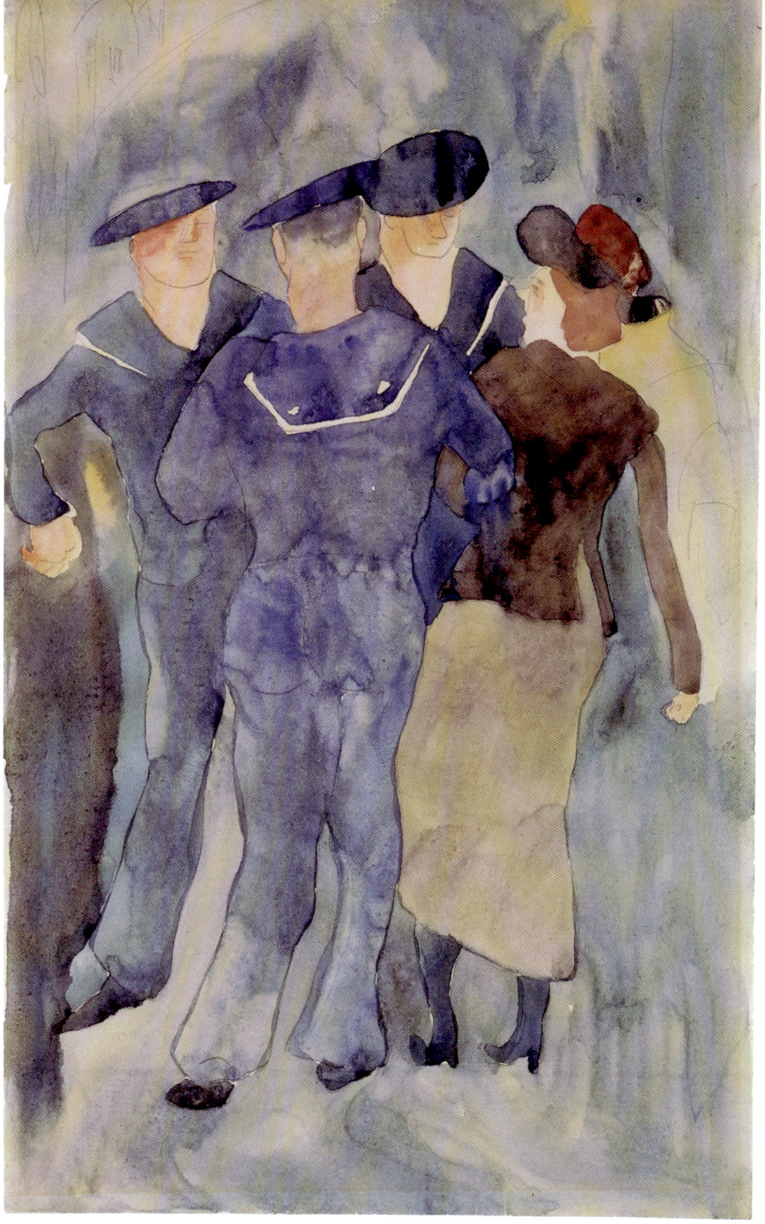

GEORGE BELLOWS

(Columbus, OH 1882–1925 New York)

Tennis at Newport, 1920
Oil on canvas (44 1/2 x 54 in.)
Signed lower center: *Geo Bellows.*
Private Collection

ONE OF THE MOST TALENTED MEMBERS OF THE ICONOCLASTIC GROUP of artists known as the Ashcan school, Bellows had already been recognized in his mid-twenties as a prodigious talent. He earned early acclaim for his gritty views of New York City, painted between 1906 and 1918, that featured children swimming, boxing matches, and the excavation of Pennsylvania Station. After World War I, however, Bellows' imagery veered markedly toward family, friends, and their activities.[1]

Tennis at Newport demonstrates all the verve and energy of Bellows' early signature works. This time, though, the focus is on America's elite enjoying a doubles match at Rhode Island's Newport Casino, a gathering place for the Vanderbilts, Havemeyers, Astors, and other members of America's high society. Still relishing the depiction of life as he experienced it firsthand—the artist was an avid athlete and tennis player himself—Bellows found artistic sustenance in the pulse of modern life where sport and society met. He completed this painting in his New York studio in March 1920, basing the image on an oil study and pencil drawings from the previous summer, the second of two consecutive seasons he and his family spent in the adjacent rural community of Middletown, Rhode Island.

In this work, a large gallery of fashionable spectators watches the major tennis event of the season, the Newport Lawn Tennis Club Invitation Tournament. Some line the grass court in the foreground, standing or seated in chairs, as was the custom at Newport; in the distance, other viewers, indicated by daubs of pigment, fill the two-story veranda of a shingle-style structure designed by McKim, Mead, and White in 1880. The men's natty boaters and blazers and the women's gaily colored frocks and parasols capture the leisure, prosperity, and ebullient mood of a summer season that also marked the signing of the Treaty of Versailles, ending World War I. The suspended balls above the net, which were used to keep track of game and set, are among the details Bellows included to characterize the competitive, yet social, ambience of a sport first introduced in the United States during the Gilded Age. The Newport Casino played a leading role in the growing popularity of the sport as the site of the national championships until 1915, when it ceded the honor to Forest Hills, New York. JM

1 For an overview of Bellows' life and career as a painter, see Michael Quick, et al., *The Paintings of George Bellows* (New York: Harry N. Abrams, Inc., in association with the Amon Carter Museum and the Los Angeles County Museum of Art, 1992).

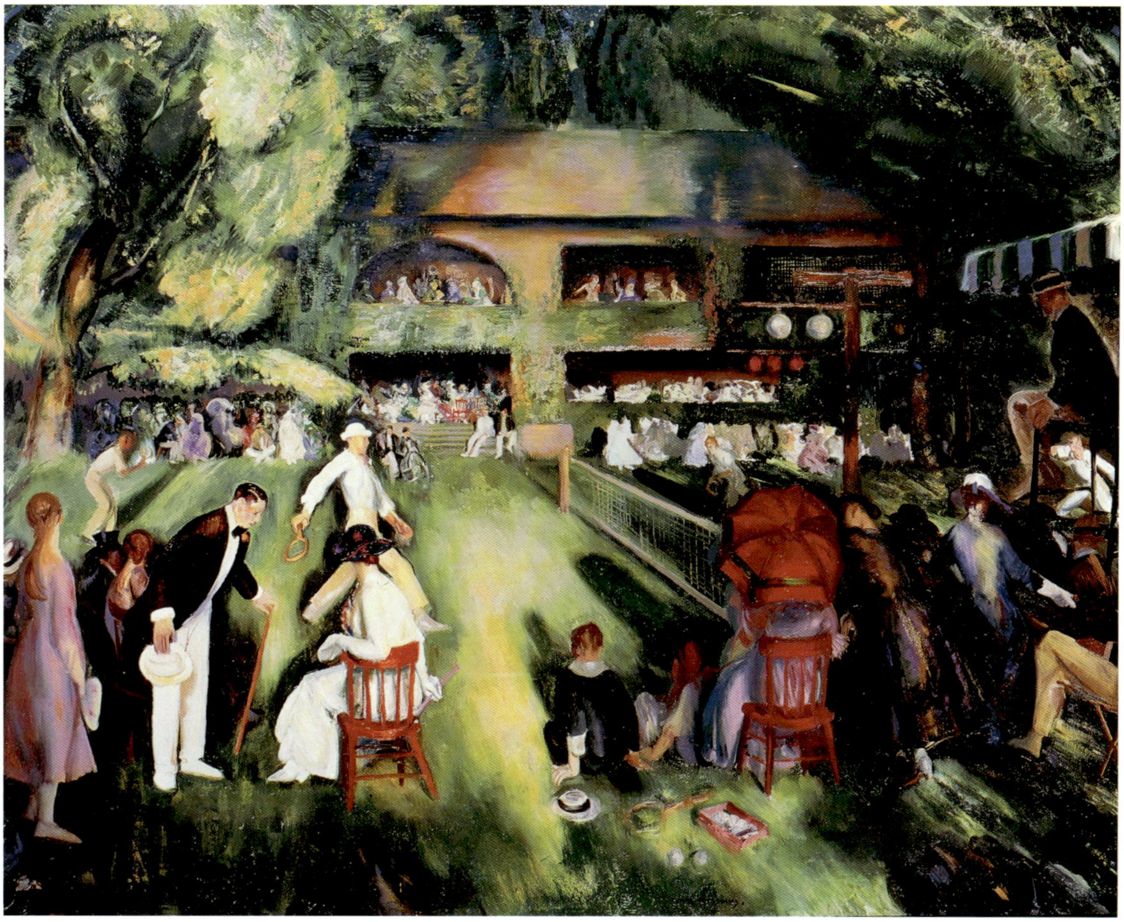

JOHN MARIN

(Rutherford, NJ 1870–1953 Cape Split, ME)

Sunset, 1922
Watercolor, graphite, and charcoal on paper (17 ½ x 21 ½ in.)
Signed and dated lower right: *Marin 22*
Eleanor and C. Thomas May

MARIN USED WATERCOLOR AS A MEDIUM for restless inquiry. Even early watercolors dating from his first trip to Europe (1905–09) display an utterly unconventional approach to handling the medium, and with it he investigated the pictorial problems of abstraction with ingenuity and fearlessness. As an artist compelled to make art that expressed what he termed "life force," Marin's remarkable gifts, especially as a watercolorist, permitted him the means to attempt such expression and, ultimately, accomplish it.

Between 1919 and 1922 Marin produced several watercolors, including *Sunset*, that used the sun's rays as a device to activate pictorial space. He painted many of these watercolors in the Stonington-Deer Isle area on Maine's Penobscot Bay, a spot he discovered in 1919 and continued to visit annually through 1928. The area would greatly influence his artistic vision.

One Marin scholar has characterized these Maine watercolors as "skyscapes" and noted how they alternate between a picturesque fidelity to nature and a schematic transcription of its components.[1] *Sunset* is among the most abstract, colorful, and vigorously painted of the series. Fully one third of the composition is devoted to sky. Here, the outsized sun, portrayed as a brilliant red circle of saturated color, hovers vibrantly above the horizon, while its rays explode outward and reflect off the terrain. Marin allows a vast, irregular field of white to remain, perhaps signifying the blinding force of the sun's glare or the whiteness of Stonington's "dream houses." At right, a sailing vessel, one of his signature motifs, is set against the horizon and isolated within a small, square block.

In his art, Marin sought what he called "a balance, a controlling of [these] warring, pushing, pulling forces."[2] He executed *Sunset* with a mixture of brushwork, augmented by touches of charcoal and graphite. Delicate, translucent washes contrast with dramatic strikes of drier, darker pigments. The effect is a rhythmic, pulsating sense of movement throughout the space. Yet, his tight, geometric control of the composition never allows the squiggles, dashes, and dots to overpower it. REL

1 Ruth E. Fine, *John Marin* (New York: Abbeville Press, 1990), 189–94.
2 John Marin, "Notes on 291," *Camera Work* 42–43 (April–July 1913): n.p.

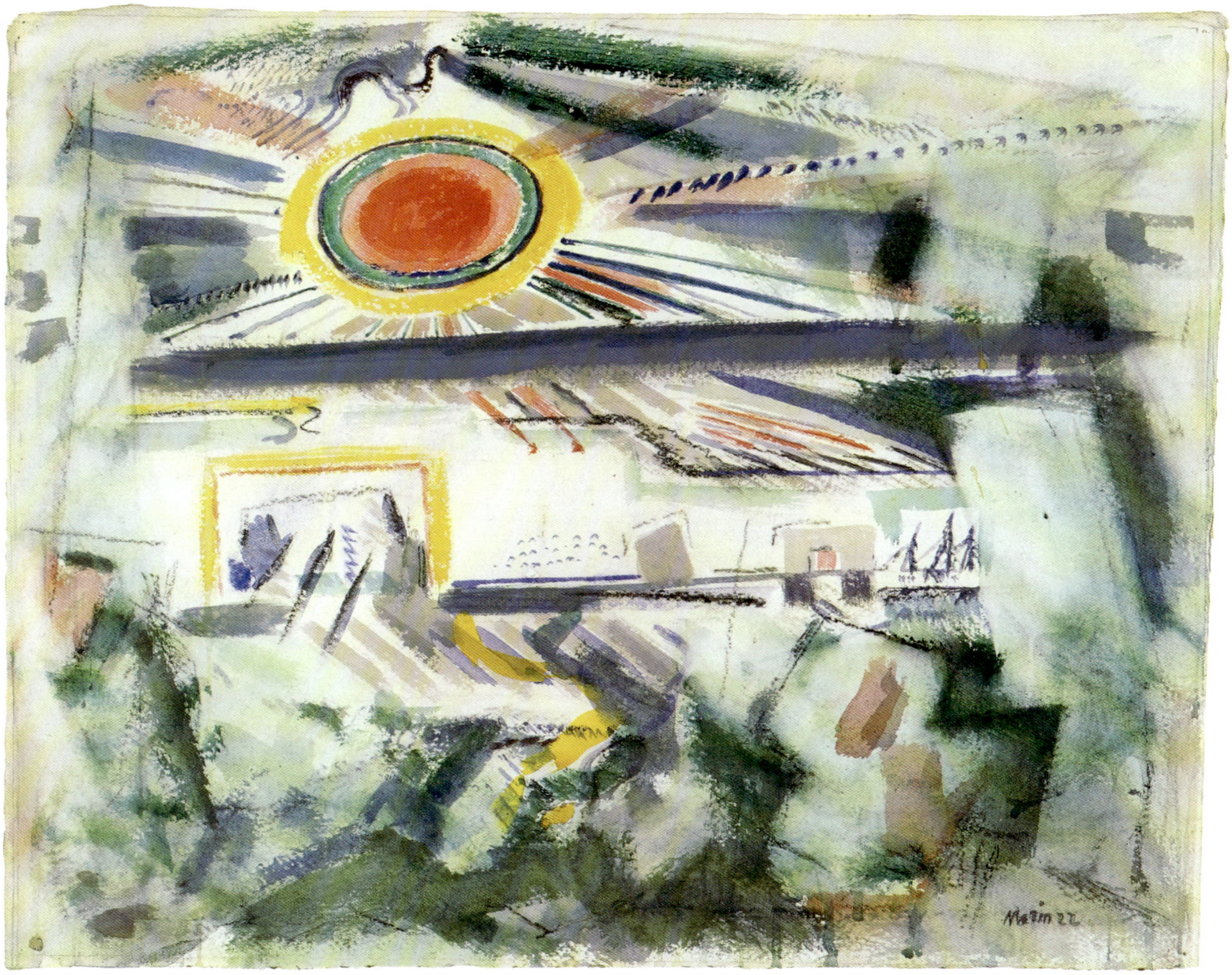
Marin 22

LAURA GILPIN

(Colorado Springs 1891–1979 Santa Fe)

Shiprock from the North Rim of Mesa Verde, 1926, printed 1929
Platinum print (4 5/16 x 6 1/4 in.)
Signed and dated on mount, lower right: *Laura Gilpin / 1929*
© 1979, Amon Carter Museum, Fort Worth, Texas, Bequest of the artist
Christopher M. Harte and Amon Burton

GILPIN BEGAN HER PHOTOGRAPHIC CAREER in the pictorialist tradition, which used soft focus to simplify the composition, soften the details, and direct the eye toward the larger components of light and dark. She learned this technique while studying at the Clarence White School of Photography in New York, but her inspiration was drawn from her native western landscape. Influenced by modern art movements to experiment with varying degrees of abstraction, it was only after Gilpin applied these theories to photographing southwestern landforms that she was able to achieve a more visually graphic presentation of her subject.

In 1924 Gilpin traveled south from her home in Colorado Springs, through the Mesa Verde National Park, to photograph Anasazi ruins. Continuing south through the Navajo lands of New Mexico, she was thrilled by the history and romance of the ancient native dwellings and landscape, and decided to prepare a photographic booklet on Mesa Verde. With this publication she established a model for all her subsequent books, which would present a study of the landscape and geology, as well as the ruins and culture of the area's inhabitants. In this way she evoked an ancient American past rooted in the landscape.

This photograph is a fine example of this approach. From a vantage point on the North Rim of Mesa Verde, Gilpin photographed the receding mesas looking toward Shiprock, the 1,700-foot-tall volcanic formation fifty miles south of the park. Although she often photographed the rock by itself, which rises majestically from the desert floor, in this image she allows it almost to disappear into the mesa in the background, becoming a ghostly shadow. In her Mesa Verde booklet, she titled the image *The Phantom Ship of the Desert* and wrote that this perspective presents the rock in its most mysterious and beautiful context. Extending the metaphor, the text describes the receding mesas as a "succession of similar promontories, jutting out into the valley like giant piers awaiting the arrival of some leviathan ship. And indeed that very ship steers its phantom course fifty miles south of the Mesa, on the vast desert sea of the Navajo reservation."[1]

BMC

1 Laura Gilpin, *The Mesa Verde National Park: Reproductions from a Series of Photographs by Laura Gilpin* (Colorado Springs: Gilpin Publishing Co., 1927), n.p.

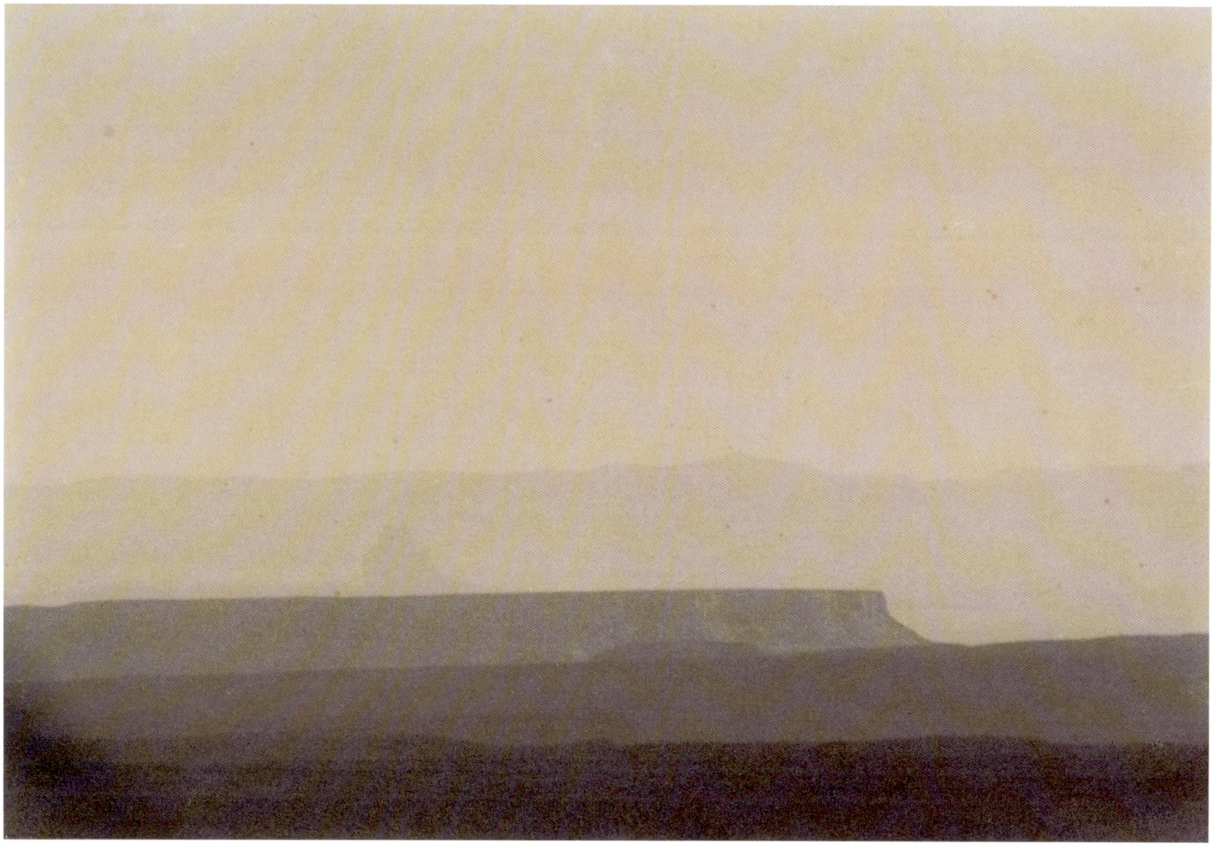

GEORGIA O'KEEFFE

(Sun Prairie, WI 1887–1986 Santa Fe)

In the face of increasing pressures as a celebrity and the wife of preeminent photographer and gallery director Alfred Stieglitz (1864–1946), O'Keeffe began a series of solo trips to Maine in the 1920s. She was ill-at-ease both with the critics' sensationalized, Freudian interpretations of her work and her husband's ubiquitous circle of associates, family, and friends. Longing for privacy, she retreated to York Beach, Maine, in the summer of 1926. It was there, inspired by the solitude and shoreline, that she began an evocative series of shell paintings that includes these stunning companion pieces.

Given O'Keeffe's frame of mind—consciously separating herself from Stieglitz—the opposing forms of *Open Clam Shell* and *Closed Clam Shell* can be seen as symbolic portraits of the artist and her husband. Other members of Stieglitz's artistic circle, such as Marsden Hartley (1877–1943) and Charles Demuth (1883–1935), had previously used abstract signs and symbols to represent portraits. Well aware of their examples, O'Keeffe had depicted a birch tree as a "portrait" of a friend in 1925.[1]

Viewed as representative portraits of the artist and Stieglitz, *Open Clam Shell* would seem to represent the latter, who was certainly the more exposed and accessible of the two personalities. O'Keeffe filled the center of this canvas with a black spermlike shape indicating its maleness, while on the upper portion of *Closed Clam Shell* she delineated rounded forms that resemble breasts. The closed casing can be seen as a metaphor for O'Keeffe's more private persona; its curved halves do not seal completely, however, suggesting a certain flexibility of temperament. The straight edges of *Open Clam Shell*, on the other hand, imply Stieglitz's unbending nature.

Both shells fill their canvases, demonstrating the close-up approach that O'Keeffe first used with floral subjects in 1924. This technique was inspired by various sources, such as her friend Paul Strand's (1890–1976) close-up photography and her former teacher Arthur Wesley Dow's (1857–1922) advice to fill compositional space. Here, her magnification of the shells exposes their exquisite shapes, while the minimal palette of opalescent, creamy whites, heather grays, and touches of soft amber simulates the pearly textures of the mollusks' exteriors.

With the striking results of these paintings, O'Keeffe was convinced she needed future solo trips. In 1929 she began her seasonal journeys to the Southwest, where she created her now landmark renderings of desert life. While these two works are poignant mementos of her Maine sojourns, they divulge more than the physical place; they embody her emotional journey as well. As she later reflected, "I find that I have painted my life—things happening in my life—without knowing."[2]

SRH

1 Charles C. Eldredge, *Georgia O'Keeffe* (New York: Harry N. Abrams, Inc., in association with the National Museum of American Art, Smithsonian Institution, 1991), 43–44.
2 Georgia O'Keeffe, *Georgia O'Keeffe* (New York: Viking Press, 1976), n.p.

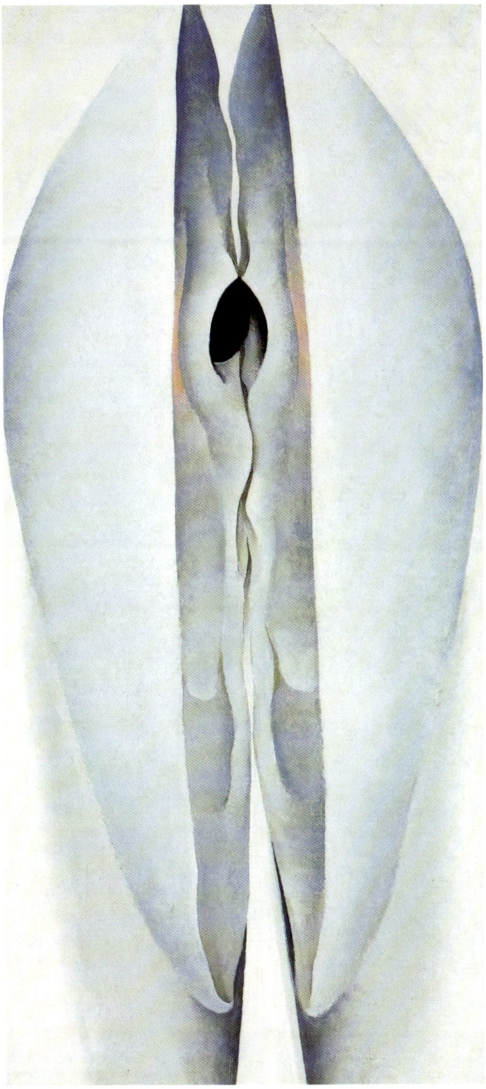

Open Clam Shell, 1926
Oil on canvas (20 x 9 in.)
Private Collection

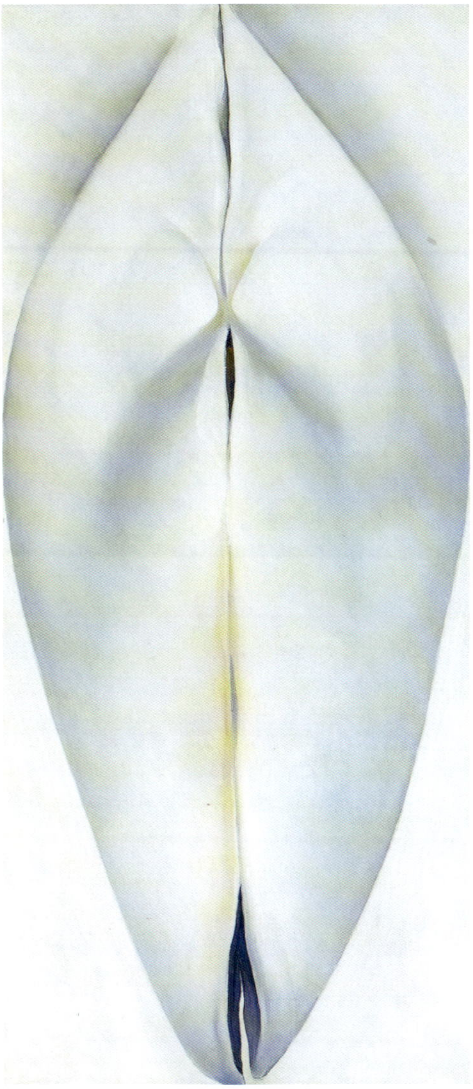

Closed Clam Shell, 1926
Oil on canvas (20 x 9 in.)
Private Collection

IMOGEN CUNNINGHAM
(Portland, OR 1883–1976 San Francisco)

Magnolia Bud, 1929, printed later
Gelatin silver print (7 1/8 x 5 1/4 in.)

Peter C. Ross and Lynda G. Loomis

ALTHOUGH CUNNINGHAM BEGAN HER PHOTOGRAPHIC CAREER when soft-focus pictorial photography was in vogue, in the 1920s she increasingly turned to a more sharp-focused, modernist style. Through a concentrated period of experimentation with floral still lifes, she developed a dedication to purity of form and clarity of detail.[1]

Flowers were perfect subjects for the photographer. While raising her children, she gardened in her spare time and could find ample photographic material in her own backyard in Oakland, California. She may also have been encouraged in this interest by other photographers. *Vanity Fair*, the photographer's favorite magazine, published Charles Sheeler's (1883–1965) *Zinnia and Nasturtium Leaves* in May 1920 and Edward Steichen's (1879–1973) *Lotus, Mount Kisco, New York* in July 1923. The greatest influence on her floral studies, however, was her friendship with a German prince, Egon von Ratibor (1886–1939), who renamed himself James West, partly because of his devotion to the American West. A horticulturist working on the creation of the University of California at Berkeley's botanical garden, West introduced Cunningham to the California Horticultural Society and went with her on field trips to photograph unusual plant subjects.

From 1923 to 1925, Cunningham worked to complete an extended study of magnolia blossoms and gradually simplified her compositions to focus more on their exquisite form and essence. Among the oldest trees in the world, magnolias are evergreens and can grow to heights of ninety feet. Their gigantic flowers, which bloom throughout the summer and fall, have six to twelve fleshy petals and can be as large as ten inches across.

Typically, Cunningham did not photograph the blooms in her garden, but brought them into the house to eliminate distractions by isolating them against a blank background. She let them fill the entire negative, and she focused sharply on the subjects to emphasize their details. Two versions from this magnolia series—one that focuses on an open blossom and another that looks closer at its core—have become her best-known images. But this lesser-known study of an unopened bud is perhaps an even more elegant interpretation of the purity of form. BMC

1 For biographical information on Cunningham, see Richard Lorenz, *Imogen Cunningham: Flora* (Boston: Little, Brown, and Co., 1996).

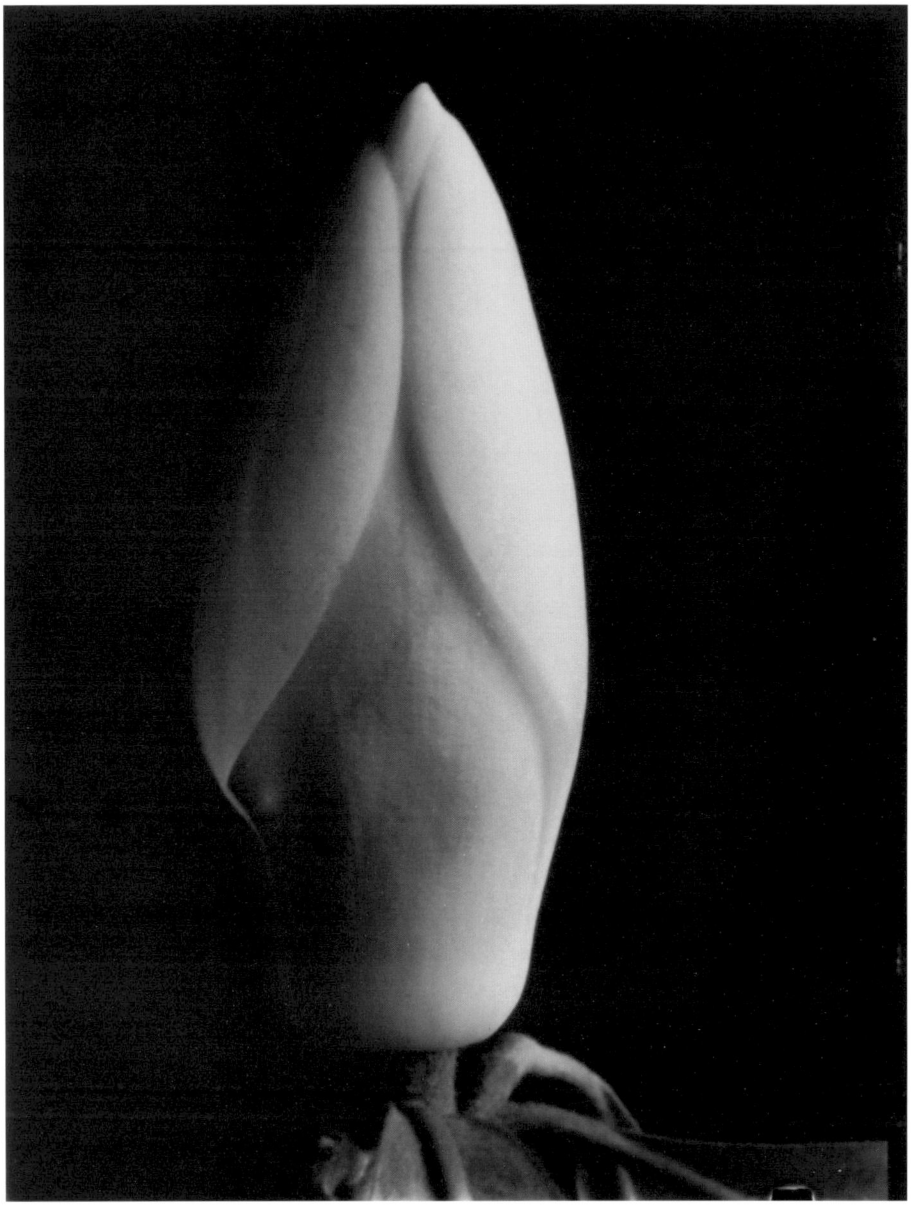

STUART DAVIS

(Philadelphia 1892–1964 New York)

Café, Place des Vosges, 1929
Oil on canvas (29 x 36 ½ in.)
Signed lower right: *Stuart Davis*

Carolyn and Roger Horchow

BY THE TIME DAVIS WENT TO PARIS IN 1928, he was already one of America's most progressive talents. As a student, he had mastered a gritty realist style and, in the 1910s, had rapidly assimilated techniques from postimpressionism and cubism. Just prior to going abroad, he created a dynamic series of abstract paintings; but the visual influence of Paris inspired him once again to alter his style.

In *Café, Place des Vosges,* Davis shifted away from strict abstraction to more recognizable forms. Recalling his work in the City of Light, the artist once said, "The actuality was so interesting I found a desire to paint it just as it was."[1] To capture the spirit of this scene in the Place des Vosges, a seventeenth-century plaza of brick and stone houses, Davis assumed a vantage point in the central square. From there, he could look across the street to a café in a building with the address of number "7" inside a box of green and multihued gray. He then successfully consolidated the entire setting into a cohesive plane, demonstrating his command of cubist principles. The yellow sign on the far left of the building, which reads "Sens Interdit" (one-way), would have actually faced to the right to alert drivers to the correct traffic flow around the plaza. Although he includes such details as the tilted red and blue cones—which indicate that tobacco is for sale—elaborate architectural features are distilled into sparse forms. The keystones above the arch and the glass panes along the façade are minimized in scale and distinguished by simple, gridlike hatching. Through the archway on the left is the entrance to the café, where a fan-shaped screen was used to protect outdoor patrons from the elements. Davis' choice of glowing pink to illuminate this spot seems to suggest his fondness for a place where he likely spent countless hours writing letters home and conversing with other artists.

The flattened rectangularity of this image suggests a postcard, a souvenir of a trip Davis later referred to as the "one outstanding event in [his] artistic life."[2] No wonder, then, that *Café, Place des Vosges* represents a critically important stage in the gestation of Davis' wholly original style, one that deftly balanced realism with abstraction and distinguished him as one of America's most important modernists.

SRH

1 James Johnson Sweeney, *Stuart Davis*, exh. cat. (New York: Museum of Modern Art, 1945), 20; quoted in Patricia Hills, *Stuart Davis* (New York: Harry N. Abrams, Inc., 1996), 86.
2 Stuart Davis, "Self-Interview," *Creative Art* 9, no. 3 (September 1931): 211.

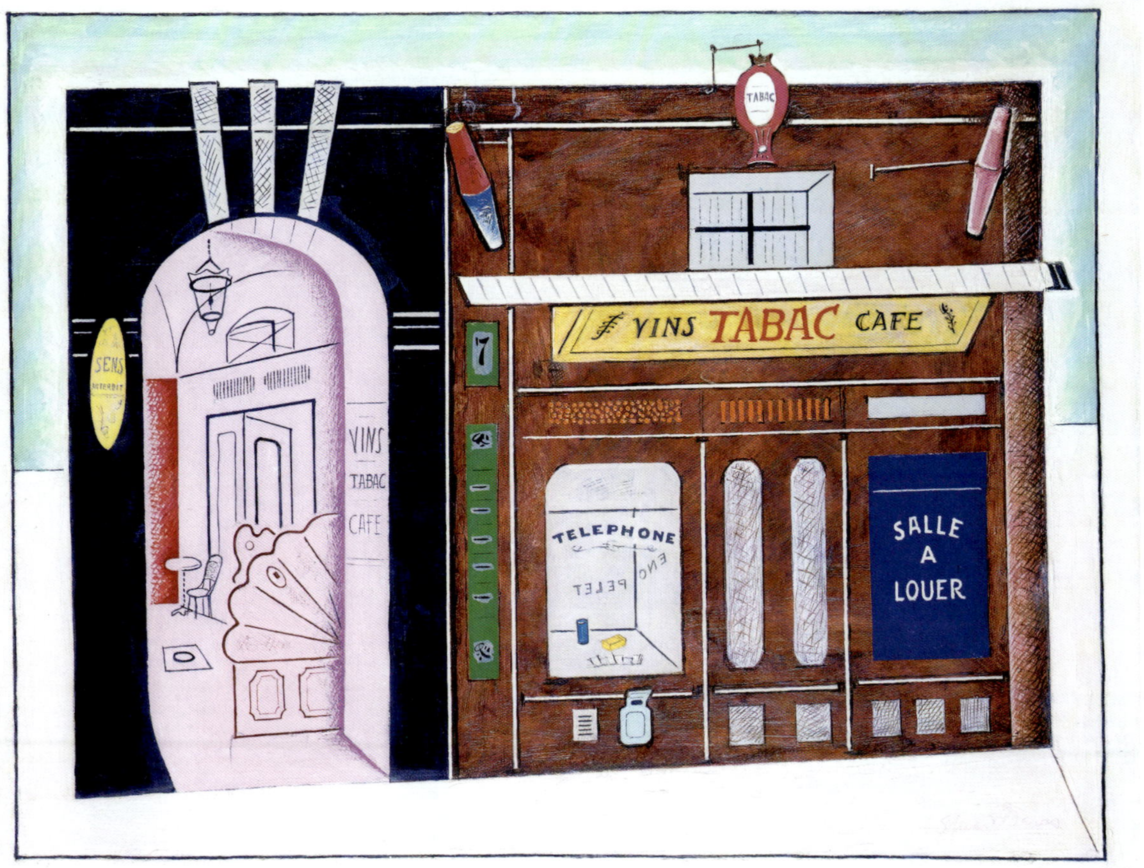
TABAC
VINS TABAC CAFE
7
SENS
VINS
TABAC
CAFE
TELEPHONE
SALLE
A
LOUER

RAYMOND JONSON

(near Chariton, IA 1891–1982 Albuquerque)

Abstract Two, 1929
Oil on canvas (24 x 15 in.)
Signed and dated lower left: *Jonson 29* [incised]
Mr. and Mrs. B. Michael Chitty

WHAT BEGAN FOR JONSON AS A MYSTICAL EXPERIENCE in 1911 ultimately led to his heading up the Transcendental Painting Group, an organization of artists devoted to nonrepresentational painting, established in New Mexico in 1938. His art was a search for spiritual fulfillment; it involved a lengthy period of experimentation, and it began with repeated drawings of the same natural forms, which he refined into patterns and gradually transformed from recognizable elements into solid shapes built upon a strong color note.

Jonson developed a design theory—he called it a "unifying principle"—to determine pictorial space. He once wrote, "I have always felt that there should be a governing sense of arrangement, that is, that a composition usually should have order and most often a simple basic motive of spaces, and interesting variety of shapes and spaces, a balance of line direction."[1] Throughout the late 1920s and 1930s, he experimented with his theory by working serially on a particular theme or symbol.

Abstract Two is one of ten works from the *Digits* series executed in 1929–30. Jonson created each painting in the series around an immutable symbol represented by a specific color. For this work, the artist protracted the numeral "2" into a highly schematized, yellow figure whose lower legs bend backward as if kneeling in prayer and whose arms coil forward. Some elements recall a naturalistic setting, while others are thoroughly attenuated and abstracted. The figure never fully merges with its surrounding space but rather sets it in motion. The design's rhythmic power is further enhanced by the repetition of the numeral to create small echoes throughout the canvas.

Jonson was a meticulous craftsman. His works seem constructed, rather than painted, and his patterned surfaces evoke the texture of weaving, perhaps inspired by Native American textiles. In some areas he applied a heavy impasto, in others a lighter dappled effect. Their jewel-like appearance is partly the result of his use of luminous colors, which recall the gelatins he used while working at the Chicago Little Theatre as a lighting designer in the teens and early twenties.

Jonson considered his work on the *Digits* series a breakthrough, a complete release from the fundamental format for landscape painting: "Here I believe I have or am touching on an approach to realization."[2] Indeed, it was only when he no longer felt compelled to represent nature in his art that he arrived at a clear artistic and spiritual purpose. REL

1 Ed Garman, *The Art of Raymond Jonson, Painter* (Albuquerque: University of New Mexico Press, 1976), 58.
2 Ibid., 84.

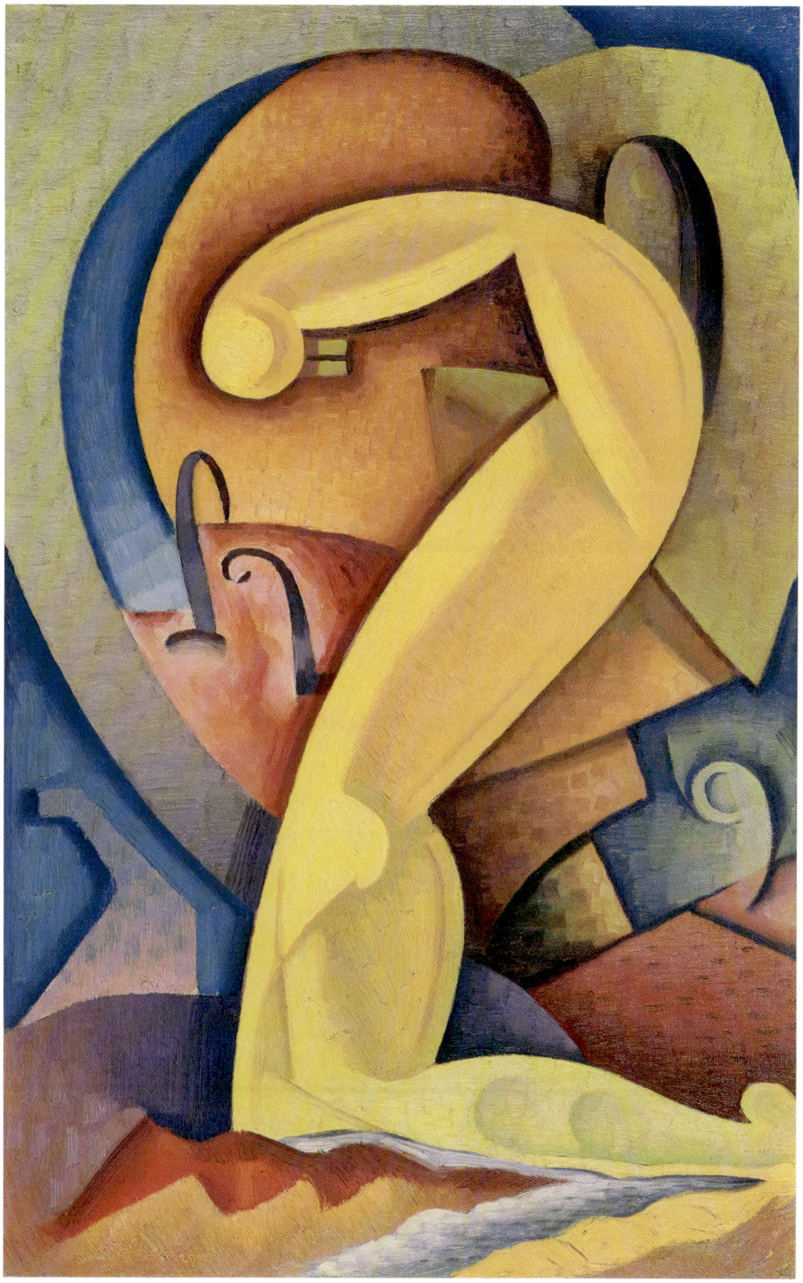

EDWARD HOPPER

(Nyack, NY 1882–1967 New York)

House by an Inlet, 1930
Oil on canvas (28 x 38 in.)
Signed lower left: *EDWARD HOPPER*
Marie and Hugh Halff

WITH THE PURCHASE OF THEIR FIRST AUTOMOBILE in 1927, Hopper and his wife, Josephine, began traveling throughout New England during what would become their annual summer excursions away from Manhattan. They spent several seasons in Gloucester, Massachusetts, and toured Maine's small coastal villages before beginning to summer routinely on Cape Cod in 1930. This canvas was executed in Hopper's New York studio in February 1930 and bears the distinct impress of these locales.[1]

House by an Inlet is a signature work. The theme of the lonely house, empty and still, figured prominently in his art after the early twenties. Scholars consider such paintings "house portraits," which the artist used as metaphors for human experience and emotion. Occasionally, Hopper identified these solitary houses or gave the paintings titles to mark their locations and the time of day. Here, however, the house remains unknown, making its silence all the more mysterious. Silhouetted against the sky, it stands starkly on a bank of sandy soil, approachable only by a narrow strip of land at the left. The shades are uniformly lowered, compelling viewers to look for signs of human habitation.

The overarching theme of this painting is a specific, transitory moment of light. The sun's rays are not blazing, activating a sharp play of shadows, but muffled, further accentuating a sense of reticence. Pallid light imparts a uniform coolness throughout the composition, and Hopper's sprightly touches of color, such as the cerulean for the water, prevent the light from stifling the scene. In their journals, the Hoppers recorded the painting initially as a "pale picture, opalescent morning" and later as a "grey but luminous—white house on dull day. . . . All shadows muted."[2] While the clouded sky is severed by a stretch of blue that runs diagonally across the canvas, this too reads as enigmatic, for viewers cannot know what course the clouds will take.

House by an Inlet is a remarkable distillation of thought and emotional content. In painting, Hopper relied upon his memory and struggled to prevent the act of painting at the easel from interfering with it. In a noted interview with Brian O'Doherty, the artist remarked upon picture making as "a long process of gestation in the mind and arising emotion."[3] The idea of a solitary house standing eerily upon an embankment may not be easily read as a metaphor for life, but here, in the curious arrangement of forms and the odd cropping of the scene to place viewers in the middle of the water, the painting reveals an underlying emotional complexity. REL

1 Gail Levin, *Edward Hopper: A Catalogue Raisonné*, vol. III (New York: Whitney Museum of American Art in association with W. W. Norton & Co., 1995), 196.
2 Ibid., 196.
3 Brian O'Doherty, "Portrait: Edward Hopper," *Art in America* 52 (December 1964): 77.

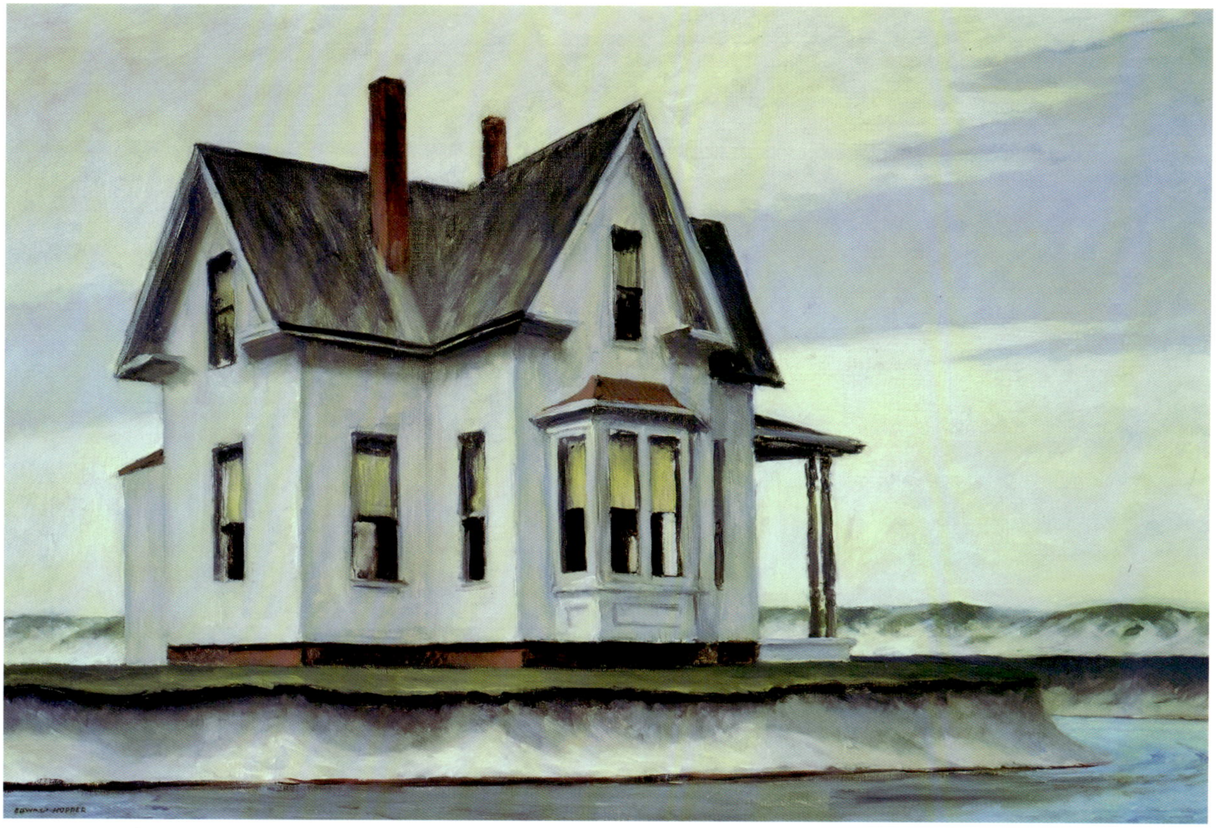
HOPPER

EDWARD WESTON

(Highland Park, IL 1886–1958 Carmel, CA)

Pepper No. 30, 1930
Gelatin silver print (9 7/16 x 7 1/2 in.)
Signed and dated lower right: *EW 1930*

Gernsheim Collection, Harry Ransom Humanities Research Center, The University of Texas at Austin

LIKE OTHER CALIFORNIA PHOTOGRAPHERS OF THE TIME, Weston began his photographic career producing soft-focus pictorial studies. However, by the 1920s he found them increasingly unsatisfying and began a photographic quest for purity of form. Well aware of the work his friend and colleague Imogen Cunningham (1883–1976) was doing with flowers, Weston turned instead to fruits and vegetables, preferring the nuances and imperfections of their flesh to what he perceived as the perfection of floral form.

Between 1927 and 1937, when he received a Guggenheim Fellowship and traveled throughout the West, Weston photographed primarily at home and in his studio. While he frequently went on location to do commercial portraits, he favored photographing small objects in his studio, where he could use his 8-by-10-inch view camera and better control the natural light. To achieve even lighting and vividly depict three-dimensional form, Weston initially photographed his subjects against muslin that filtered light from behind. However, he was much happier with the results when he placed the objects in a funnel that reflected light into the shadows. He photographed his first pepper in 1927, and he soon became obsessed with the vegetable's sinuous qualities. Sonya Noskowiak, his student and lover, brought him new examples every day. In 1929–30, he made forty-three negatives of peppers—thirty of them during a concentrated, four-day session.

Weston thought of these photographs as both portraits of individual vegetables and as representations of an absolute "pepper-ness," as he phrased it. On August 8, 1930, he wrote about the image here in his daily journals, which were later published: "It is classic, completely satisfying,—a pepper—but more than a pepper: abstract, in that it is completely outside subject matter. It has no psychological attributes, no human emotions are aroused: this new pepper takes one beyond the world we know in the conscious mind."[1] This particular image became his most popular, and he made at least twenty-five prints of it.

BMC

1 Nancy Newhall, ed., *The Daybooks, Volume II, California* (Rochester, N.Y.: George Eastman House, 1961), 181.

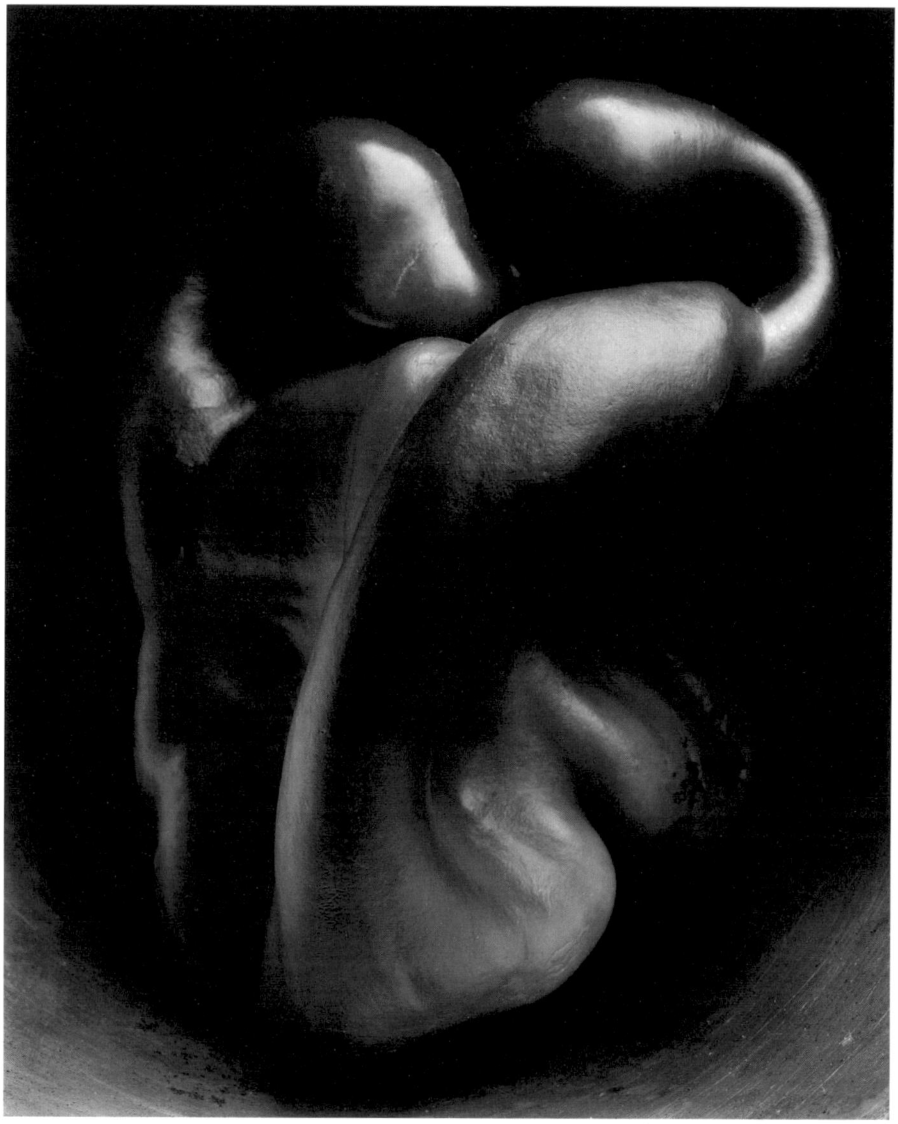

CHARLES BURCHFIELD

(Ashtabula Harbor, OH 1893–1967 West Seneca, NY)

Winter Landscape with Stream, 1931
Watercolor on paper (23 x 34 in.)
Signed lower right: *CEB* [monogram]
Private Collection

Burchfield's watercolor scenes often inhabit the quiet junctions of the landscape and the periphery of America's small towns, initially in his native Ohio and, after 1925, in Gardenville, New York, a suburb of Buffalo. The artist enjoyed long walks in the country in all seasons, and the watercolors that resulted resonate with a combination of lyricism and nostalgia.

Winter Landscape with Stream likely illustrates Buffalo Creek, a small tributary not far from his Gardenville home.[1] The water, trees, and snow-laden landscape in the work form alternating dark and light diagonal bands, united by the artist's remarkable ability to convey winter's unique light and atmosphere. The elevated perspective creates a high horizon line of neatly compacted buildings. This underscores the individuality of Burchfield's viewpoint, as do the expressive, long purple shadows cast by bare trees upon the glistening snow and the radiant stars—a favored motif suggesting spiritual symbolism—shimmering across the water's surface. Burchfield's appreciation for the seasonal cycles in a scene often included a suggestion of sound, such as the melodious trickle of the partially frozen stream in an otherwise still and silent landscape.

Burchfield's deep reverence for classical music furthered the fusion of his inner vision with the American landscape. Shortly before making *Winter Landscape*, he acquired the first available recording of Jan Sibelius' (1865–1957) Second Symphony. This release marked the beginning of a decade of widespread interest in the Finnish composer among Americans seeking their own cultural identity through vernacular artistic forms. Burchfield, too, felt a kinship with the great composer who, in response to the Russian threat of repressive political control of Finland, had written rhapsodic music about his homeland. Burchfield sought a similar conjunction of truth and beauty in order to convey "the great epic poetry of Midwest American life, and my own life connection with it."[2]

The year he created this work, Burchfield wrote in letters to his friends of his yearning to achieve a richer awareness of his origins: "As an artist grows older, he has to fight disillusionment, and learn to establish the same relation to nature as an adult as he had when a child. . . . That is my struggle now."[3] In its breadth of statement and heartfelt associations, Burchfield's watercolor becomes a personal archetype of small-town Middle America that approaches the grandeur of a great symphony.

JM

1 Nancy Weekly, Head of Collections and the Charles Cary Rumsey Curator, Burchfield-Penney Art Center, Buffalo, N.Y., in a letter to the author, April 1, 2002.
2 Charles Burchfield, "On the Middle Border," *Creative Art* 3, no. 3 (September 1928): xxx.
3 John I. H. Baur, *The Inlander: Life and Work of Charles Burchfield, 1893–1967* (Newark: University of Delaware Press, 1982), 192.

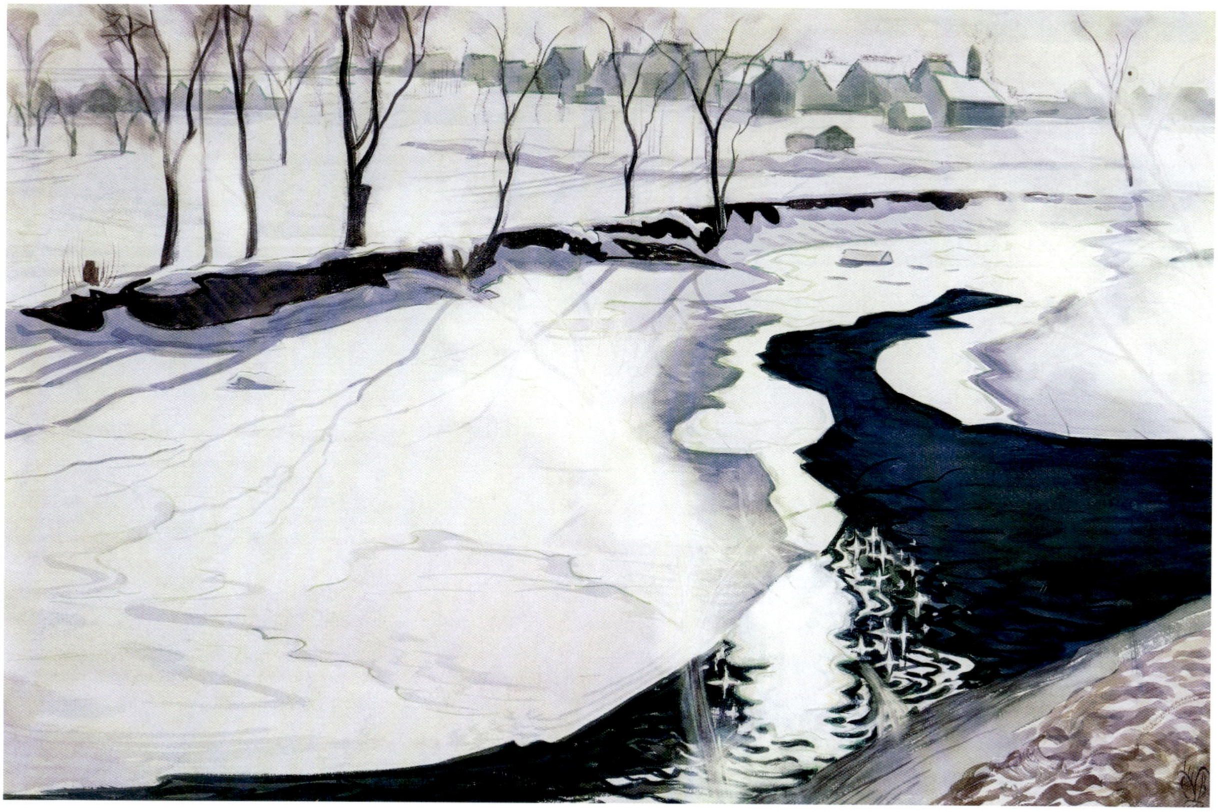

THOMAS HART BENTON

(Neosho, MO 1889–1975 Kansas City, MO)

Romance, 1931–32
Egg tempera and oil on panel (45 ¼ x 33 ¼ in.)
Signed lower left: *Benton*
Photo credit: George Holmes

Jack S. Blanton Museum of Art, The University of Texas at Austin,
Gift of Mari and James A. Michener, 1991

BENTON REGARDED THE SOUTH AS AN ESSENTIAL CONSTITUENT in the epic continuum of American life and history. Road trips to the area during the 1920s gave him the visual vocabulary to describe those unique regional features that would become increasingly fascinating to other artists, writers, and composers of the period. The artist's autobiography reflects his sympathies toward African-Americans in the South and the disquiet he felt over the ever-imminent threat of violent racism. His painted imagery, however, eschews overt political debate for subjects emblematic of southern labor, such as the rice harvest in Louisiana, Alabama's steel manufacturing, and the cattle, horse, and oil ventures of West Texas.

Romance reveals Benton's preference for a generalized figural type and the use of spare contextual detail to establish place. He integrates the long-limbed, softly modeled figures into the landscape through the vertical forms of the tree and chimney, while the woman's red dress provides a bright counterpoint to the painting's narrowly defined range of hues. Attired in their finest clothes, the couple stroll into the night beneath a full moon, leaving behind the day's privations. Benton's experiences with the coastal Gullah culture of Georgia and South Carolina may have inspired this work. There, the cotton pickers' seasonal work ". . . provides opportunity for courtship and at night after work the girls dress up and parade about. . . . The boys close in on them. . . . They edge off in pairs toward the palmettos or moss-draped live oaks."[1]

As his career advanced, Benton became known for subjects indelibly associated with the Midwest, but this painting's powerful evocation of the South appealed to writer James Michener (1907–1997) who, in 1962, purchased it directly from the artist after seeking him out at his Kansas City home. Michener enjoyed a bout of whiskey drinking with the artist and Harry S. Truman, two men Michener admired for their populist politics. The meeting occurred the same year that Michener ran unsuccessfully for Congress from Pennsylvania. This experience evoked sentiments parallel to Benton's own, for Michener had come to appreciate the nation as "a carefully assembled mosaic whose individual pieces require close attention."[2] *Romance* was among the over 200 twentieth-century paintings that Michener and his wife donated to the University of Texas. JM

1 Thomas Hart Benton, *An Artist in America* (New York: R. M. McBride & Co., 1937), 171.
2 James A. Michener, *The World Is My Home: A Memoir* (New York: Random House, 1992), 188. Michener described his acquisition of the painting in Lawrence Grobel, *Talking with Michener* (Jackson: University Press of Mississippi, 1999), 116.

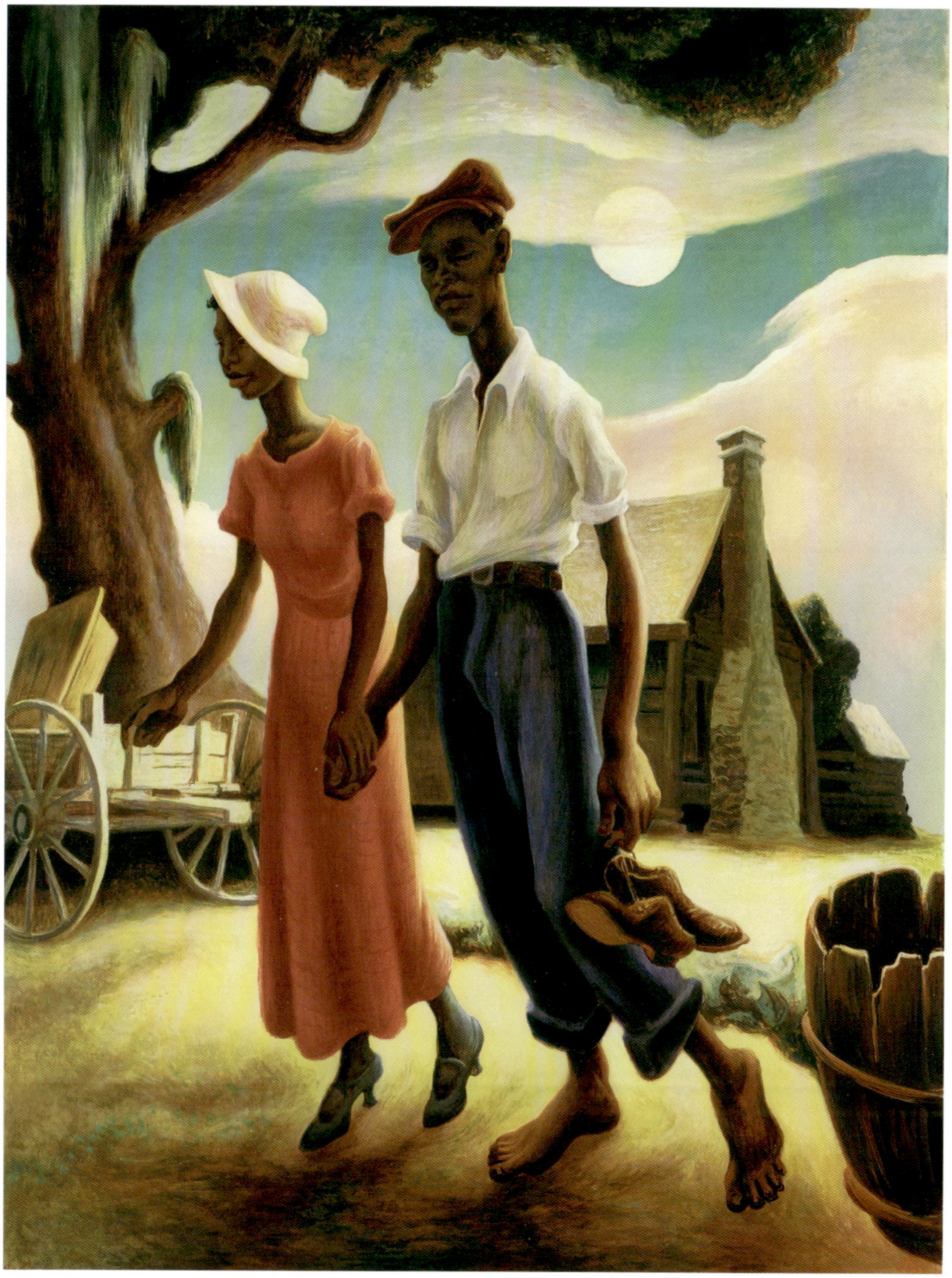

PAUL STRAND

(New York 1890–1976 Orgeval, France)

Christo with Thorns, Huexotla, Mexico, 1933
From *Photographs of Mexico*, 1940
Photogravure (10 5/16 x 8 1/8 in.)
© 1940 Aperture Foundation, Inc., Paul Strand Archive
Gernsheim Collection, Harry Ransom Humanities Research Center, The University of Texas at Austin

LIKE OTHER ARTISTS AND INTELLECTUALS OF THE TIME, Strand was sympathetic to the ideals of the Mexican Revolution. Wishing to personally witness the Mexican Renaissance—the cultural flowering that occurred in the decades following the war—he drove to Mexico City in the fall of 1932 and remained until 1934. The work he completed there culminated in *Photographs of Mexico* (1940), a portfolio of twenty photogravures that remains one of the most beautiful photographic portfolios ever produced.

Strand arrived in Mexico at the invitation of Carlos Chávez, an official who directed government support toward art projects. Chávez appointed Strand his chief of photography and cinematography and instructed the artist to make a report on both the arts and the teaching of arts and crafts in the state of Michoacán. Traveling with Velásquez Chávez, Carlos' nephew and an art teacher, Strand photographed throughout the central states of Hidalgo, Puebla, Mexico, Oaxaca, and Tlaxcala. Impressed and inspired by the people's emotional strength and faith, Strand photographed anonymous individuals on the streets, as well as religious artifacts in churches. He was especially drawn to *bultos*, carved figures of Christ and the Virgin Mary, believing they demonstrated the spiritual component of the people and the talent of their artisans. In his 1933 report to Chávez, Strand wrote that the handcrafted figures took on "beauty, dignity, and meaning," and that he hoped to do the same in his own work.[1]

After returning to the States, Strand produced 250 copies of the portfolio. He chose the photogravure process because its richness of tonality could simulate the appearance of his original platinum prints. In 1967 the collection was published again, in an edition of 1,000 copies, as *The Mexican Portfolio*. Strand's leftist politics led him to depict Mexico and its workers with sympathy in this body of work. Alluding to the connection between the sacred and the secular in Mexican culture, by juxtaposing *bultos* images of the Passion of Christ with portraits of peasants, he posited a Christlike nobility, dignity, and humility in the people's everyday struggles. BMC

1 Maren Stange, ed., *Paul Strand: Essays on His Life and Work* (New York: Aperture, 1990), 116.

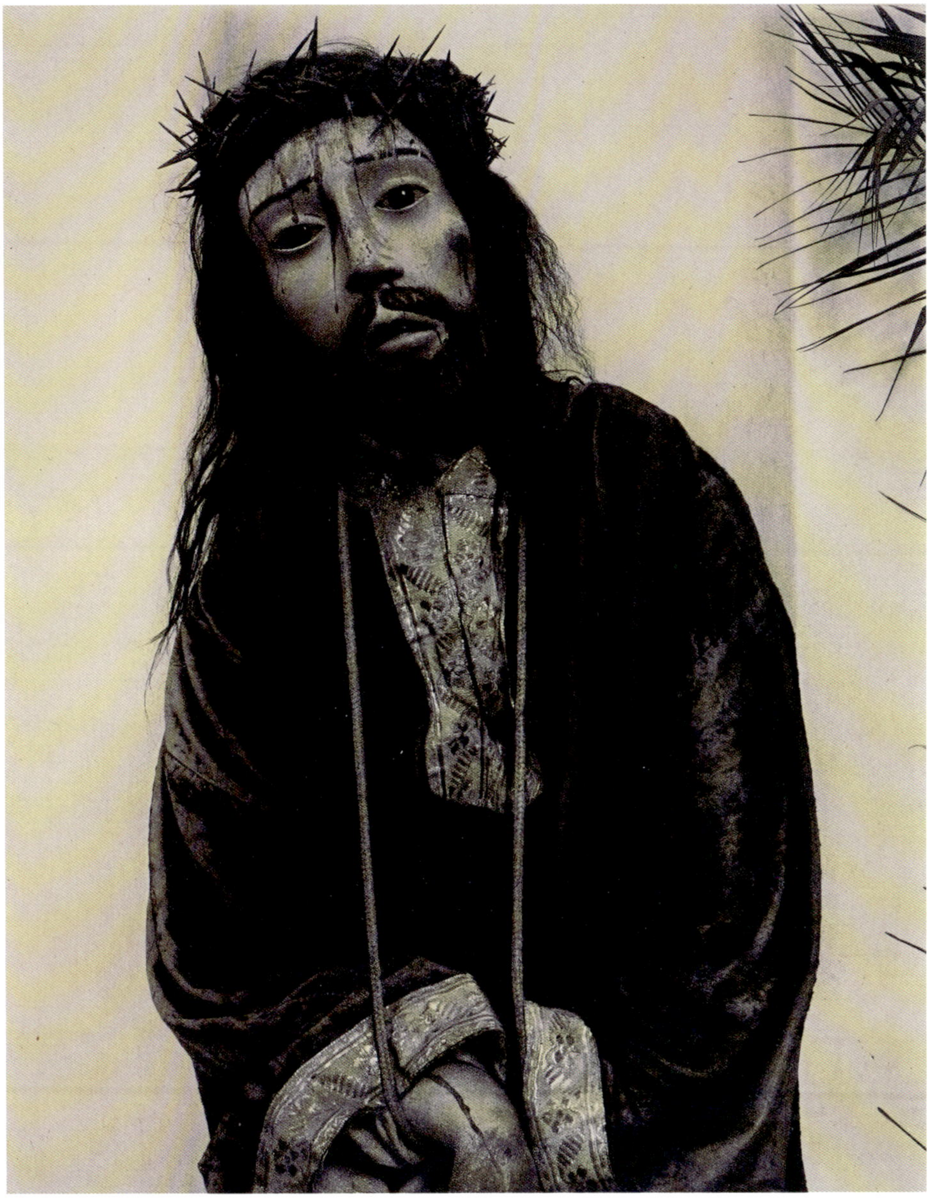

ADOLF FASSBENDER

(Grevenbroich, Germany 1884–1980 Newton, NJ)

City, Thy Name Be Blessed, 1934
Gelatin silver print (16 1/4 x 11 5/8 in.)
Signed and inscribed on mount, lower right: *Adolf Fassbender*; lower left: *City, Thy Name Be Blessed*

Peter C. Ross and Lynda G. Loomis

FASSBENDER WAS A LEADER OF THE SECOND GENERATION of photographers who advocated the handcrafting of photographs through extensive manipulation in the darkroom. Although most leading fine art photographers, like Alfred Stieglitz (1864–1946), had turned away from this style in the teens, it remained popular in camera clubs and exhibition salons well into the mid-twentieth century. Defending the benefits of exercising complete control over the process, Fassbender defined the photographic artist as one who "uses the mechanical light-sketch as a foundation and by technical manipulation. . . is able to recreate and rebalance the values of light and shade until by the very ingenuity of his appreciative treatment, an artistic creation results."[1]

After emigrating from Germany in 1911, Fassbender enjoyed an early career in portraiture and commercial photography in New York. He closed his studio in 1928, shortly after beginning to exhibit his photography in salons. He taught photography at the Brooklyn Institute of Arts and Sciences from 1930 to 1935 and wrote extensively about the medium throughout the 1930s, submitting many articles on photographic manipulation to journals like *Camera Craft*. The year he made this photograph, the artist had a one-person exhibition at the Camera Club of New York and became one of 100 charter members of the Photographic Society of America, which would become the country's largest organization of amateur photographers.

Commenting on his photograph of nuns in front of the skyline of New York City, Fassbender described the successful effect of the image: "I was able to portray the materialistic creation of man in stone and steel dwarfed by the heavenly grandeur overhead. The heads of nuns, bowed in prayer, seem to be blessed by the great slanting beams of sunlight."[2] In an October 1936 article in *Camera Craft*, he revealed how he had arrived at the final result. First, while on a boat returning from Nova Scotia, he made many exposures of the nuns, the shore, and the cloud formations. He then made a transparency from two different negatives by masking them during the exposure, then applying extensive handwork to the transparency to remove the distracting chimneys, water towers, and the nuns' hands holding their hoods down in the heavy winds. Finally, he used chalk to introduce the sun's rays and thus completed the final negative from which this print was then made. BMC

1 Adolf Fassbender, quoted in Christian A. Peterson, *The Pictorial Artistry of Adolf Fassbender* (Nutley, N. J.: Fassbender Foundation, 1994), 13.
2 Ibid., 15.

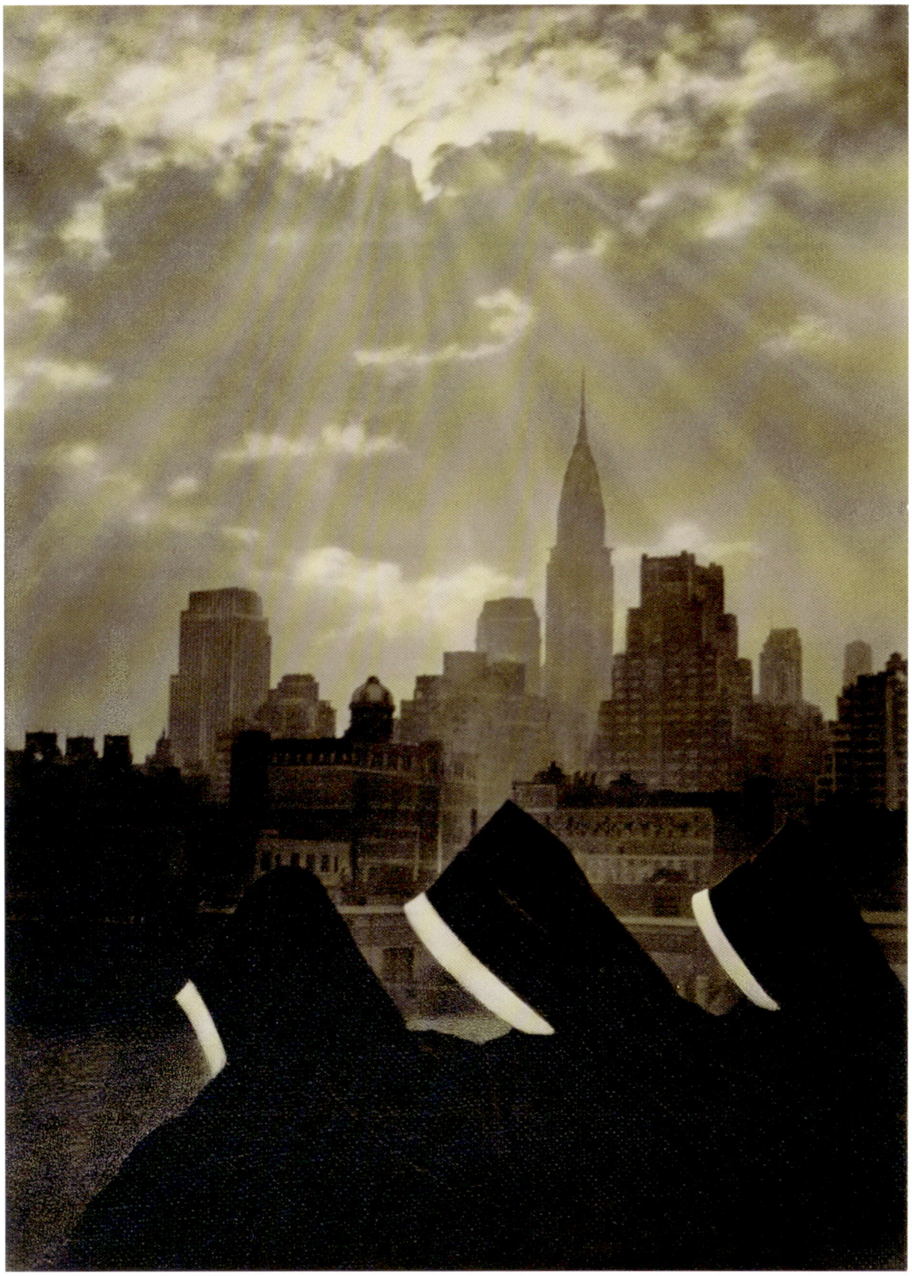

WINOLD REISS

(Karlsrühe, Germany 1886–1953 New York)

Bullhead, ca. 1934
Pastel and tempera on paper (52 x 30 in.)
Signed lower right: *WINOLD/REISS*
Burlington Northern Santa Fe Corporation

CASUALTIES OF WESTERN EXPANSION and years of inconsistent federal Indian policies, the Blackfoot Indians of Montana that Reiss encountered during eleven summer sojourns held tightly to vestiges of their traditional culture. Among the sweeping changes they had endured was the rapid attrition of their lands from the 1870s to the 1890s. They ceded property to the Great Northern Railway Company and then to the United States government for the establishment of Glacier National Park, which opened in 1910. In 1927 the president of the Great Northern, Louis W. Hill Sr. (1886–1948), commissioned Reiss, a successful East Coast interior designer and artist, to record these once-powerful people of the northern plains, by then confined to a reservation near Browning, Montana.

Reiss' portraits captured his reverent attitude toward the Blackfeet and helped satisfy his lifelong quest for an authentic western experience, fueled by romantic tales of America he had heard as a boy in Germany. The colorful regalia worn by Bullhead in this drawing was increasingly rare, for by the date of this work the Blackfeet had been wearing modern dress for some time. Bullhead, a medicine man, wears his signature half-red, half-yellow horn headdress, once worn only in battle.[1] It is adorned with brass bells and weasel-tail pendants, which were symbols of high stature. The colorful and geometric beaded designs favored by the Blackfeet adorn Bullhead's garments and the ceremonial bag for the simple wooden-handled pipe that was used to seal important agreements.

Reiss' sensitive portraits appeared on calendars, travel literature, and playing cards as promotional icons for the enterprising railroad in their efforts to lure tourists to the spectacular scenery of Glacier National Park.[2] Employing the Blackfeet to serve as tour guides for the seasonal visitors and to live in tipis on the grounds of the company's grand park lodges further perpetuated this successful advertising campaign. Bullhead's reflective countenance and relaxed posture, reinforced by a decorative fluid blue line alluding to Reiss' famed art deco interiors, convey both the pride and resignation that attended the stark contrast between the past and present of all Native Americans. JM

1 The headdress is now in the collection of the Denver Art Museum.
2 Reiss' drawing of Bullhead appeared on the Great Northern Railway Company's 1938 calendar.

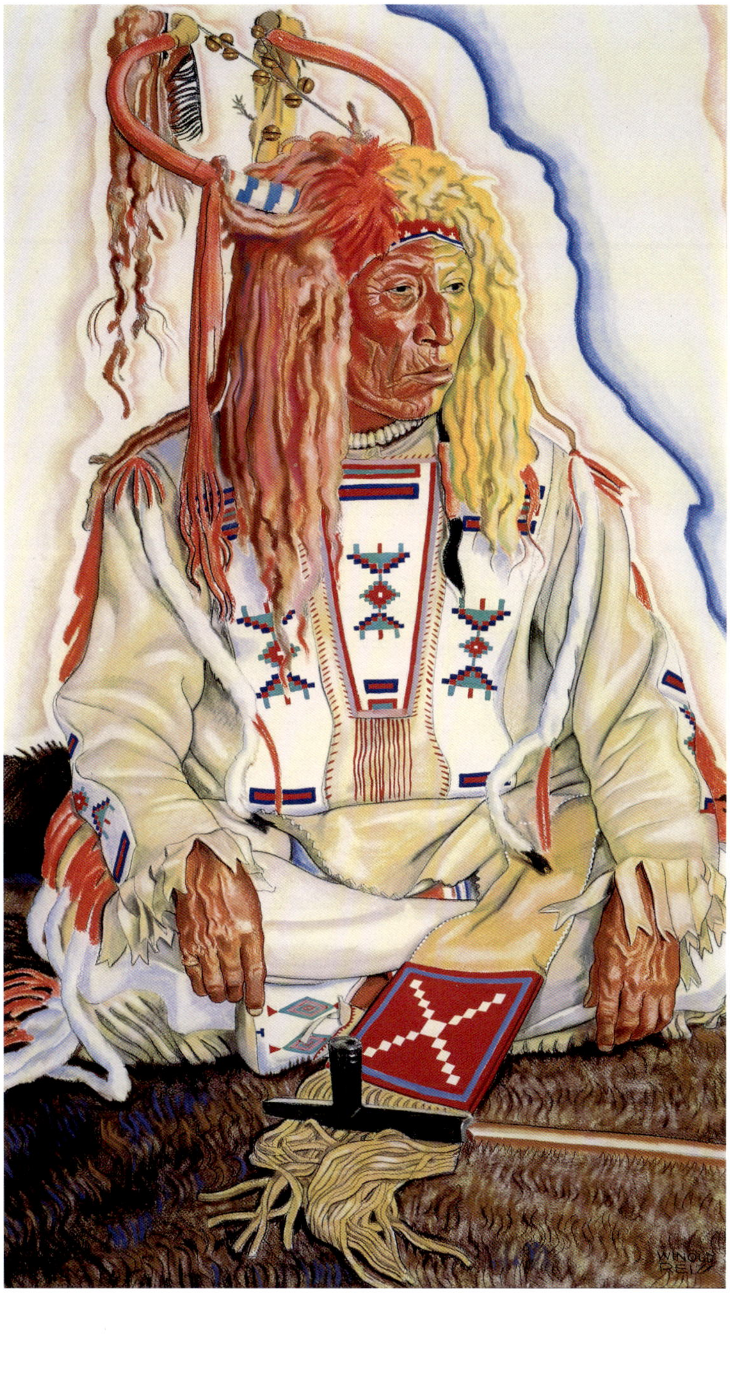

WALKER EVANS

(St. Louis 1903–1975 New Haven)

Floyd Burroughs' Bedroom (Tenant Farmhouse), Hale County, Alabama, 1936
Gelatin silver print (7 15/16 x 10 in.)
Signed on reverse, lower right: *Walker Evans*
The Menil Collection, Houston

WITH HIS STRAIGHTFORWARD COMPOSITIONS and distinctly American subject matter, Evans ushered the documentary style into the arena of fine art photography. Hired by the Resettlement Administration (later called the Farm Security Administration or FSA) in the fall of 1935 to document the effect of the Great Depression on the country, Evans was the only FSA photographer to use a tripod-mounted, 8-by-10-inch camera. The equipment demanded careful precision but allowed him to exercise great control over the composition of his images.

During the summer of 1936, Evans left the FSA program to travel with his friend, the writer James Agee (1909–1955), while collaborating with him on an article about tenant farmers for *Fortune* magazine. The resulting work remains the most memorable of Evans' long career. In Hale County, Alabama, Agee and Evans stayed for three weeks in the home of Floyd Burroughs, interviewing and photographing three area tenant families. Evans made fewer than 100 images during the project, many of which focused on rooms in the farmers' homes, which fascinated him. Although *Fortune* rejected the article, Agee and Evans expanded and published their work in the book *Let Us Now Praise Famous Men* (1941). Critical response to their collaborative venture was light and only 600 copies sold; when it was republished in 1960, however, its time had come. The book garnered extensive attention and has since become recognized as one of the most important American publications of its kind.

Although Evans is known for his lack of artifice and preference for strict adherence to the actual scene, he did on occasion rearrange objects for the sake of the image, a practice evident in this photograph. Agee's text describes the bedroom depicted here as having two beds set parallel to each other, with their headboards flush against the rear wall. Evans rearranged the furniture for this photograph, ostensibly to ensure that the foot- and headboards would stand out against the wood grain. Additionally, while Agee's text describes the bed linens as old, stale, and moist, Evans' photograph portrays them as clean and white, indicating that he manipulated the image in the darkroom to achieve greater contrast. He clearly wanted to show that despite their poverty, the sharecroppers did not succumb to their harsh environment, but maintained a simple order and beauty in their lives. His rosy depiction went only so far. The flies on the bed were mistaken by the printers as dust spots to be removed from the negative before publication, but Evans insisted that the "spots" remain.[1] BMC

1 James C. Curtis and Sheila Grannen, "Let Us Now Appraise Famous Photographs: Walker Evans and Documentary Photography," *Winterthur Portfolio* 15, no. 1 (Chicago: University of Chicago Press, Spring 1980): 16–17.

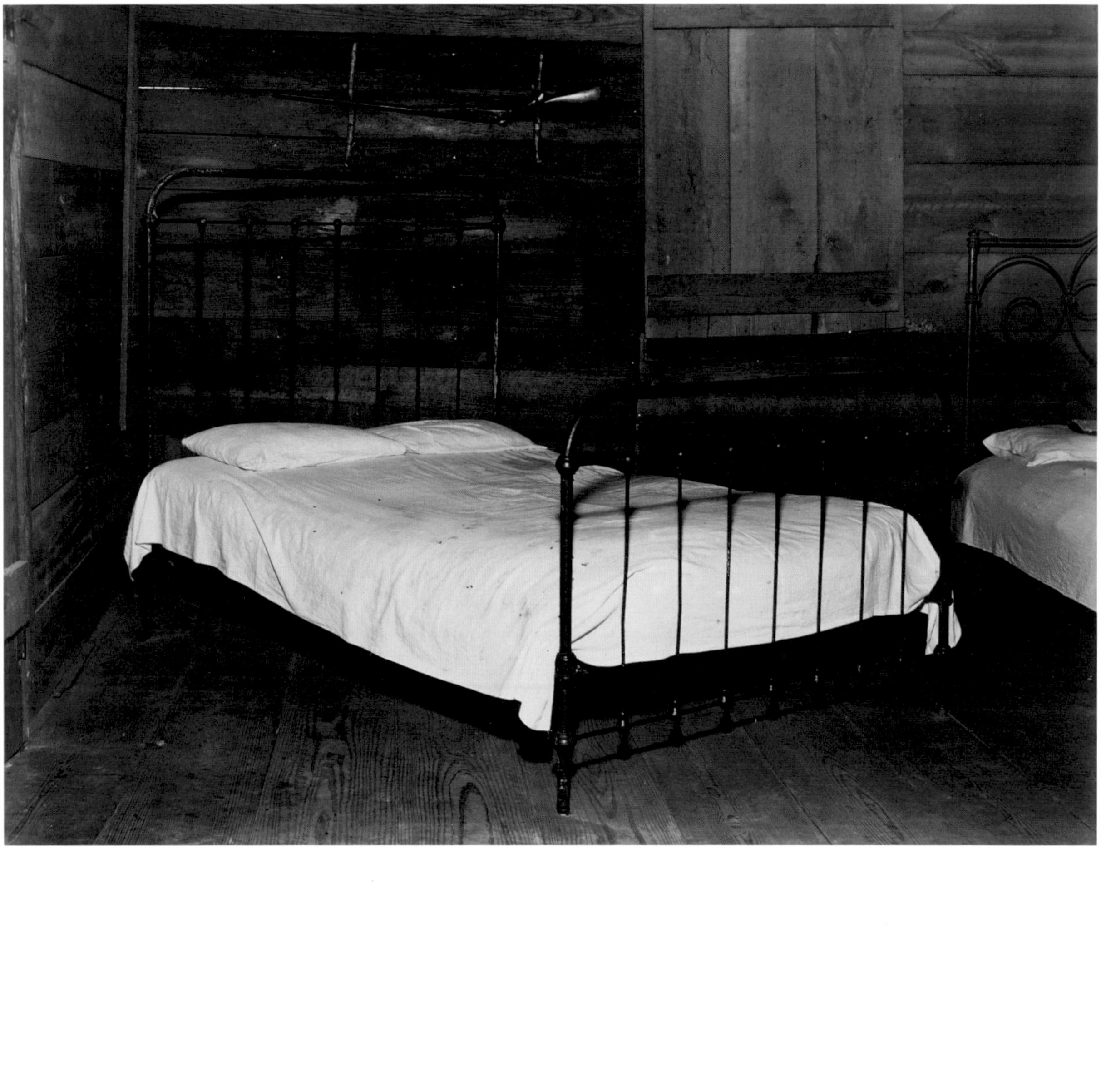

GEORGE L. K. MORRIS

(New York 1905–1975 Stockbridge, MA)

Crescendo, 1936
Oil on canvas with collage (31 ½ x 41 in.)
Signed lower right: *Morris*
Private Collection, Dallas, Texas

IN THE 1930S, AT A TIME WHEN REALISM DOMINATED the visual arts, Morris became one of the decade's most fervent spokesmen for abstraction. He helped organize the American Abstract Artists group and wrote articles that defended the viability of nonfigurative art against critics who disparaged it as elitist and irrelevant. He argued that geometric abstraction could provide order and stability in the midst of chaotic times; having studied in Paris, he believed that cubist-inspired styles were the most appropriate means of expressing modern, contemporary life.

In *Crescendo* Morris applied these artistic convictions to the vanguard opera *Elektra* by German composer Richard Strauss (1864–1949). Morris' interest in Strauss was perhaps the result of his recent marriage to artist/singer Suzy Frelinghuysen (1912–1988), who was a fledgling opera soprano in 1935. Both had experienced the opera since their youth, but music was Frelinghuysen's passion. In the late 1940s, she became an acclaimed vocalist after a breakthrough role in one of Strauss' operas.

When *Elektra* debuted in 1909, it was hailed as a musical tour de force. Strauss had collaborated on the piece with librettist Hugo von Hofmannsthal (1874–1929), who devised the lyrics as a Greek tragedy. Elektra, the main character, is consumed with avenging the death of her murdered father, Agamemnon. Strauss conveyed the story's escalating tensions through a series of continuous crescendos. One of these climactic cadences clearly inspired Morris to search for visual equivalents to evoke its sound.

Crescendo eloquently suggests the score's upsurge of musical tone through colorful overlapping planes. Although Morris layers them within a shallow, cubist space, these black, red, blue, gold, and white forms suggest the orchestra's swelling sounds. Black, V-shaped "notes" simulate the reverberation of loud, piercing tones while semicircular golden hues evoke a soft timbre. Shades of blue, green, and brown balance the color spectrum, and the interspersing strips of red seem to allude to the violent tenor of the opera.

To acknowledge the inspiration for the painting, Morris includes a piece of *Elektra*'s sheet music and inscribes the title in the upper-right corner in ascending and descending capital letters, like notes on a staff. A music critic remarked that in the midst of one of *Elektra*'s climactic passages, Strauss' orchestration remained "rational, lucid, clean, without redundancy or sensationalism."[1] The same might be said for Morris' intellectual and vibrantly abstract translation. SRH

1 Derrick Puffett, ed., *Richard Strauss: Elektra* (Cambridge, England: Cambridge University Press, 1989), 144.

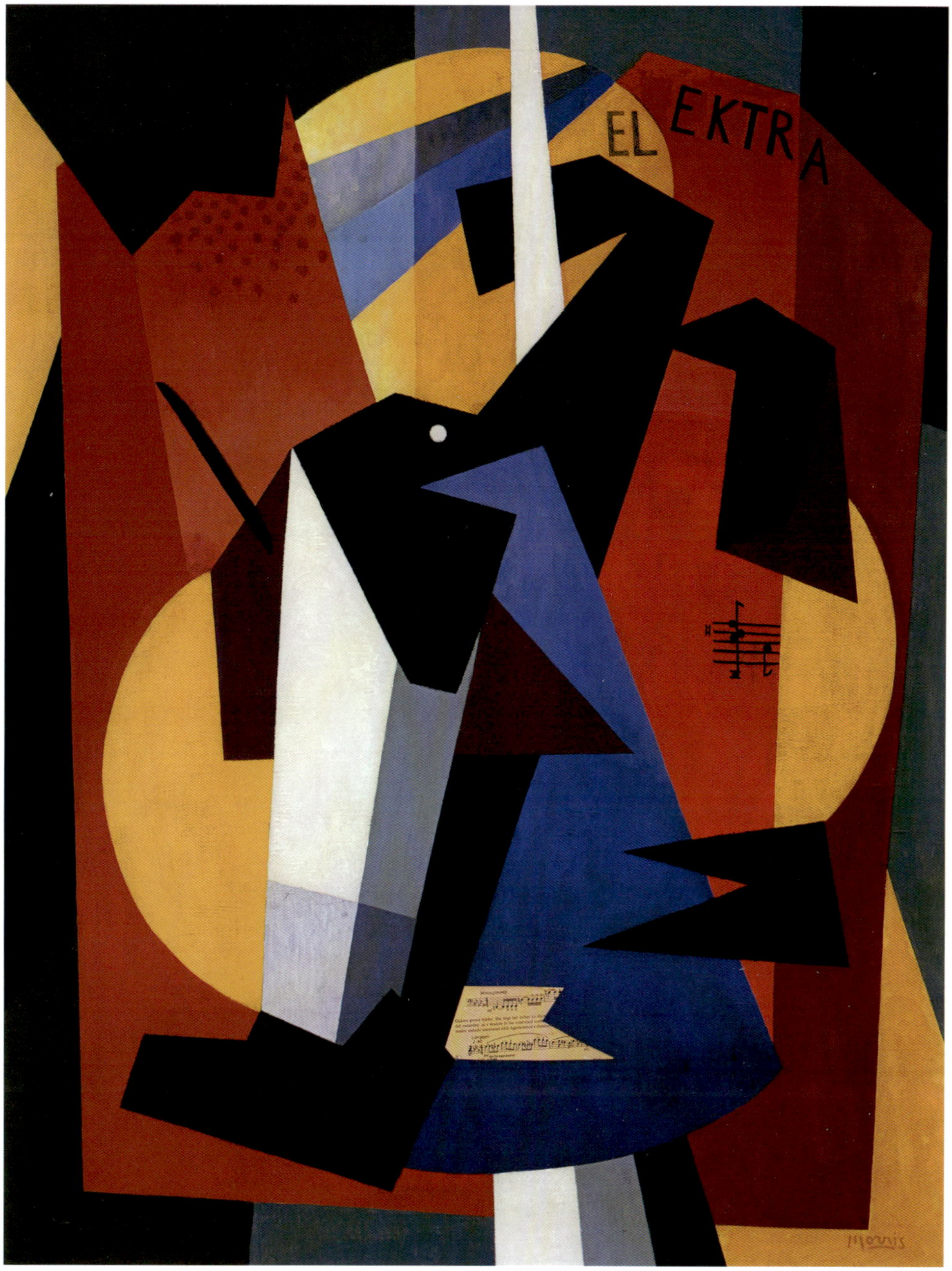
EL EKTRA

RUSSELL LEE

(Ottawa, IL 1903–1986 Austin, TX)

Mr. and Mrs. John Landers, Tenant Farmers, at the Back Door of Their Farmhouse, Near Marseilles, Illinois, 1937
Gelatin silver print (6 1/2 x 9 9/16 in.)
Signed on reverse: *Russell Lee*
Wittliff Gallery of Southwestern & Mexican Photography,
Southwest Texas State University/San Marcos, Texas

A RENOWNED DOCUMENTARY PHOTOGRAPHER, Lee was born and grew up in Ottawa, Illinois, less than ten miles from where he made this photograph. After studying chemical engineering, he became manager of a roofing factory in Kansas City, but he left there in 1929 to study painting. While at the Art Students League in New York City, he became concerned that he was not developing his painting skills fast enough. His initial thought was to use a camera to capture the fleeting images he wanted to paint, but as he photographed he became increasingly captivated by the medium's immediacy.[1]

Early on, Lee realized the power of the camera to capture and convey the country's social and economic conditions. After discovering, in 1936, that a federal agency called the Historical Section of the Farm Security Administration was hiring photographers to document the effects of the Great Depression on the American people, Lee approached Roy Stryker (1893–1975), who was in charge of the program, for a job. The agency did not yet have a photographer working in the Midwest. Aware of the importance of depicting the breadbasket of the country, Stryker hired Lee to photograph tenant farms there. Lee began in Iowa and proceeded to Indiana and Illinois, where he photographed near his hometown. In Marseilles, a small industrial community on the Illinois River, Lee photographed the Landers' farm. A group of mortgage note holders owned the farm, and, concerned more for their financial situation than for the plight of the farmers, they had foreclosed on the Landers' mortgage. Lee photographed the farm buildings in their various states of disrepair, but knew that the effectiveness of such documentation depended on his ability to put a face on the story. By photographing the Landers in front of their dilapidated farmhouse, he drew attention to the human element at the center of the troubled tenant-farming system. This image is a perfect illustration of how, even in his earliest images, Lee employed his signature style: a straightforward approach, attention to detail, and devoted sensitivity to humanity. BMC

1 For biographical information on Lee, see F. Jack Hurley, *Russell Lee, Photographer* (Dobbs Ferry, N.Y.: Morgan & Morgan, 1978).

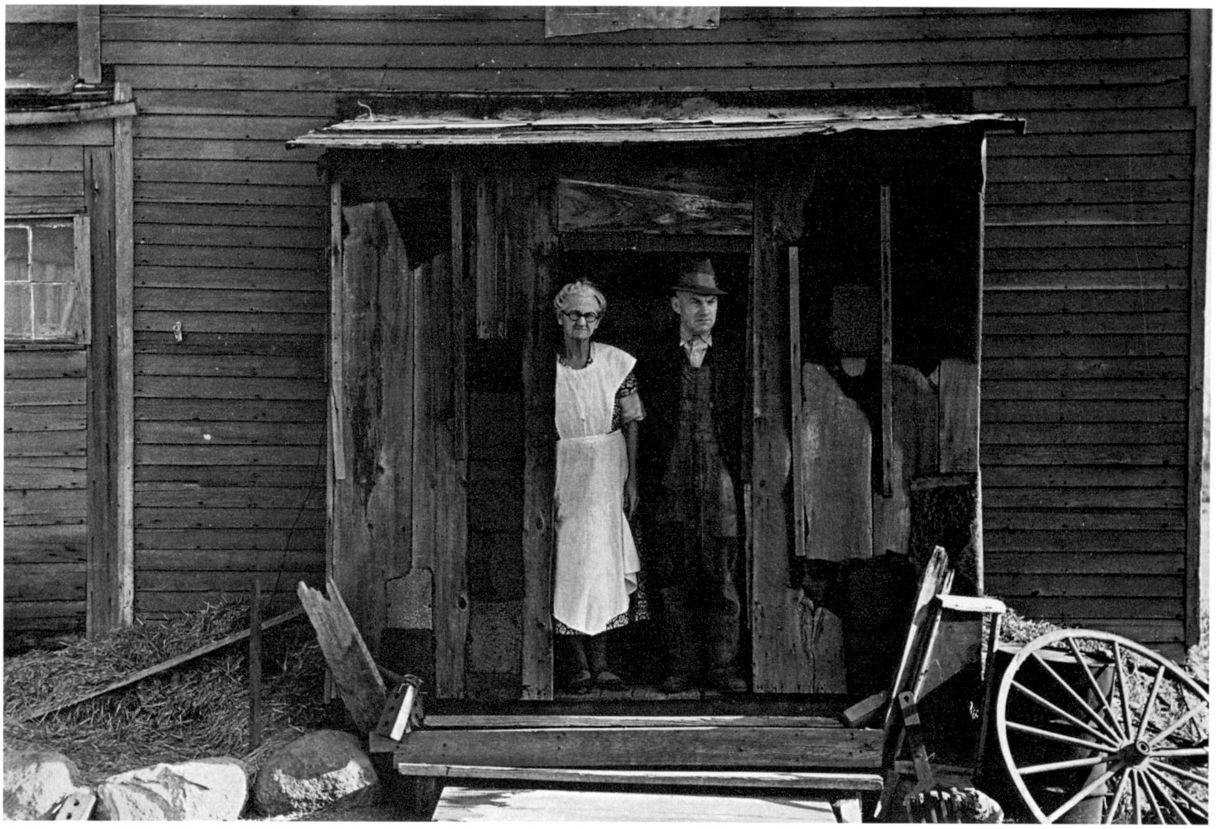

WRIGHT MORRIS

(Central City, NE 1910–1998 Mill Valley, CA)

Gano Grain Elevator, Western Kansas, 1940
Gelatin silver print (9 7/16 x 7 7/16 in.)
Signed lower right: *Wright Morris*
Photo permission: Josephine Morris
Michael H. Marvins

A NATIVE OF NEBRASKA, MORRIS DEVELOPED AN ACUTE APPRECIATION for the rural landscape of the Midwest, an aesthetic that imbued the style and subject matter of both his writing and his photography. While attending college in California, he began to photograph and write short, poetic story fragments. In 1938, when his wife was offered a job teaching school in New England, the two embarked on a cross-country tour to the East Coast, a trip he later described as a revelation in which he perceived the American landscape as "crowded with [the] ruins" of homes, towns, and farms abandoned during the Great Depression.[1] He resolved to record these relics through his work.

By 1939 Morris had begun combining text and photographs in a manner that treated each as equals. A carefully measured textual passage on one page was accompanied by a photograph on the facing page, each one telling its own story, neither directly illustrating nor describing the other. Indeed, in most of the pairings the text frequently bore little or no relation to the specific photographs opposite it. Calling such unions "photo-texts," Morris believed that the mind would naturally weave the two elements together into a complex tapestry of interpretation.

Morris' photographs depict structures and artifacts that set the stage for the lives that flash briefly through his words; the people are invisible, but their presence is understood through their relics. When photographing these relics in the abandoned landscape, he often chose a direct, frontal stance—as in this depiction of a grain elevator—letting the subject speak for itself, with no interpretation. He later wrote of this image, "As I drove south, I caught glimpses of an arrow that pointed at the sky, like a rocket on its pad, the moon its destination. As I moved closer I saw the staggered tiers of a grain elevator approximately in scale with the landscape. The freight train at its base was hardly visible. . . . An almost high noon light, filtered through an overcast, revealed the ripple in the sheet metal attached to the structure's surface. This enhanced the reflected shimmer of light. Near the top, appropriately enigmatic, the four letter word GANO."[2] The image, for Morris, was symbolic of a yearning to escape the flatness of the land. He included it in his first photo-text, *The Inhabitants* (1946), which along with his subsequent photo-texts would greatly influence later photographers. BMC

1 Wright Morris, *Structures and Artifacts: Photographs 1933–1954* (Lincoln: Sheldon Memorial Art Gallery, University of Nebraska, 1975), 112.
2 Wright Morris, *Photographs & Words* (San Francisco: Friends of Photography, 1982), 33.

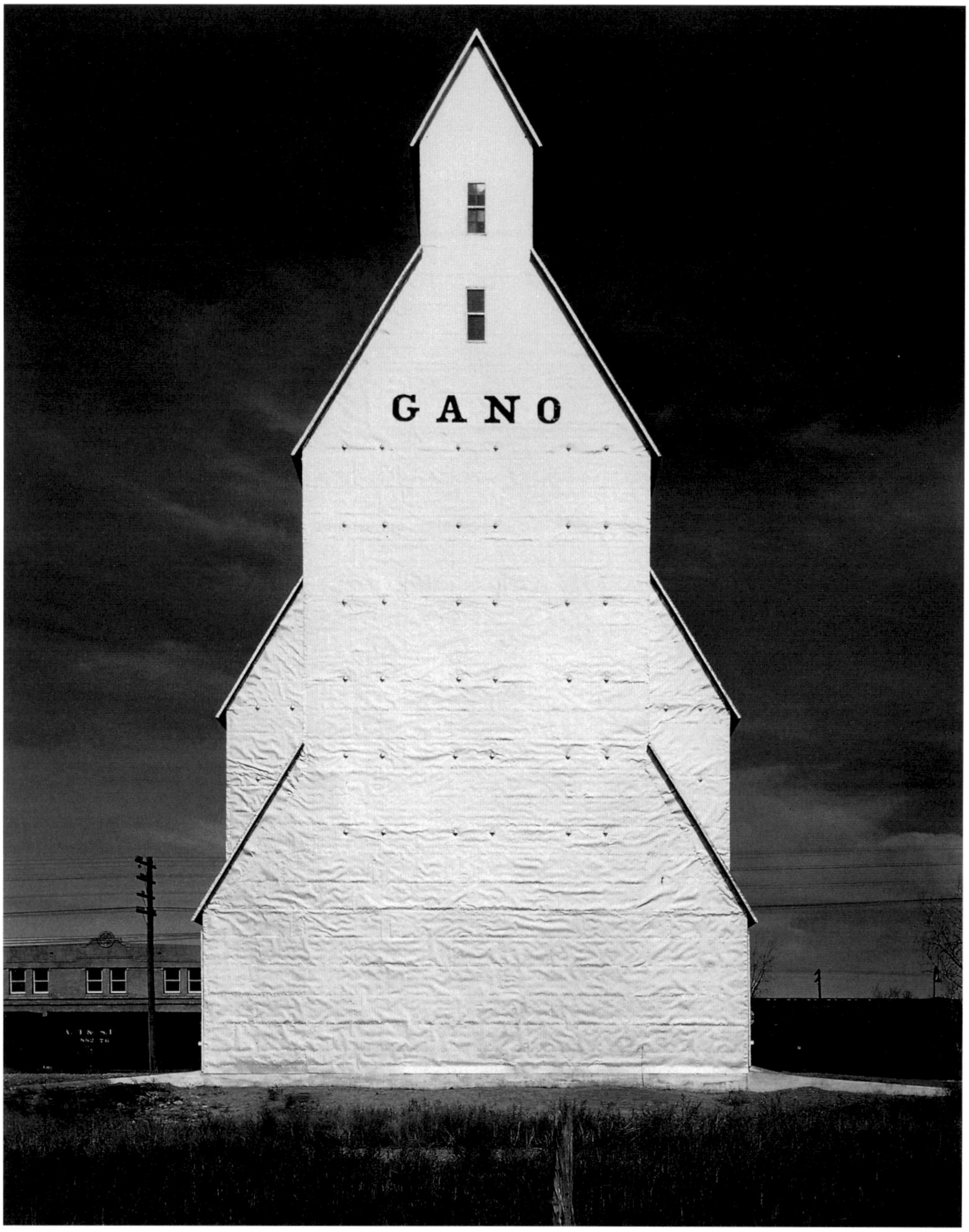
GANO

REGINALD MARSH

(Paris 1898–1954 Dorset, VT)

Pink Elephant, 1943
Oil and Maroger on board (29 x 35 in.)
Signed and dated lower right: *REGINALD MARSH '43*
Susan H. Albritton

SINCE HIS DAYS AS AN ILLUSTRATOR OF VAUDEVILLE and burlesque shows for the *New York Daily News* in the 1920s, Marsh had been attracted to public forms of entertainment. No place inspired him more than Coney Island, which he frequented in the summers to sketch and photograph pictorial ideas. It was most likely on one of these trips, while visiting his favorite park there, Steeplechase, that Marsh found the inspiration for *Pink Elephant*.

He has recreated in this work that park's infamous Blowhole Theater, an elaborate open-air fun house that made visitors' follies the source of entertainment. The principal attraction involved a dwarf, dressed as a clown, who whisked unsuspecting women over blowholes, at which point a man seated atop a pink elephant released a blast of air that raised their skirts. Nearby, rotating barrels were rigged to appear as if they could tumble down at any moment.

While Marsh included on this canvas many of the actual details of the show, such as the painted scenery with the six-foot-high playing cards and the crimson papier-mâché pachyderm, his interpretation evokes a strange dreamscape. The figures appear to occupy a transient world, more reverie than reality. The artist also introduces unexplainable grisaille figures: one cleans the elephant's leg and another, with beard and straw hat, stands in the background. The latter figure may represent Walt Whitman (1819–1892), whose love of all things American included Coney Island. Marsh was aware of Whitman's fondness for the place, and he had already included the poet in another of his paintings.[1]

It was through works like *Pink Elephant* that the shy, unassuming Marsh could express his fantasies, particularly those about women. He often portrayed them as voluptuous, alluring, and unattainable types rather than as individuals. In this painting, he transforms the main attraction of the clown pulling the woman over the blowhole into a peep show of unrestrained exhibitionism. The elephant's trunk takes on phallic symbolism next to the nudity of the young girl and other women, whose figural proportions recall the robust forms found in the paintings of the Old Masters. For Marsh, the crowds at Coney Island resembled the "great compositions of Michelangelo and Rubens."[2] But his Renaissance forebears focused on religious and historical themes; as *Pink Elephant* reveals, Marsh believed modern life possessed a drama worthy of such great art. SRH

1 Lloyd Goodrich, *Reginald Marsh* (New York: Harry N. Abrams, Inc., 1972), 268.
2 Reginald Marsh, "Let's Get Back to Painting," *Magazine of Art* (December 1944): 296.

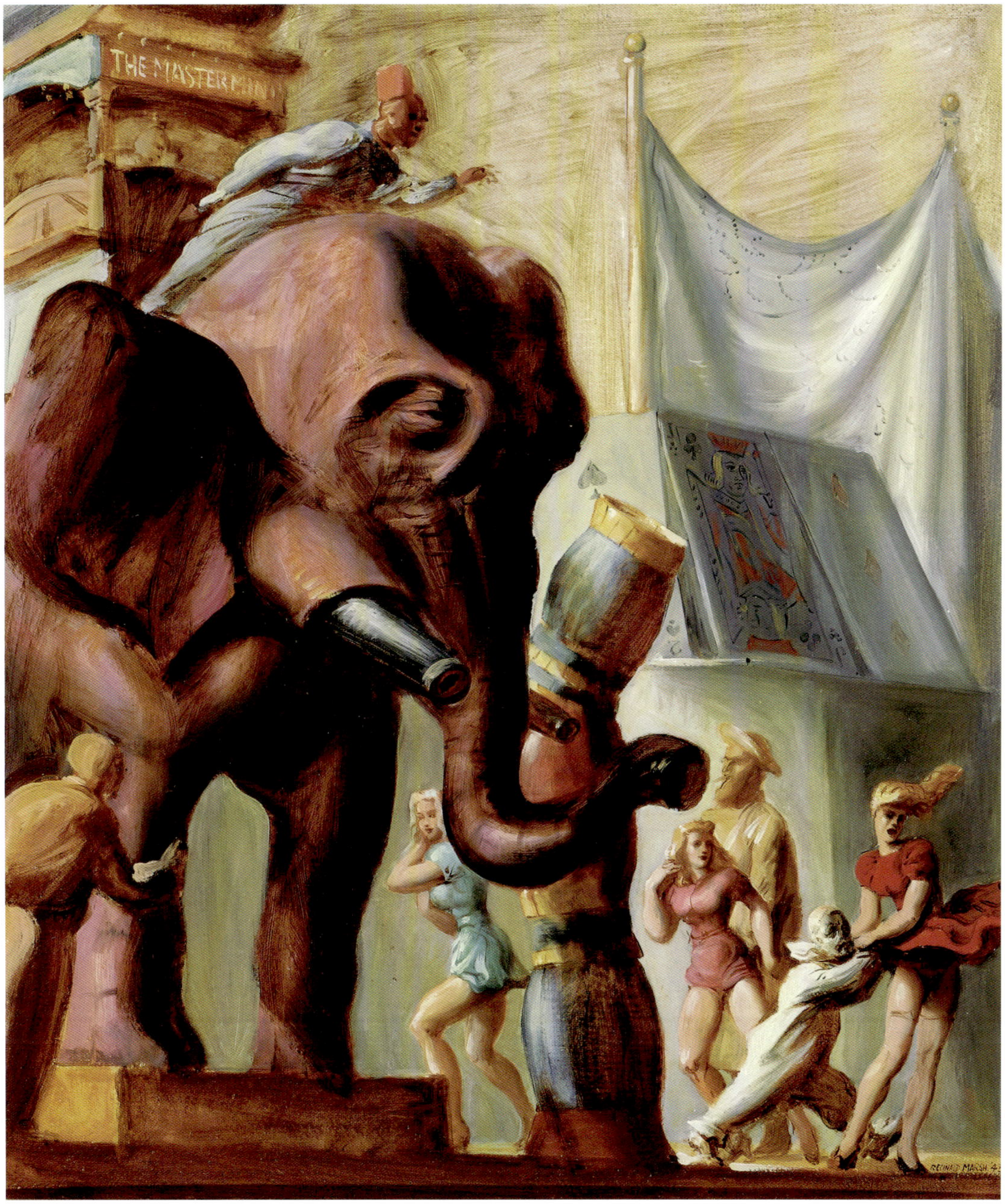
THE MASTERMIND

MICHAEL G. OWEN JR.

(Dallas 1915–1976 Portland, OR)

Leadbelly, 1943
Black serpentine (12 in. high)
Dallas Museum of Art, Mr. and Mrs. Tom Gooch Fund Purchase Prize,
Twelfth Annual Texas Painting and Sculpture Exhibition, 1950–1951

WHILE THE FOLK AND BLUES SINGER Huddie "Leadbelly" Leadbetter (1885–1949) sat for Owen on New York City's Lower East Side in 1943, he played his guitar and sang. The session lasted five hours. Leadbelly was then on the cusp of fame, having developed a sizable following and the respect of fellow folksingers, such as Woody Guthrie, Pete Seeger, and Burl Ives. He was a naturally gifted musician who possessed a seemingly limitless repertoire. His violent past had already made him a legend and included two terms of hard time in southern penitentiaries for murder, as well as the miraculous pardons he received supposedly because of his talent.

Relatively little is known about Owen's career, and only a small body of his work has been recorded thus far. Born in Dallas, he attended the Art Institute there from 1932–35 and later moved to Greenbelt, Maryland, outside of Washington, D.C. He lived his last years in Corvallis, Oregon, blind and disabled from multiple sclerosis.[1]

For this extraordinary sculpture, Owen first roughed out a portrait of Leadbelly in clay, based upon photographs. He finished the model during his session with the singer in New York, and it then became the basis for the completed work, carved from a piece of black serpentine. Richly executed, the head is slightly stylized to convey Leadbelly's powerful build, massive features, and supple flesh. Owen's textural treatment of the hair enlivens what is otherwise the satiny black surface of the stone. It is an utterly convincing, forceful likeness of a spirited man acquainted both with rough times and the bitter side of life.

When the work was acquired by the Dallas Museum of Art in 1950, Owen expressed regret that the singer had not lived to enjoy his popularity. Just months after Leadbelly's death, the Weavers' recording of his song "Goodnight Irene" climbed to number one on the music charts and sold two million copies.

REL

1 For biographical information on Owen, see Rick Stewart, *Lone Star Regionalism: The Dallas Nine and Their Circle* (Dallas: Dallas Museum of Art, 1984), 183–84.

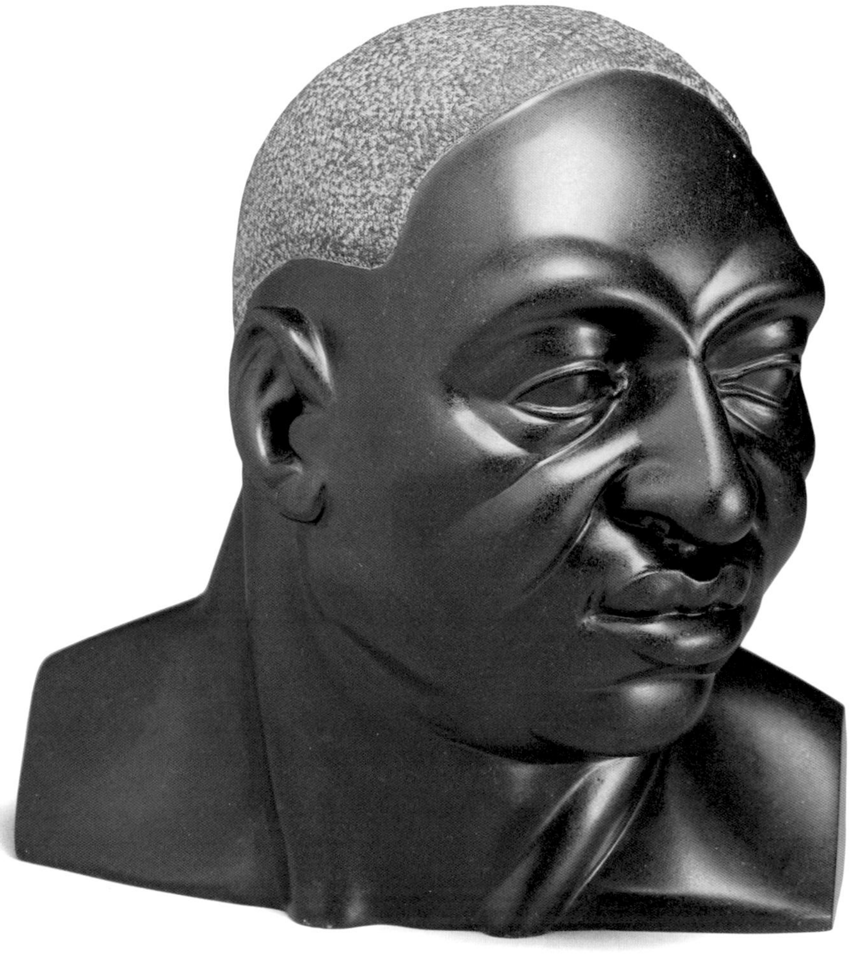

ARSHILE GORKY

(Khorkom, Armenia 1904–1948 Sherman, CT)

L'Amour du fusil neuf [Love of the New Gun], 1944
Oil on canvas (29 3/4 x 37 3/4 in.)
Signed and dated upper left: *A Gorky / 44*

The Menil Collection, Houston

GORKY PAINTED *LOVE OF THE NEW GUN* during an extraordinarily innovative period marked by an intense study of the natural world. Although his life ended prematurely at age forty-four, when depression and ill health led him to commit suicide, the final five years of Gorky's career, a period that witnessed both the decline of surrealism and the stirrings of abstract expressionism, proved to be his finest. Gorky's imagery bridges these two enormously significant movements that dominated the American avant-garde during the mid-twentieth century. Influenced by friends among those European surrealists who had immigrated to New York during World War II, Gorky conveyed a dreamlike sensibility through his paintings and drawings. Simultaneously, his distinctive imagery looked forward to the randomness and spontaneity that characterizes abstract expressionism.

Love of the New Gun expresses Gorky's emotional response to nature as experienced at his in-laws' farm in Loudoun County, Virginia, where he and his young family lived for much of 1944. The countryside recalled the fields of his homeland, Armenia, which he had left as a teenager when the Turkish government attempted to wipe out his people through massacre or deportation. Twenty-five years later, Gorky's poetic interpretation of his environment, both present and past, entailed the creation of enigmatic, symbolic shapes that originated in the depths of his psyche. His compositions loosely refer to the intersection of verticals and horizontals that distinguish the landscape format, combined with organic forms suggestive of the natural world. Here, gravity drags the thinly applied paint downward, prefiguring the drip technique associated with abstract expressionism. These veils of vibrant color intersect gracefully with a weblike network of fluid grey lines. The overall effect underscores the paradox of Gorky's great oils of 1944, which contain individual forms whose specific references remain obscure and unrecognizable.[1]

In 1945, *Love of the New Gun* was one of nine masterpieces featured in Gorky's first solo exhibition at the New York gallery of Julien Levy (1906–1981). French poet André Breton (1896–1966), who in 1924 had first articulated the surrealist concept of transcending reason, created salient yet often inscrutable phrases for the works in the exhibition, invoked by Gorky's running commentary about the works as he showed them to the Frenchman. Not all of the oils in the exhibition sold, and *Love of the New Gun* remained in Levy's private collection for many years, awaiting the larger audience that attended the posthumous celebration of Gorky's genius. JM

1 See Michael Auping, et al., *Arshile Gorky: The Breakthrough Years* (Fort Worth: Modern Art Museum of Fort Worth in association with Rizzoli, 1995).

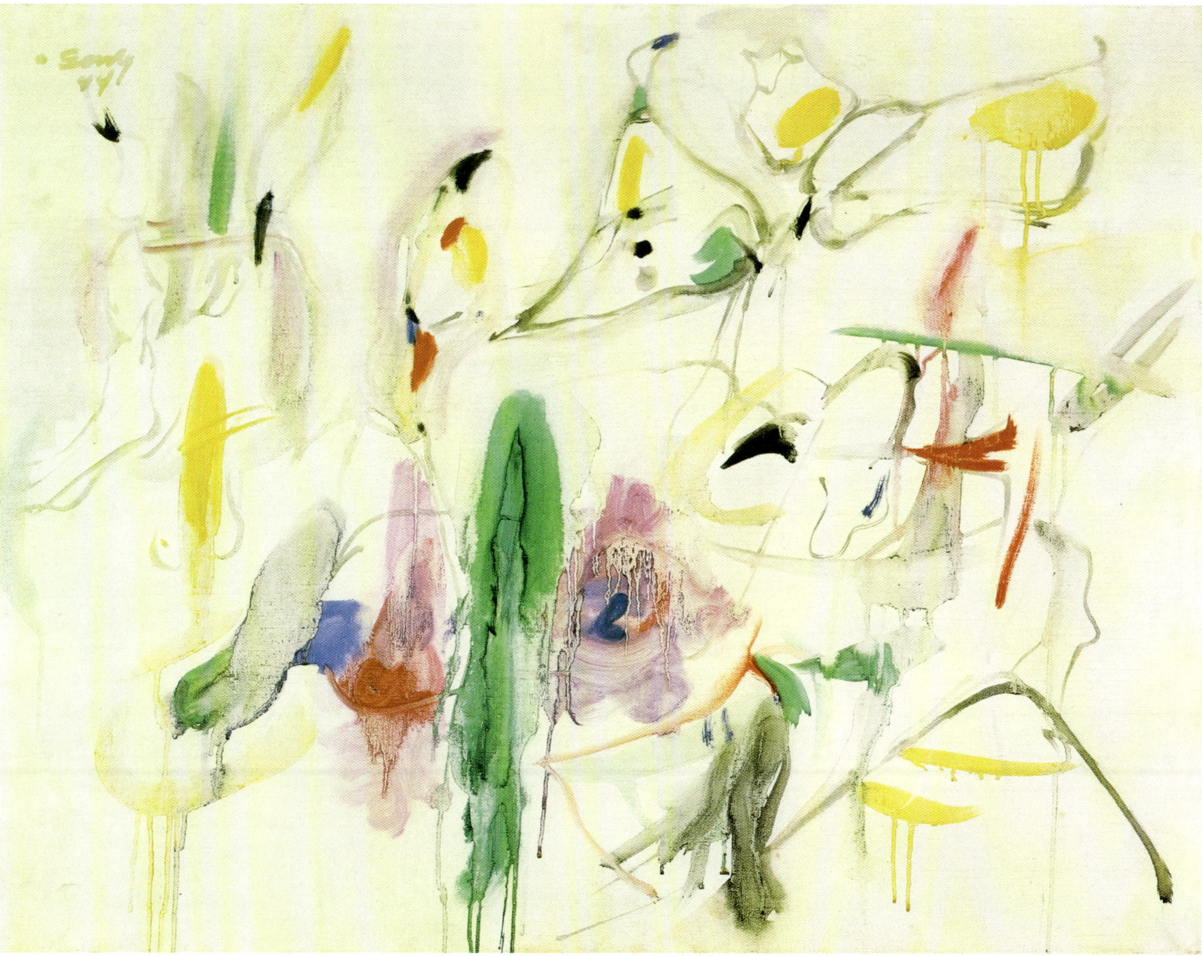

DAVID SMITH

(Decatur, IN 1906–1965 Bennington, VT)

House in a Landscape [Rural Landscape with Manless House], 1945
Welded steel etched with acid (18 1/8 in. high)
Signed and dated back edge of upper ledge: *David Smith 1945*
Photograph by: David Heald, The Solomon R. Guggenheim Museum

The Patsy R. and Raymond D. Nasher Collection, Dallas, Texas

SMITH BEGAN HIS CAREER AS A PAINTER but shifted to sculpture when he realized the medium better suited his forceful temperament. In the early 1930s, the artist discovered the aesthetic possibilities of welding steel after seeing sculpture by Pablo Picasso (1881–1973) and Julio González (1876–1942). The use of industrial methods toward artistic ends appealed to Smith, who had worked as a welder in a plant that built locomotives and M-7 tanks.

While virtually all of Smith's pieces are abstract and informed by European modernist movements such as cubism and surrealism, he believed that such works could be perceived and understood by everyone on some level. "We meet on grounds of equality in the unconscious mind," he noted.[1] *House in a Landscape* is a work that owes much to surrealism. The piece was created two years after the critic Clement Greenberg (1909–1994) predicted that Smith would become one of America's greatest artists.[2] The sculptor was in the midst of one of his most inventive and prolific periods, living on a farm in Bolton Landing, New York, where he was building a new home and studio. Perhaps inspired by this project, Smith seems to have translated his visions of domesticity and nature into this elusive and personal sculpture.

Connoting the "landscape" of the title, two trees balance the general composition of this work, and the vertical piece that stands between them suggests a house. The square frame on the right evokes a window with windblown curtains that curl upward to reveal a figure that consists primarily of an arm and hand, which holds a ball. Another arm holding a ball protrudes from the lower left of the central structure. Smith considered such abstract forms to be manifestations of his unconscious, which he presented in his work as meaningful symbols.

Described as a man of ferocious energy, Smith welded many brilliant forms in metal, but his artistic vigor exacted a toll on his personal relationships. At the time of this work's creation, the artist was morose and struggling with his first marriage, which would end in 1950. His tension seems palpable in the distorted figures, jagged trees, and spiky protrusions of the sculpture. Yet the artwork as a whole seems to maintain a sense of mystery. As Smith once remarked, "If you ask why I make sculpture, I must answer that it is my way of life, my balance, and my justification for being."[3] SRH

1 David Smith, "On Abstract Art," in Garnett McCoy, ed., *David Smith* (New York: Praeger Publishers, 1973), 39.
2 Clement Greenberg, "American Sculpture of Our Time: Group Show," *Nation* 156, no. 4 (January 23, 1943): 141.
3 David Smith, "Statement," in McCoy, 63.

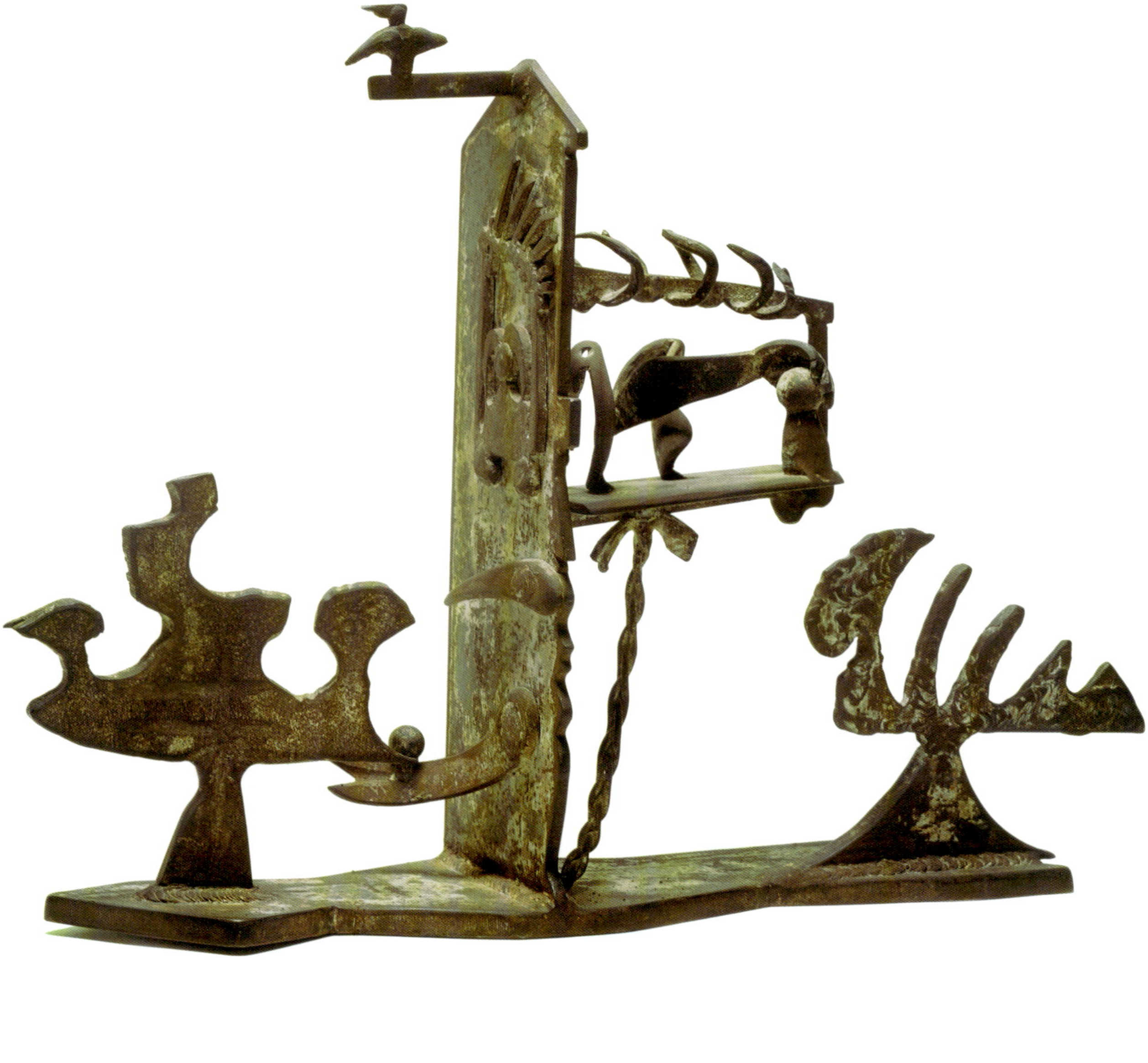

O. WINSTON LINK

(Brooklyn 1914–2001 South Salem, NY)

Hot Shot Eastbound, Iaeger, West Virginia, 1956
Gelatin silver print (16 x 20 in.)
Copyright O. Winston Link Trust
Courtesy of SBC Communications Inc.

ROBERT FRANK

(Zurich 1924)

Bar–Gallup, New Mexico, 1955–1956
Gelatin silver print (11 7/8 x 7 7/8 in.)
Signed, dated, and inscribed, lower left: *Gallup New Mexico 1956*; lower right: *R. Frank*
Copyright Robert Frank, *The Americans,* courtesy Pace/MacGill Gallery, New York
Paul Brauchle

THESE TWO PHOTOGRAPHS WERE TAKEN LESS THAN A YEAR APART, yet they could scarcely be more different. Frank, a naturalized citizen born in Switzerland (p. 129), and Link provide here opposing views of the nation's culture in the 1950s. They also illustrate two extremes of photographic technique and style from that era.

Link had been a railroad buff since early childhood, and from 1955 to 1960 he documented the last days of the steam-powered locomotive, an integral part of American culture that was fast disappearing from the landscape. He traveled over 2,500 miles along the Norfolk & Western line, the last Class I railroad line to use steam engines, producing thousands of views of locomotives. For many years he had practiced commercial photography and was adept with all the photographic tools of his craft, a talent that allowed him to completely control the image-making process. He meticulously planned a shoot ahead of time, researched the location, and controlled and synchronized the lighting with elaborate flash setups.

On August 2, 1956, Link photographed a freight train hauling merchandise to Norfolk, Virginia, as it traveled through Iaeger, a small town at the southern tip of West Virginia. A No. 1242 coal-fired steam locomotive—in Link's opinion the most beautiful engine ever built—was pulling the train, so the photographer had taken extra precautions in planning the shot. The tracks passed alongside the screen of a drive-in theater, itself an icon of 1950s American culture, so the artist chose a camera location that would record the train in the background, just beyond the screen. His 4-by-5-inch Graphic view camera, with a wide-angle lens, allowed the foreground couple in the convertible, as well as the train and movie screen in the rear, to all be in sharp focus. Link made a separate exposure of the movie as a plane filled the screen so that he could add it to the print later. As the train passed by, he fired

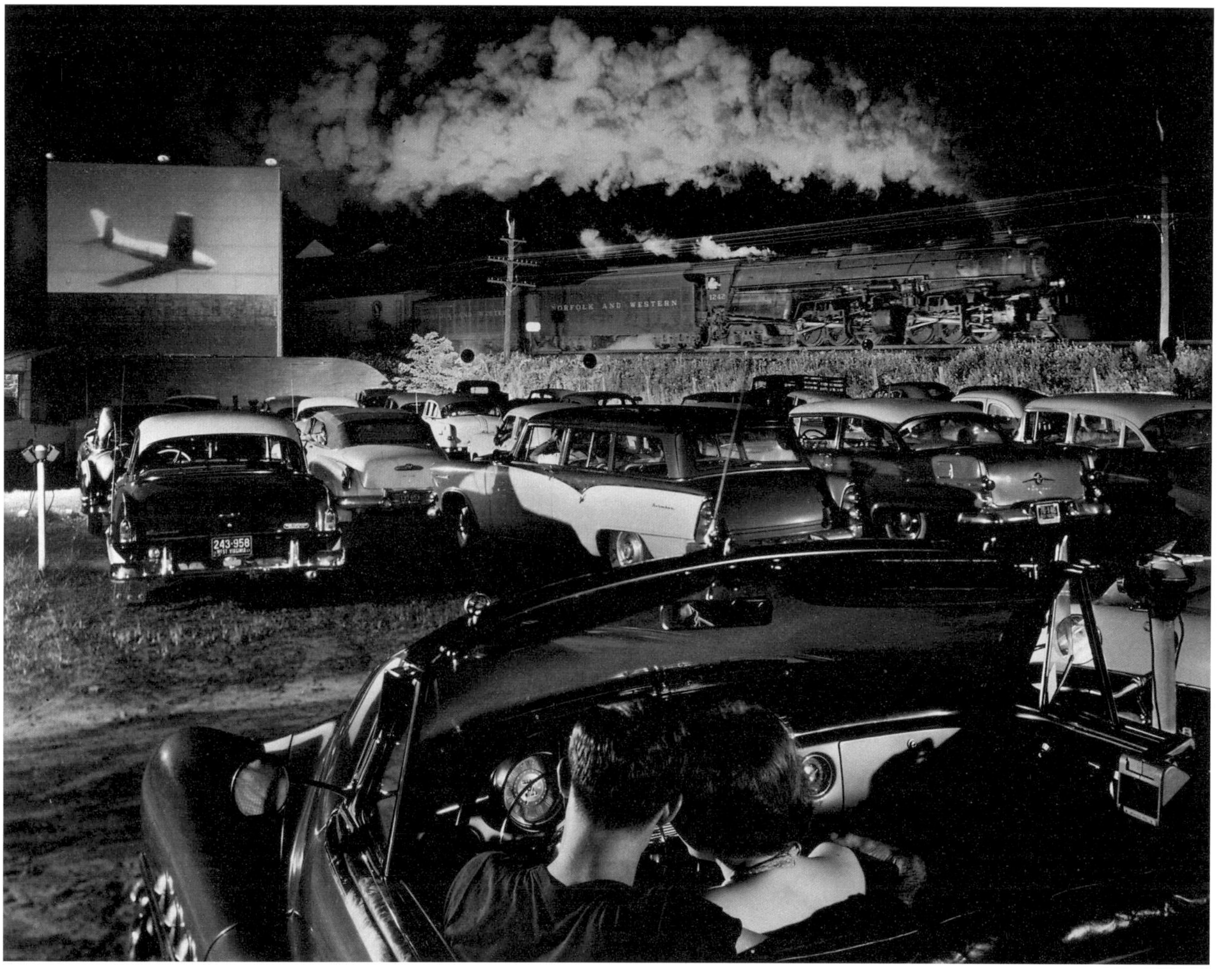
NORFOLK AND WESTERN
243·958

forty-three flash bulbs simultaneously, illuminating the scene as he exposed the film. The final image transports the viewer into a surreal landscape dominated by the train's anomalous presence.

In contrast to Link's highly choreographed image, Frank's photograph is a spontaneous reaction and has much in common with improvisational jazz and abstract expressionism. Frank immigrated to the United States in 1947 but continued to travel and live abroad until 1953. When he took this photograph two years later, he was still experiencing American culture as somewhat of an outsider. He applied for and received a Guggenheim Fellowship in 1955 (the first European photographer to be awarded the fellowship) and detailed his intent to document scenes that signified American civilization through the eyes of a naturalized citizen.

After buying a five-year-old Ford, Frank began his odyssey in 1955, traveling down the East Coast to Florida and then across the southern states to Los Angeles. He stopped there for the winter and processed his film. Rather than planning his route according to what he wanted to see and attempting to carefully compose images according to the photographic style then in vogue, he responded intuitively to what he found. He disregarded other traditional photographic rules as well, such as keeping the light behind the camera and the foreground in focus. Using a 35mm Leica and literally shooting from the hip, Frank revolutionized camera aesthetics in a manner described by the poet Allen Ginsberg as "spontaneous glance, accidental truth."[1]

When Frank's ground-breaking book, *The Americans*, was published (1958 in France, 1959 in the United States), critics were struck by the sense of alienation and violence projected through the photographer's subjective style. In the 1958 *U.S. Camera Annual*, Frank responded to those who claimed his view of America was a negative one, writing that his feelings toward his adopted country were necessarily complex and his photographs had to reflect that complexity. "Life for a photographer cannot be a matter of indifference. Opinion often consists of a kind of criticism. But criticism can come out of love. It is important to see what is invisible to others. Perhaps the look of hope or the look of sadness."[2]

In *Bar–Gallup, New Mexico*, the neon and fluorescent lights cast a ghostly pallor over the scene, and the tilted frame implies a lack of balance. Peering past the towering dark figures in the foreground toward the menacing-looking cowboys beyond, the viewer feels uneasy, an outsider in an unfriendly bar. While Link's paean to the days of steam locomotion offers a nostalgic look at the country's perceived age of innocence, Frank's photograph hints at the subconscious neurosis that was about to break upon the nation's consciousness in the 1960s.

BMC

1 Allen Ginsberg, "Robert Frank to 1985—A Man," in *Robert Frank: New York to Nova Scotia* (Houston: Museum of Fine Arts in association with Little, Brown, and Co., 1986), 74.
2 Robert Frank in *U.S. Camera Annual*, 1958 (New York: Camera Publishing Corp., 1967): 115.

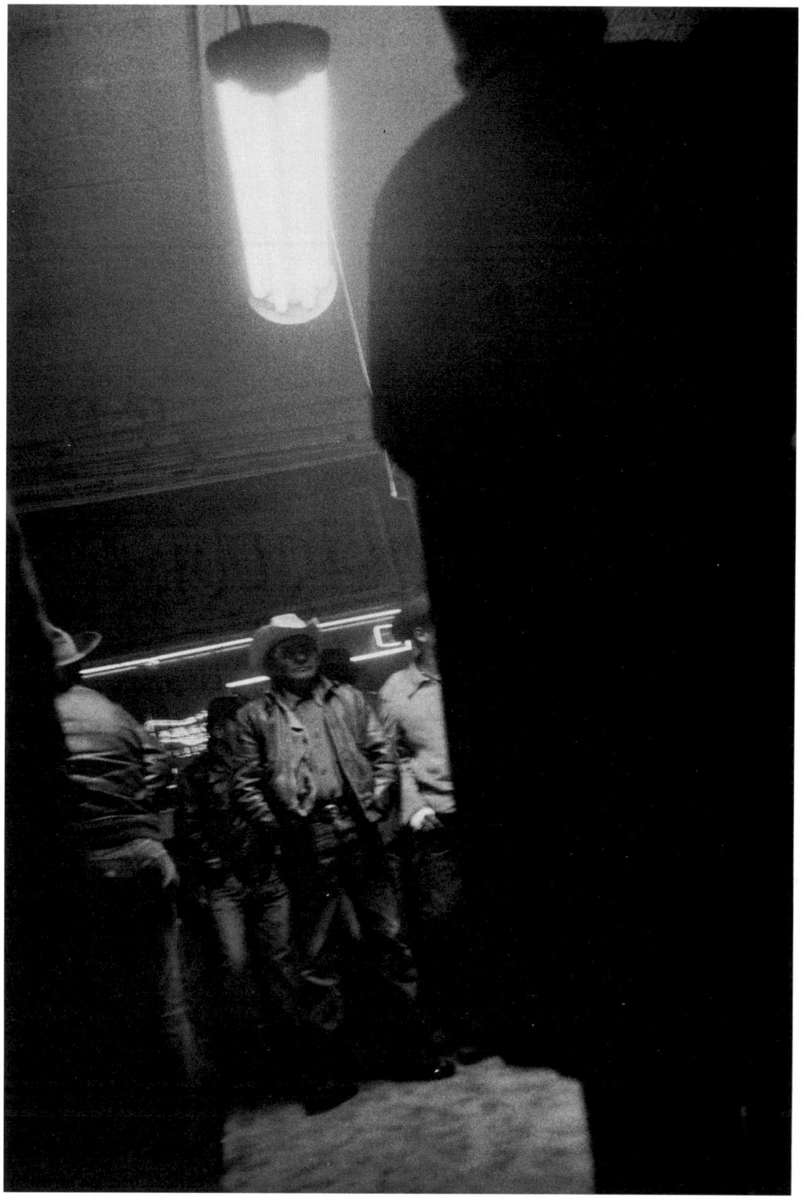

ANSEL ADAMS

(San Francisco 1902–1984 Carmel, CA)

Aspens, Northern New Mexico, 1958; printed 1976
From *Portfolio VII*
Gelatin silver print (18 x 22 3/4 in.)
Signed lower right: *Ansel Adams*

Joseph W. Gray, M.D.

ADAMS WAS DRIVING NEAR THE CREST of the Sangre de Cristo Mountains in New Mexico with his wife, Virginia, and two assistants when he came upon this group of aspen trees nestled in the forest's shadow. The light cast a cool, quiet impression on the area, infusing it with a soothing serenity. It was a crisp autumn day, and the aspen leaves were a vibrant yellow against the green trunks and russet shrubs. To make the leaves stand out against the background and to better convey the coolness of the woods, Adams photographed the scene from across the road, using a longer lens to eliminate the sky and a yellow filter to lighten the leaves. In this way he made the scene look sunlit, even though it was in shadow. With his 8-by-10-inch view camera, Adams made two exposures: a vertical and this horizontal view.[1]

This is a perfect example of how Adams exercised remarkable control over the tonal values in his work, turning understated scenes into emotionally charged statements. He wanted his prints to evince the magic of being in nature and to foster a realization of the need to preserve these special places. To communicate this message to as broad an audience as possible, Adams worked to publish his images for large distribution, at the same time ensuring that the tonal values of those reproductions carried his intended emotional message.

Adams first published this photograph, both on the book jacket and as the final image, in the groundbreaking Sierra Club publication *This Is the American Earth* (1960), the first in the club's Exhibit Format series. The print run of 10,000 copies sold out within ten months, dramatically increasing the club's membership. Adams also published limited-edition portfolios of his photographs and, through them, broadened the market for his work. When he included this image in his *Portfolio VII* (1976), he printed it even more dramatically, making the leaves and the trunks seem to glow as they emerge from the shadow.[2]

BMC

1 Ansel Adams, *Examples: The Making of 40 Photographs* (Boston: Little, Brown, and Co., 1983), 61–63.
2 Ansel Adams, with an introduction by John Szarkowski, *The Portfolios of Ansel Adams* (Boston: Little, Brown, and Co., 1983), vii–xii.

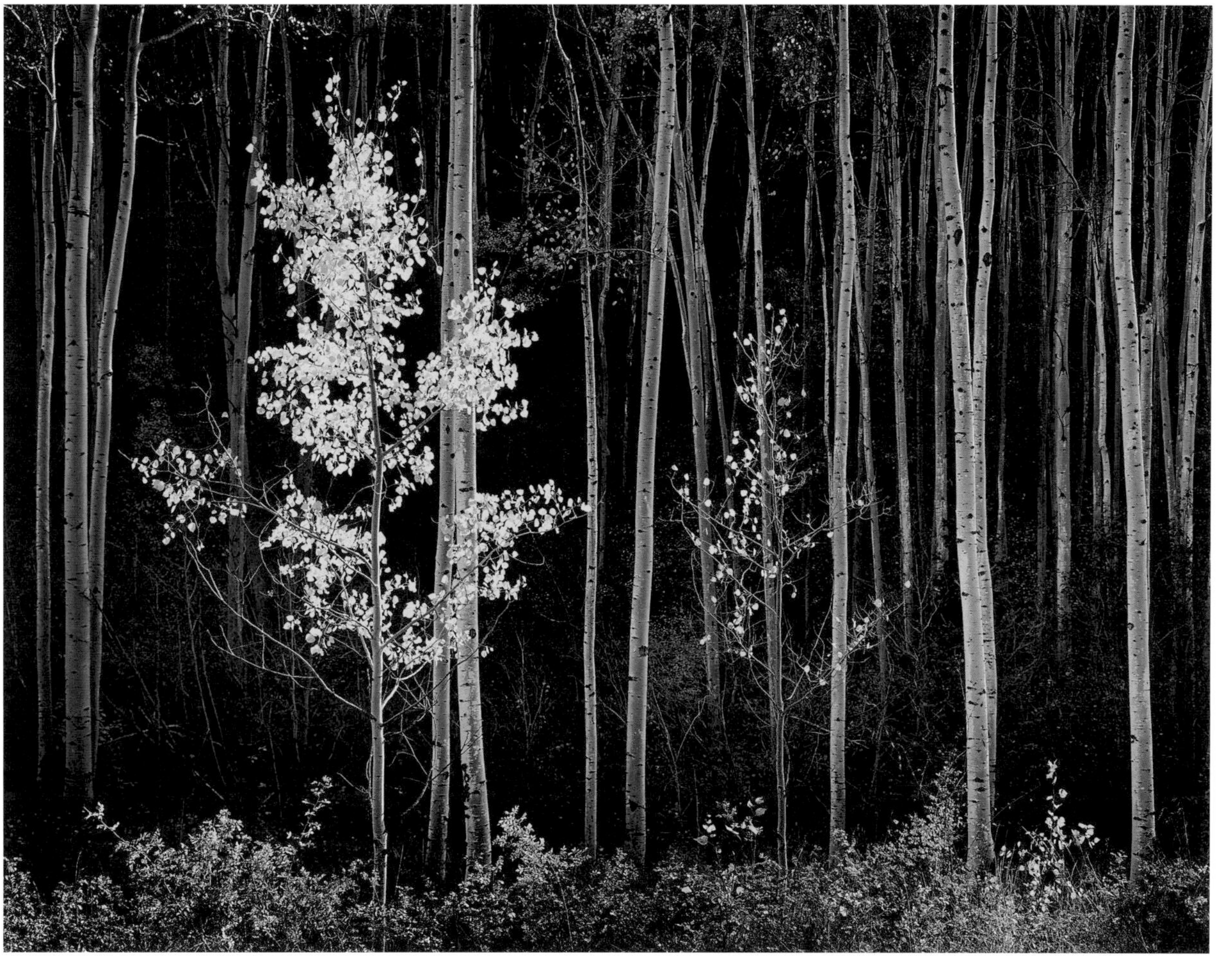

MINOR WHITE

(Minneapolis 1908–1976 Boston)

Windowsill Daydreaming, 1958
Gelatin silver print (11 7/8 x 9 1/8 in.)
Signed, dated, and inscribed, lower right: *Minor White*;
on reverse, at bottom: *"Windowsill Daydreaming" Rochester, NY 1958 Minor White*
Reproduction courtesy The Minor White Archive, Princeton University.

Paul Brauchle

ONE OF THE MOST INTROSPECTIVE PHOTOGRAPHERS of the twentieth century, White equated the act of photographing with striving toward mystical awareness. He subscribed to Alfred Stieglitz's (1864–1946) theory of equivalence, which asserted that the photographic image could serve as an "equivalent" of the artist's inner experience. But to this philosophy White also added a complex blend of Christian mysticism, Zen Buddhism, Jungian psychology, and the tenets of G. I. Gurdjieff (1872?–1949), whose writings are a call to spiritual awakening. Believing that to photograph is "to be," White was convinced that an image could not only stand as an equivalent, but be possessed of the power to convey spiritual meaning.

White championed this philosophy through his own photography, curatorial work, publishing, and teaching. One of the most influential photography educators of the mid-twentieth century, he held teaching positions at the California School of Fine Arts in San Francisco, the Rochester Institute of Technology, and the Massachusetts Institute of Technology. In both Rochester and Boston, White always had a number of students living with him in a large apartment, and he thereby spread his philosophy even outside the classroom. In 1952 he founded the highly influential photography journal *Aperture* and served as its editor until 1975.

While living in Rochester at 72 Union Street, White kept a 4-by-5-inch view camera set up on a tripod adjacent to a window in the front room. He maintained a constant relationship with it, frequently looking through it whenever he passed by. On July 20, 1958, while eating breakfast, he noticed that the light from behind him cast a profile of his wire chairs and bounced off neighboring glass onto the wall, creating the extraordinary circular light pattern seen here. He later explained that the true meaning of the photograph did not necessarily reflect the reality of the subject matter. "Again the affirmation that visual occurrences around me reflect something of my inner state and that when they are photographed become like signposts along the way. . . . I had not perceived the 'coming in' when seen, nor in the negatives; the proofs showed me what was unmistakably the revealed moment. 'It had taken over' without my being aware. I was left to discover the occurrence in the photograph."[1]

BMC

1 Minor White, "Memorable Fancies," July 20, 1958, the Minor White Archive, The Art Museum, Princeton University.

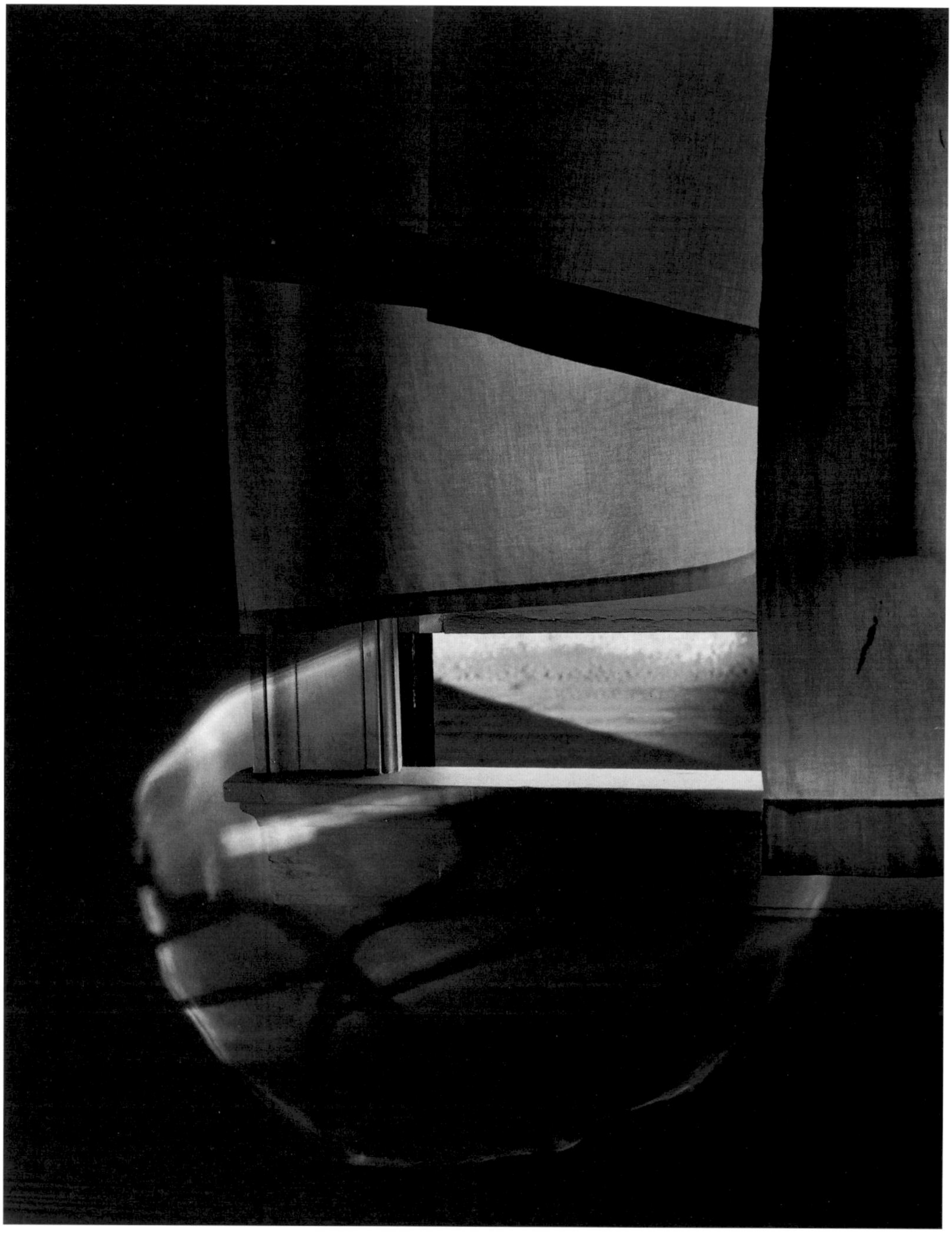

AARON SISKIND

(New York 1903–1991 Providence)

San Luis Potosi 16, 1961
Gelatin silver print (13 5/8 x 18 in.)
Signed, dated, and inscribed, lower right: *Aaron Siskind*; lower left: *San Luis Potosi, Mexico 1961*;
on reverse, upper center: *San Luis Potosi 16 1961/Aaron Siskind*

Paul Greenberg

"THE INTERNAL DRAMA IS THE MEANING OF THE EXTERIOR EVENT," Siskind wrote in 1945, explaining why he had abandoned his earlier documentary style in favor of formal abstraction.[1] Influenced by abstract expressionism, he began to work outside the documentary approach, which had left him wanting more. He soon discovered that by using the same techniques of straight photography—selectively framing details of reality in sharp focus—he was able to craft visual metaphors that went beyond the literalness of the subject and instead encouraged a subjective interpretation. Through his work and through teaching, Siskind thus created an alternative form of photography that became a major influence on the field in the mid-twentieth century.

Although he thought of photography as a way to order the world and believed it could lead to meaning in both the world and himself, Siskind did not want his photographs to dictate a specific message to the viewer; rather, he wanted to create images that would invite viewers to discover their own meanings in his work. So he chose not to use recognizable psychological symbols, but instead to isolate separate shapes and components in the picture frame, implying a narrative relationship between them. As a result, his works often defy interpretation and delve into exploring the mysteries of symbolism.

In 1961, prior to assuming his new position as head of the department of photography at the Chicago Institute of Design, Siskind spent the summer traveling in Mexico. He found the country offered fertile ground for his abstractions, and he would return there several times over the course of his life. The abundance of Catholic imagery, the language difference, and the rich history evident in the urban architecture all alluded, for Siskind, to the mysteries of humanity. He was fascinated by the aged city walls and the way that deterioration and the passage of time left behind fragments of torn posters and faded lettering. Photographing these collage-like configurations of overlapping history, Siskind frequently included the letter "a" as a reference to himself. BMC

1 Aaron Siskind, "The Drama of Objects," in *Minicam Photography* 8, no. 9, 1945, 20–23, 93–94, quoted in Nathan Lyons, ed., *Photographers on Photography* (Englewood Cliffs, N. J.: Prentice-Hall, Inc., 1966), 97.

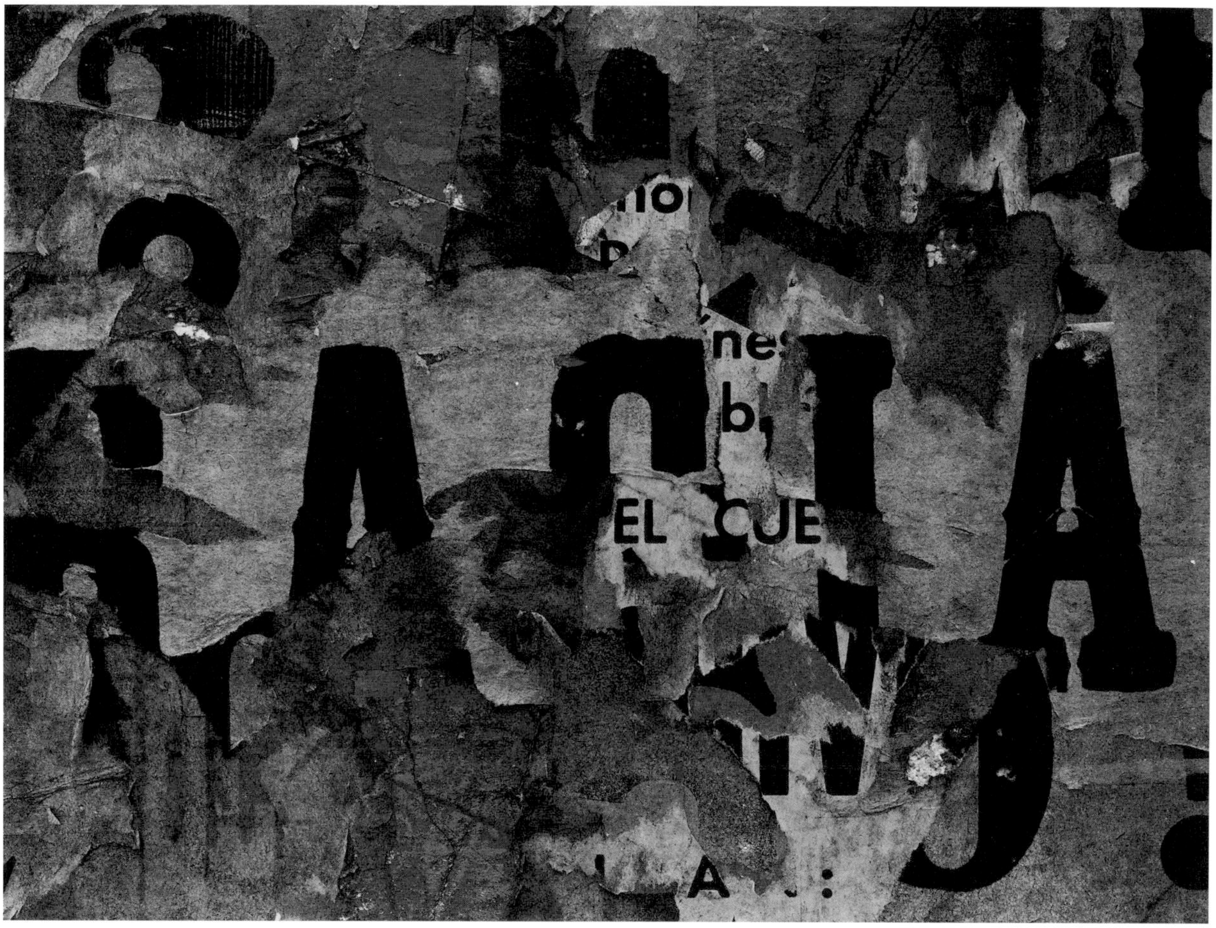

WAYNE THIEBAUD
(Mesa, AZ 1920)

Shelf Pies, 1961
Oil on canvas (24 x 18 in.)
Signed lower right: *Thiebaud* [in graphite] / *Thiebaud* [incised]
Mr. and Mrs. W. A. Moncrief Jr.

THIEBAUD'S IDIOSYNCRATIC ARTISTIC VOICE FOUND its first mature expression in 1961, the year he painted *Shelf Pies* in his northern California studio. When shown in New York and San Francisco in 1962, the artist's paintings of foodstuffs were enthusiastically received, and their exhibition launched his career as one of the foremost artists of the era. Thiebaud's singular images featured hot dogs, cakes, ice cream, candy, and other commonplace fare presented in a conventional setting, evoking what might be perceived as a quintessentially self-indulgent American lifestyle.

Despite the work's ostensible straightforward simplicity, *Shelf Pies*, like other paintings in the series, reveals a complex array of ideas and estimable technical mastery. Although the pieces of pie, arranged by flavor, march in regimented rows across the composition, they are highly individualized in their fabrication. Unexpected coloristic touches of blue and red appear as reinforced borders along the edges of pie slices and plates. The artist mixed the same vivid colors into the white pigment that describes the meringue atop the pie slices on alternating shelves, providing a rich liveliness to what otherwise might read as inert similitude. The shadows cast by the pie wedges also vary, from the luminous turquoise of the top row to vivid blue at the bottom, each falling to the right of the triangular wedge of pie to designate a bright light entering the composition from the left. The pies appear from varying perspectives as they recede from top to bottom; these shifting angles reveal the contents of the glass case from an elevated viewpoint, as if seen from above.

When he painted *Shelf Pies*, Thiebaud drew upon a variety of life experiences, not only as a practicing painter since the mid-1940s, but as a stage designer, cartoonist, illustrator, and advertising graphic designer. In these occupations he learned about theatrical presentation and was challenged to create salient characterizations of consumer goods. Not unlike many successful advertising campaigns, Thiebaud's ubiquitous and familiar objects—in this instance, pie—conjure up a range of ironic or nostalgic personal associations, in the artist's words, "from mom's home cooking to pie in the sky."[1] Above all, this celebration of solid, abstract forms in the guise of a subject matter as abstruse as it is conventional reflects the joy the artist took in the act of painting. Thiebaud's thick, gestural brushwork is as luscious as its subject. JM

1 Kathan Brown, *Ink, Paper, Metal, Wood: Painters and Sculptors at Crown Point Press* (San Francisco: Chronicle Books, 1996), 34.

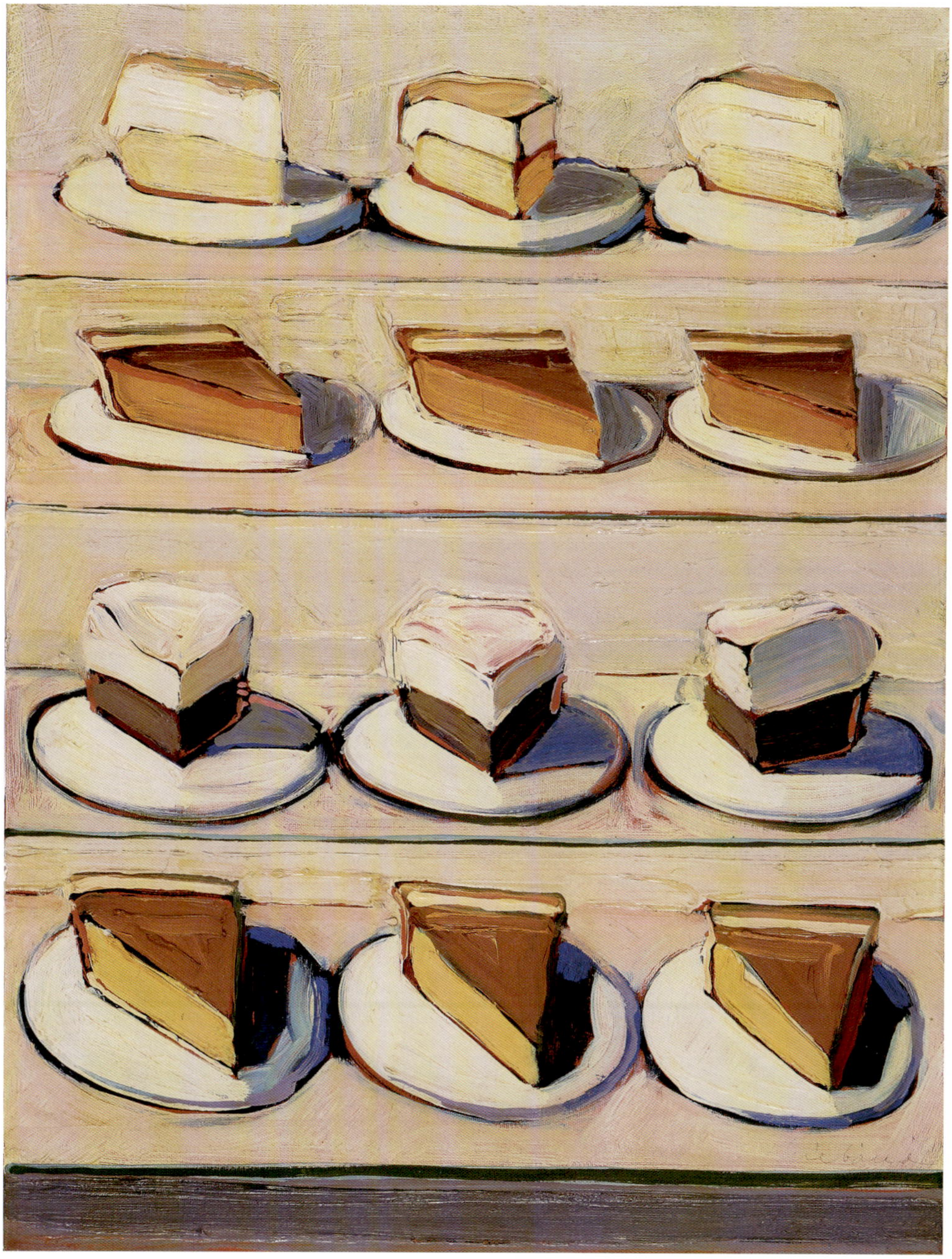

PAUL CAPONIGRO

(Boston 1932)

Redding, Ct., 1968, printed later
Gelatin silver print (16 3/4 x 22 1/4 in.)

Lorine and David H. Gibson

ALTHOUGH SOME PHOTOGRAPHERS LOOKED TOWARD NEW STYLES of photographing in the 1960s, many remained loyal to established traditions. Caponigro is representative of those photographers who persisted in affirming the relevance of making eloquent statements about the landscape, inspiring a new generation of photographers to do the same.

Caponigro's relationship with nature began in childhood, when each day outdoors was filled with the miracles of discovery. Although he initially planned to pursue a musical career, he studied piano at Boston University College of Music for only one year before taking up photography as his preferred creative medium, convinced that he could thus achieve a closer relationship with nature. His instinct proved true. "By looking at nature, through the photographic process," he would later say, "I discovered forms and dimensions in the landscape I'd only vaguely sensed before."[1]

At age twenty-five, Caponigro moved to Rochester, New York, to live and study with photographer Minor White (1908–1976). From White he learned to photograph meditatively and, in so doing, capture an intense visualization within a moment of stillness. He also began to espouse this approach to photography, first through assisting White as he taught workshops in San Francisco and Portland, Oregon, and then through his own workshops and university courses across the country.

Caponigro's landscape photographs encourage reflection and introspection, and they convey the need for relationship with the natural world. He made this image on a bridge overlooking the Little River in Redding, Connecticut, during the last light of day. Although the print is a realistic depiction of the scene, there appear to be two distinct photographs in evidence, separated by a nearly horizontal line across the middle. The bottom half of the photograph captures distorted reflections on the water's surface; the top half depicts the overall setting of the river winding through the forest. By situating the small waterfall near the center of the frame, Caponigro creates a tension between the dreamlike foreground and the recognizable reality of the background, poetically evoking the transcendence he passionately believed could be found in nature. BMC

1 Paul Caponigro, quoted in *Landscape: Theory* (New York: Lustrum Press, 1980), 60.

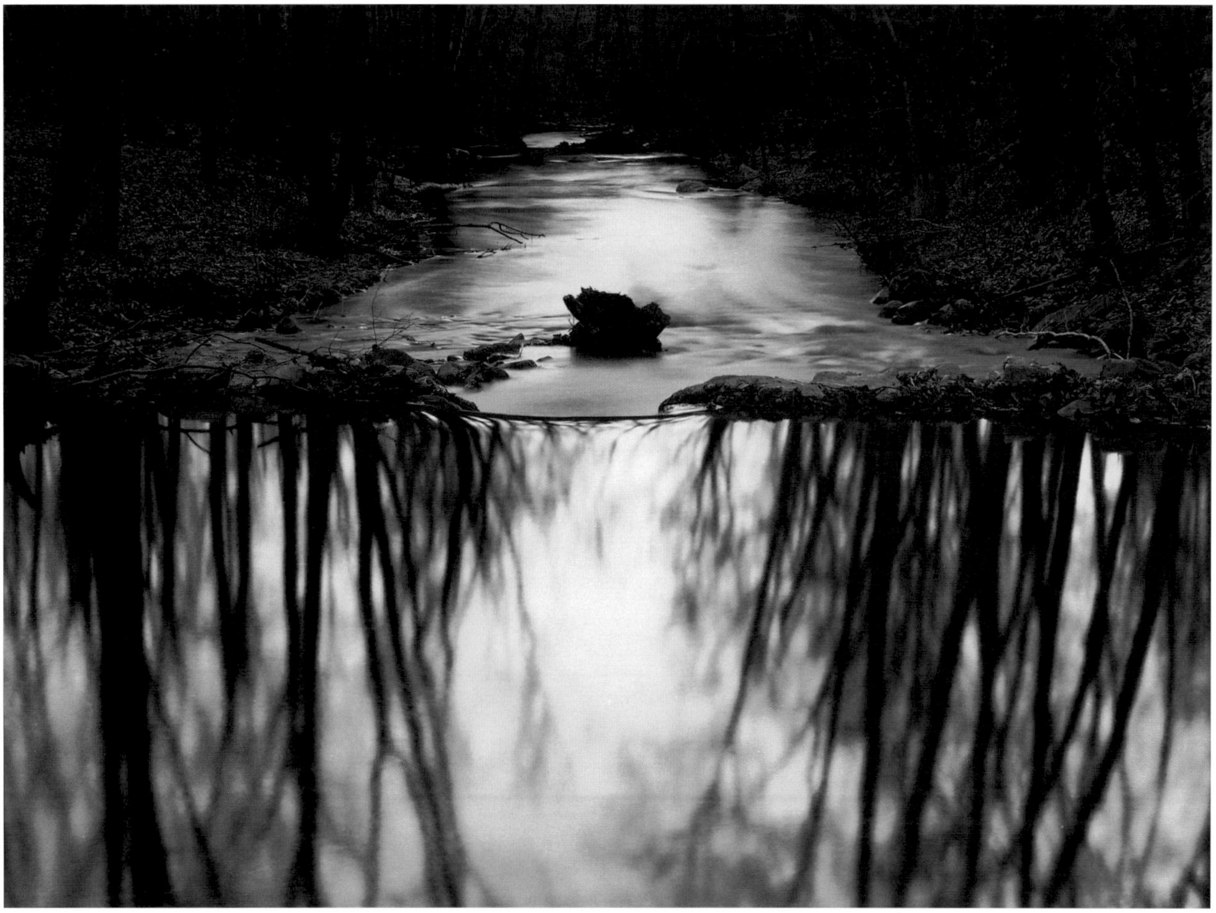

GARRY WINOGRAND

(New York 1928–1984 Tijuana, Mexico)

Los Angeles, California, 1969
Gelatin silver print (8 1/2 x 12 3/4 in.)
Signed on reverse: *Garry Winogrand*

Paul Brauchle

MORE THAN ANY OTHER PHOTOGRAPHER IN THE 1960S, Winogrand redefined the way we look at the social landscape. He viewed public spaces as theaters where the tragedies and comedies of life are played out, and time and again he turned his camera to these subjects.

By focusing on how people act together in these spaces, Winogrand revealed the confusing urban world of modern times. His work was first exhibited in the Museum of Modern Art's seminal exhibition *The Family of Man* (1955). From that point on, he was included in many major exhibitions there and at the George Eastman House in Rochester, New York. He was awarded the first of three Guggenheim Fellowships in 1964 to make "photographic studies of American life," then received his second in 1969 to photograph "the effect of the media on events."[1]

A Winogrand photograph presents a disordered reality, a dizzy, tilted view filled with visual noise. He achieved this signature style using a 35mm camera with a wide-angle lens, which allowed him to photograph subjects close-up as he walked through crowds. He photographed with a "machine gun" approach, exposing film rapidly, without composing or framing the scene and without knowing how the final image would appear. He often said, "I photograph to find out what something will look like photographed"—the antithesis of the pre-visualization philosophy popularized by photographers like Ansel Adams (1902–1984).[2]

In this image, made at the corner of Hollywood and Vine in Los Angeles, three women hold center stage as they make their way down the sidewalk, following the shafts of light and shadow created by the strong backlighting. Their "big hair," miniskirts, and high heels fit in perfectly with the surrounding neighborhood, recognized as the center of the world's entertainment capital, with motion picture, television, and recording studios nearby. But the more disturbing elements and dynamics of the real world often find their way into Winogrand's photographs. Here, in the women's sideways glance at a wheelchair-bound beggar, the glitz and artificiality of Hollywood collide with gritty street reality, and the viewer is left with a sense of unease at the incongruity of these elements. BMC

1 John Szarkowski, *Winogrand: Figments from the Real World* (Boston: Little, Brown, and Co., 1988), 249–50.
2 From Dennis Longwell, ed., "Monkeys Make the Problem More Difficult: A Collective Interview with Garry Winogrand," *Image* 15, no. 2 (July 1972), 4; quoted in Szarkowski, 23.

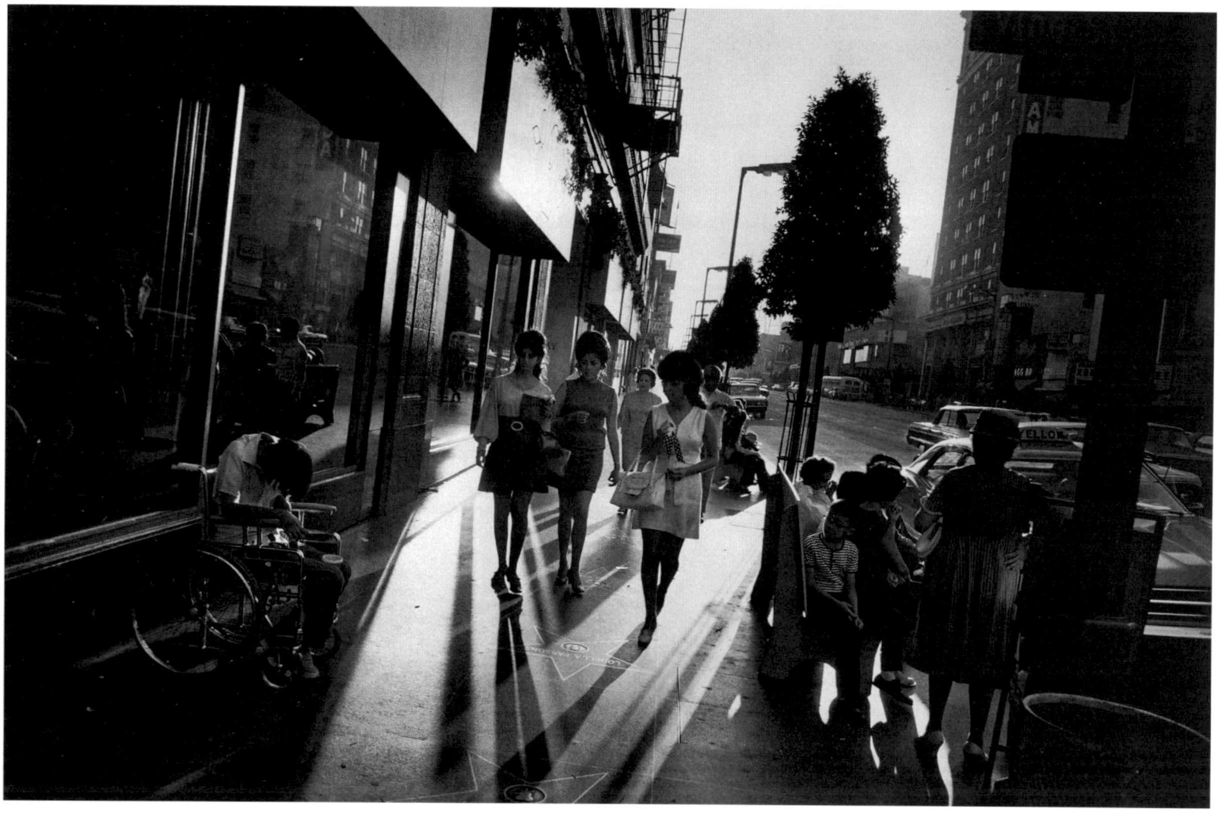
YELLOW

About the Authors

Patricia Junker is curator of paintings and sculpture at the Amon Carter Museum. She is the principal author of *John Steuart Curry: Inventing the Middle West* (1998), for the Elvehjem Art Museum, University of Wisconsin–Madison, and *Winslow Homer, Artist and Angler* (2002), coproduced by the Fine Arts Museums of San Francisco and the Amon Carter Museum. She is coauthor of collection catalogues for the Fine Arts Museums of San Francisco, the Smith College Museum of Art, and the Amon Carter Museum. Her 1990 exhibition catalogue for the Memorial Art Gallery of the University of Rochester, *Winslow Homer in the 1890s: Prout's Neck Observed*, was awarded the 1991 Henry Allen Moe prize for scholarship by the New York State Historical Association.

Rebecca E. Lawton is assistant curator of paintings and sculpture at the Amon Carter Museum. She is a contributing author to *Refining the Imagination: Tradition, Collecting, and the Vassar Education* (1999) and author of *Heroic America: James Daugherty's Mural Drawings from the 1930s* (1998).

Barbara McCandless, curator of photographs at the Amon Carter Museum, is the author of *Equal before the Lens: Jno. Trlica's Photographs of Granger, Texas* (1992). She is coauthor of *Photography in Nineteenth-Century America* (1991), *New York to Hollywood: The Photography of Karl Struss* (1995), *An American Collection: Works from the Amon Carter Museum* (2001), and *Singular Moments: Photographs from the Amon Carter Museum* (2001), all four of which were produced for the Amon Carter Museum.

Jane Myers is chief curator at the Amon Carter Museum. She is the principal author of *Revealed Treasures: Works on Paper from the Amon Carter Museum* (2001), and coauthor of *Stuart Davis: Graphic Work and Related Paintings with a Catalogue Raisonné of the Prints* (1986), *George Bellows: The Artist and His Lithographs, 1916–1924* (1988), and *An American Collection: Works from the Amon Carter Museum* (2001), all four of which were produced for the Amon Carter Museum. She is also coauthor of the exhibition catalogues *The Paintings of George Bellows* (1992), for the Amon Carter Museum and the Los Angeles County Museum of Art, and *The Shores of a Dream: Yasuo Kuniyoshi's Early Work in America* (1996) for the Amon Carter Museum.

Shirley Reece-Hughes has worked as a curatorial assistant for both the Dallas Museum of Art and the Amon Carter Museum. She is a contributing author to *The Dallas Museum of Art: A Guide to the Collection* (1997), *Revealed Treasures: Watercolors and Drawings from the Amon Carter Museum* (2001), and the forthcoming collection catalogue of the Albrecht-Kemper Museum of Art in Saint Joseph, Missouri. She recently completed her PhD coursework in art history at the University of Kansas, where she received a Henry Luce Foundation American Art Research Grant for her dissertation work on the artist David Bates.

Rick Stewart is director of the Amon Carter Museum. His publications for the museum include *Charles M. Russell: Sculptor* (1994), which won the National Cowboy Hall of Fame's Western Heritage Award for Outstanding Art Book. He is coauthor of the exhibition catalogues *Eyewitness to War: Prints and Daguerreotypes of the Mexican War, 1846–1848* (1989), which was named the Outstanding Publication of the Year by the American Historical Print Collectors Society, and *Carl Wimar: Chronicler of the Missouri River Frontier* (1991). He is also coauthor of *An American Collection: Works from the Amon Carter Museum* (2001).

Artist Index